The Temptation of
Innocence

Pascal Bruckner

The Temptation of Innocence

—

Living in the Age of Entitlement

Algora Publishing
New York

Algora Publishing, New York
© 2000 by Algora Publishing
All rights reserved. Published 2000.
Printed in the United States of America
ISBN: 1-892941-56-2
Editors@algora.com

Library of Congress Cataloging-in-Publication Data 00-010706

Bruckner, Pascal.
[Tentation de l'innocence. English]
The temptation of innocence : living in the age of entitlement / by
Pascal Bruckner.
 p. cm.
Includes bibliographical references.
 ISBN 1-892941-56-2 (alk. paper)
1. Responsibility. 2. Entitlement attitudes. 3. Civilization,
Modern—20th century. I. Title.
BJ1452 .B7813 2000
170'.9'049—dc21
                              00-010706

Algora Publishing
wishes to express its appreciation
for the assistance given by
the Government of France
through the Ministry of Culture
in support of the preparation of this translation.

New York
www.algora.com

Table of Contents

"Everyone is guilty but me."

Céline.

THE INCREDIBLE SHRINKING MAN

On the deck of a motorboat, a man is sunning himself. Suddenly, he's splashed by a curtain of spray, sprinkled with droplets that leave his skin with a pleasant tingling feeling. He towels himself off without giving it much thought. He soon notices that he is a couple of inches shorter. His doctor conducts a thorough examination, finds nothing out of the ordinary, and admits that he has no explanation. The man goes on getting smaller every day. The people around him seem to grow; his wife, who used to come up to just above his shoulder, is now a head taller than he is. She soon leaves this runty little husband. He takes up with a dwarf in the circus, with whom he shares his last human passion before she, too, transforms into a giantess. He keeps on shrinking and reaches the size of a doll, then a tin soldier, until he finds himself confronted by his own cat — an adorable kitty who has become a tiger with immense eyes and who stretches her paw at him, sharp-edged talons extended. Later, having taken refuge in the cellar, he faces a monstrous spider. . .

In this science fiction novel, Richard Matheson offered a striking metaphor of the insignificant individual struck by his smallness. Compared to the vastness of the world and the multitude of other beings, we are all pygmies crushed by how gigantic the world has become. We are all shrinking men.[1]

"Nothing but the earth" exclaimed Paul Morand, in the 1920's, with the offhanded tone of the dandy who has just completed a world tour, already finding it too small and sighing, afterwards, for new frontiers, new drugs. The whole world, we could say today: for the unification of the planet by technology, by communication links, and by the weapons of mass destruction render all of humanity co-present to itself at all times. This immense achievement has a terrible flip side: we find ourselves potentially burdened with, and informed about, everything that takes place at every instant.

The "global village" is only the sum of the constraints that subject everyone to the same externality from which we strive to protect ourselves — for want of being able to master it. This interdependence of humanity, and the fact that remote acts have incalculable repercussions for us, are suffocating. The more the media, trade, and exchanges bring continents and cultures closer together, the more overpowering becomes the pressure of all upon each; we seem to have been dispossessed of ourselves by a chain of forces over which we have no influence. The planet has contracted so much that the distances that used to separate us from our peers have been reduced to negligibility. The net has closed in, causing a sense of claustrophobia and almost of incarceration. Demographic explosions, mass migrations, ecological catastrophes, you would think that human beings were falling all over each other. And what was the end of Communism but the irruption, on the international scene, of the innumerable? Human tribes are legion and all of them, delivered from the totalitarian yoke, aspire to recognition. But no one can remember their names! Thus the voiceless plea that each one, on a globe that is full as an egg, raises to heaven: Deliver us from the others (which should be understood as: Deliver me from myself)!

I call *innocence* the disease of individualism; it consists in trying to escape the consequences of our own acts, attempting to enjoy the advantages of liberty without suffering any of the disadvantages. It is expanding in two directions — *infantilism* and *victimization*, two means of escaping the trials of being, two strategies for achieving happy irresponsibility. In the first, innocence must be understood as a parody of the insouciance and ignorance of youth; it culminates in the figure of the perpetually immature, the lifelong adolescent. In the second, it is synonymous with otherworldliness, meaning the absence of culpability, the incapacity of doing evil, and it is embodied in the figure of the self-proclaimed martyr.

What is infantilism? Not just the need for protection (which is, in itself, legitimate) but the transfer into adulthood of the attributes and the privileges of childhood. The child, in the West, has been our new idol for the past century — our little household god, he who is permitted everything in exchange for nothing — and now he embodies (at least in our fantasy) that model of humanity which we would like to reproduce at every stage of life. Infantilism combines a desire for security, and boundless greed, and it shows up as a desire to be in charge but without being willing to be subjected to the least obligation. The concept is so highly charged, it so strongly colors every aspect of our lives, because it has two objective allies in our society, two allies which continuously feed it and secrete it: consumerism and entertainment. Both are founded on the principle of constant surprise and endless satisfaction. The essence of this "infantophilia" (which should not be confused with a real interest in childhood) could be summarized by the formula: you don't have to give up anything!

As for victimization, that is the tendency of the citizen coddled by the capitalist "paradise" to think of himself in terms of the model of a persecuted people, especially at a time when crises sap our confidence in the benefits of the system. In a book on the West's guilty conscience, I once defined support of the Third World as the tendency to blame all the problems of the young nations of the southern hemisphere on the old colonial metropolises. For the Third World to be innocent, the West had to be absolutely guilty; it was transformed into an enemy of humankind.[2] And certain Westerners, especially those inclined toward the Left, liked to flagellate themselves, taking a special pleasure in describing themselves in the worst terms. Since then, support for the Third World has declined as a political movement. Who could have predicted that it would show up again as a mindset (with all of us, now, as the victims), and be propagated so rapidly among the middle classes? Nobody wants to be held responsible anymore; everyone aspires to being taken for an underdog, even if he hasn't suffered any particular difficulty.

And what goes for the private person goes for minorities, and for whole countries throughout the world. For centuries, men struggled to broaden the idea of humanity in order to include in the great common family those races, those ethnic groups, those categories who were downtrodden or reduced to servitude: Indians, Blacks, Jews, women, children, etc.. The task of restoring dignity to denigrated or subjugated populations is far from being completed; perhaps it never will be. But running parallel to this immense labor of civilization (if civilization is indeed the progressive constitution of mankind into an ensemble), is a process of division and fragmentation. Whole groups, even nations, call for special treatment in the name of their misfortune. There is no comparison, in either cause or effect, between the complaints of the great puerile adult of the rich countries, the miserable hysteria of certain groups (whether feminists or male chauvinists), and the deadly strategy of nations or terrorist groups (like Serbia or the Islamists) that hold high the banner of martyrdom in order to assassinate their enemies with impunity while appeasing their lust for power. However, each on his own level regards himself as a victim who is owed reparations, an exceptional case marked with the miraculous stigmata of suffering.

Infantilism and victimization, while they may sometimes overlap, are not the same thing. They differ from each other as the mild differs from the severe, the insignificant from the gravely important. Nonetheless they consecrate the paradox of the contemporary individual, who is exaggeratedly concerned for his independence but who still demands to be taken care of and assisted, who seeks to play both the dissident and the baby, and to speak the double language of nonconformity and insatiable demand. And just as the child, due to his weak constitution, has rights that he will lose as he grows up, the victim, due to his distress, deserves comfort and compensation. Playing the child when one is adult, and playing miserable when one is prosperous, are both ways of seeking advantages that one does not deserve, ways of indicating that other people owe us something. Should I add that these two pathologies of modern times are not inevitable but are only trends, and that we might dream of other ways of being that would be more authentic? But failure and fear are inherent in freedom. The Western individual is by nature a wounded being; the price he pays for his foolish pride (in wanting to be himself) is that he will always feel an essential precariousness. Our societies have abolished the support that tradition used to provide and we are no longer certain of our beliefs; thus, the event of adversity, we are forced to take refuge, so to speak, in magical ceremonies, easy substitutions, and recurrent complaints.

Why is it scandalous to feign misfortune when nothing actually stands in your way? Because then, you usurp the place of the truly afflicted. They, indeed, ask for neither exemptions nor privileges — simply the right to be men and women like everyone else. Therein lies all the difference. The pseudo-desperate want to be different, they claim preferential treatment in order not to be confused with ordinary humanity; the truly desperate call for justice, just so that they can become human. So many criminals don the guise of the victim just to be able perpetrate their crimes in all good conscience, to be innocent bastards.

Finally, this exaltation of the distressed (Nietzsche noted that it was inherent in Christianity, which considers itself guilty, to divinize the victim), this special consideration for the weak (which he called the morality of the slave, and which we will call humanism) degenerates into a perversion when it is transformed in the charitable ideology into a love of indigence for indigence's sake, into a universal victimization in which only sufferers are offered up to our kind consideration, never culprits.

At this change of millennia when the governments of the oppressed have, for the most part, transformed themselves into regimes of terror and arbitrary rule, a persistent suspicion hovers over the afflicted, who are suspected of wanting, in their turn, to become the oppressors, to take their revenge. The historical Left (as distinct from certain pretenders), having taken up the torch of evangelism, succeeded in imposing on the entire political world the viewpoint of the handicapped; but in the aftermath of the revolution it too often fell short, when the former-exploited inevitably transmuted into a new exploiter. Liberation movements, revolts, uprisings, civil wars seem dedicated to despotism, to reproducing iniquity. What's the point in rebelling, only to recreate the same structure, or worse? And the great crime of Communism is that it discredited the claims of the victim for so long. That is the problem: how can we continue to aid the oppressed without allowing the victim's role to be confiscated by all kinds of impostors?

Footnotes

1. Richard Matheson, *The Shrinking Man*, Lightyear Press, 1997.
2. Pascal Bruckner, *Le Sanglot de l'Homme Blanc*, "L'Histoire immédiate", Seuil, 1983.

PART ONE

IS BABYHOOD MAN'S FUTURE?

CHAPTER ONE

THE VICTORY OF THE INDIVIDUAL,

OR

CROWNING THE KING OF DUST

> "If I could have chosen not to be born, I certainly
> would not have accepted existence under such ri-
> diculous conditions."
> Dostoyevsky, *The Idiot.*

The individual forms the backbone of modernity, in Europe,
and like modernity it is born in perplexity. Stepping out of the
Middle Ages, where social order took precedence over private individuals, he arrived at the dawn of the Modern Era to see the private person gradually winning out over any form of collective organization. Buoyed by the Christian notion of personal salvation,
ennobled by the Cartesian rupture — which assigned to the *cogito*
alone the exercise of knowledge and reflection — the individual is
a recent product of our societies; he arrived on the scene only between the Renaissance and the French Revolution. Following
Tocqueville, we generally celebrate the individual as the result of
liberation from two forces: tradition and authority. He rejects the
first in the name of freedom and the second in the name of egalitarianism, the basis of democracy. Refusing to allow his behavior
to be dictated by an external law, he supposedly strives to leave
behind the mental slavery that used to bind human existence to
the past, to the community or to a transcendent figure (God, the

Church, Royalty). No one put it better than Kant, in his definition of the Enlightenment as man's exit "from the state of minority where he has remained through his own fault" and each one's conquest of his own autonomy, that is, the courage to think for himself without being directed by another. With the spread of the Enlightenment and the public use of reason, humanity would be ready to leave behind the crudeness of earlier times to achieve its own majority (which then became almost synonymous with modernity).

However attractive it may be, this hope was never confirmed (and never denied, either). Ever since Benjamin Constant, the individual has been problematic, not triumphant, and has been invested with the greatest expectations as well as the greatest fears. And every one of the latter-day theorists of individualism expresses a certain pessimism. The individual as a historical creation thus bounces between exaltation and distress. Released from the arbitrary nature of the ruling powers by a battery of rights that guarantee his inviolability (at least under a constitutional regime), he atones for the permission to be his own master by enduring a constant state of fragility. Until then, men had all belonged to each other through networks of relations and of reciprocity, which inhibited them but also guaranteed them a status and a place. No one was really independent; a matrix of duties and obligations intertwined each one with his close relations, and social ties were rich and varied. "The aristocracy," said Tocqueville, "made all the citizens into a long chain that extended from the peasant to the king; democracy breaks the chain, setting each link apart." Breaking up the antiquated solidarity (of the clan, the village, the family, the region) upset the entire state of affairs. Being released from any obligation and being guided only by the lantern of his own understanding, the individual loses all assurance of a place, an order, a definition. He may have gained freedom, but he has lost security, he has entered the era of perpetual torment. To some extent, he suffers from having succeeded too well.

BE YOURSELF — THAT IS, GUILTY

Rousseau's *Confessions* represents the literary birth of contemporary individualism. Much has been written since then about this oscillation between anguish and joy. And the author of *The Social Contract* shows his genius by not only having been a fundamental thinker but in having anticipated, through the narrative of his life itself, all the hopes and all the pitfalls that lie in wait for modern man. Like all those who spend their lives cleaning up their defamed honor, Rousseau writes his *Confessions* to correct and rectify the bad image that others have given him. "I knew that I was being depicted, in the public eye, with features so very dissimilar to my own and sometimes so deformed that, in spite of the bad side of which I wanted to conceal nothing, I could only win more by showing myself as I really was."[1] Refusing to cave in to public opinion, Rousseau magnified his project. "I am undertaking an enterprise that has had no example in history and which, in its execution, will not have imitators. I want to show my peers a man in all the truth of his nature; and that man will be me," (Book One, Volume I, p. 33). For this commoner, this vagrant pretends to truth as much as to singularity, and he knows that it has universal applicability. He is endlessly proud of being different. "I know my heart and I know men. I am not made like any other in existence. If I am not better, at least I am different," (*idem*, p. 33). Whereas Chateaubriand opens his *Memoirs from Beyond the Tomb* by inscribing himself within a lineage, by declaiming his genealogy: "I was born a gentleman," Rousseau claims to inaugurate a story with no other counterpart: he prefers to be unique, at his own humble level, than to be grand within tradition. Since this difference isolates him from his peers (the Jean-Jacques that others have created, in order to drag through the mud, is not him), he must work to rehabilitate himself, to repel the ill will and to show others who he is, as he feels himself to be.

Affirming oneself as a consciousness that is both close to others and yet distinct from them is, from the very start, tantamount to making oneself guilty. With Rousseau, the autobiography takes the form of a plea, of an interminable defense that we hold up to others throughout our entire life, as if we were at fault simply for existing. "We enter the lists at birth, and we exit only at death."[2] Rousseau, however — and that is the heart of his originality — mixes two culpabilities: one applies to anyone who rebels against the social order and its laws; the other, more insidious, testifies to everyone's allergy to being watched and judged by others. The first, which tends to identify the individual with the figure in revolt, with the asocial, has enjoyed an endless posterity. By stepping out from the ranks, by claiming "to be free and virtuous above destiny and public opinion and to be sufficient in and of oneself," (*Confessions*, Book Eight, Volume II, p. 100), Rousseau caused a scandal and called down upon himself the reprobation of his friends, especially, who did not forgive him for his desire to be separate. And his existence began with a separation: one Sunday, when he was sixteen years old, he came home too late from a walk outside the city and found the gates of Geneva closed; he decided to run away, for fear of being beaten. He could have stayed in his native village, with close relatives, and become "a good Christian, a good citizen, a good family man, a good friend, a good worker, and a good man in every way," (Book One, Volume 1, p. 78), but he set out down the road, challenging the fate that his birth had intended for him. Concerned "only with living freely and happily in my own way," (Book Eight, Volume II, p. 112), he would decide his own destiny, at the risk of incurring blame, not to mention anathema. "Determined to spend in independence and poverty what little time remained to me to live, I applied all the force of my heart to break the chains of opinion and to do with courage everything that seemed good to me, without worrying about other people's judgment at all. . ." (Book Eight, Volume II, pp. 106-107). He who is determined "to walk alone along a new road" must expect to suffer the jealousy and the resentment of the vulgar. Thus Rousseau is certain of universal persecution: having defied the world, he thinks that the whole world will punish him, uniting its forces against him. The danger being everywhere and nowhere, including in the kind gestures and the flattery of his close relations, his will to escape the influence of others never lets up. In writing his *Confessions*, Rousseau is actually working on his acquittal. Convening the reader as both judge and witness, he gathers evidence, presents exhibits and documents to answer the charge of being stubborn in persevering along his own path. To be oneself is to offer oneself up as both the rebel and the defendant. It is both mutiny and a justification of one's mutiny.

Especially since, having taken the first step, Jean-Jacques discovers with fright what will become the leitmotiv of all later explorers of the ego, of the division of the subject: "Nothing is so dissimilar to me as I am, myself." Noting moods, blunders, and inconsistencies which astonish him, he depicts himself as unstable, prone to unforeseeable reversals. If the other is my similar, am I then another, to myself, since I do not resemble myself? How can I be fully myself if I do not even know what I am? Rousseau has a famous predecessor in this field: discovering the inner world more than a millennium before the father of *Emile*, Saint Augustine (4th-5th century AD) also detects disorder and inconsistency in himself, but associates them with the misery of the creature crushed by the absolute power of its creator. "As for me, although under your gaze I find myself contemptible, considering myself ashes and dust, nevertheless I know something of you that I do not know about myself . . . what I know about me, I know because you enlighten me and what I do not know, I am so unaware of it that before your face my shadows become like broad daylight."[3] Man's inner world is an abyss of mystery, of the unknown, which belongs only to God: "What am I thus, O my God? What kind of being? A changing, multiform life of furious excess," (Book X-17 [26], p. 267). Trying to break through to daylight means butting up against a wall of opacity to which only the divine power holds the key. "I saw myself as nothing but sweat and embarrassment, time and again," (Book X-16 [24], p. 266). My ego is not my own, since at the deepest level of my being lies absolute otherness, divine transcendence. To delve into myself is thus to meet God, "who is more intimate with me than I am, myself," and only an act of boundless love for the Almighty makes it possible to cross the chasm, to overcome falseness, ignorance. (In this sumptuous way Augustine inaugurates the topic of mad love, of the lover who prostrates himself before his beloved and discovers that he is nothing but dust, compared to her, and judges himself unworthy of her attention. The closest intimacy signals the greatest distance, for I and the other are never on an equal footing.) These *Confessions* thus do not offer a magical spell of self-knowledge but invite us to conversion, to abandon the "pestilential sweetnesses" of the world, the false softness of pleasure, for the only reality that is genuine is that of the Divine, the holy inhabitant of my inner sanctum: "I know only this, that for me, not only outside of me but also within me, everything is worthless without you and that any opulence which is not my God is in fact a deficit," (Book XII-9 [10], p. 373). In the night of the human heart, only faith brings salvation and truth. In response to the vastness of God, believers have only one recourse: absolute worship.

It took us more than thirteen centuries to get from Augustine, inventor of introspection, to Rousseau, inventor of intimacy, and during that time Europe became largely secular. Even if the author of *La Nouvelle Héloïse* still offers allegiance to a Supreme Being, his trouble is all the greater since he retains his focus on the human dimension. His inability to justify his oscillations, his contradictions, is a source of constant affliction to him. He postulates in vain that he is the same person experiencing different states; he turns out to be a foreigner to himself, a fragmented being. He is exiled from himself. Not understanding himself, he cannot expect others to understand him any better or to manifest any indulgence toward him. The ego is some other whom I believe I know, a close relation who is the most remote from me ("I do not know what I am, and I am not what I know," the German Franciscan, Angelus Silesius, was already saying in the 17th century). Each one of us is several and these several do not communicate among themselves. We are not masters of our affects — happiness comes to us and leaves us without our wishing it — and it troubles us when it is there, and afflicts us when it leaves, as Rousseau, frightened, noted while writing, in *Confessions,* his proclamation of the refractory man. If Rousseau had said nothing but that, he would only be a successor to Montaigne, who had already depicted himself as divided, contradictory, and haunted by his pirouettes, his about-faces. But Jean-Jacques goes further: what exasperates him is having to legitimize himself for being so multiple in one unit, having to explain "the bizarre and singular assemblage of (his) heart." That, for him, is the original drama: we are never accepted as such in the innocence of our appearance. We must constantly prove what we are. Because meanwhile, a new character, infinitely less sympathetic than God, has entered the dialogue one holds with oneself: others. St. Augustine trampled on the tiny race of men to heighten the glory of the Almighty. Rousseau describes humanity without God as prey, in the worst possible torment, that of assessments, of the reciprocal judgments that men render on each other. God can be a terrible judge; at least he is only one, and He is just. With humanity I must deal with a multiform, elusive judge whose sentences can strike me at any moment without my being able to answer. *Being born means having to compare.*

IN THE DOCK

Thus, a second form of guilt eats away at the individual: not that of the troublemaker who rises up against the established order (what could be more conformist in our day than seeing oneself as a rebel, a nonconformist?) but of the defendant, who lives under the gaze of the others and never escapes their spirit of inquisition. Others prevent me from enjoying myself in all quietude, that's the problem: their cold gaze, their acerbic comments that dissociate me from my own existence. St. Augustine set out to establish man's absolute indebtedness to God, "in respect to whom no one will ever discharge what He has, without any obligation, given us," (Book IX-13 [36], p. 245).

Rousseau discovers in a more terrible way the hell of modern man: I am indebted to the others, all the others, before whom I must give an accounting. Even if our "true self is not entirely complete in us," even if one never manages, in this life, "really to be oneself without the concord of the other," the latter is first of all the one who talks about me without my knowledge, who objectifies me and by so doing, locks up me in an image. It is an intolerably arbitrary condition thus to be removed from oneself, to be defamed and trammeled, and that there should be so great a distance between one's sense of oneself and the sense that others have of you. I thus collapse under the weight of a vague accusation that I cannot formulate, since it is addressed directly to the fact that I am: *existence is an expiation*, one must pay continually for having the audacity to speak in the first person. The jury of the others never renders a final verdict: while I might never be condemned, I am never exonerated, either, to my very last breath. What Rousseau invents (and which will enjoy an astonishing fortune), is this: the desire to be oneself is not only an attempt to know oneself, it is the aspiration to be recognized by the others (to borrow a page from Hegel), i.e. to put oneself under the pitiless eye of his prosecutors.

If the trial has become the model learning tool in the democratic age, the human adventure reduced to its bare bones, we owe it to Rousseau. Like him, we see the courts as the place to defend the most important cause, that is, our very self. Forced to make our case, we must seek our contemporaries' approval, convince them, move them; we place our fate in their hands. That is our secular hell, our first judgment, which is considerably worse, in a sense, than Christianity's last judgment. For fear of being misunderstood, Rousseau will go as far as to haul himself before the jury (by writing his *Dialogues*), resuming all the criticisms that have been addressed to him, the better to pardon himself and to describe himself as a worthy and virtuous being. This is the mad dream of de-fanging the other, eluding the other's authority. And Rousseau's communion with nature is the exact counterpart of his divorce from mankind. Since I do not belong to myself, since I am scattered among the others, since I am composed of all that they say and think of me, I must constantly take control of myself again, reunify myself. Not only by taking up again that strangeness that I am for myself, and stamping it with the seal of my personality, but also by recovering the fragments of my being that have been scattered among the others. This is disturbing work: for delivering oneself to "the foolish judgments of men" means transforming one's existence into an eternal apology, it means trying to control, to rectify the image of oneself that floats in the world and makes us prisoners in the open air.

Rousseau is so full of himself that he sees the Other only as an occupier, and sees his presence, diffuse as it may be, as a judgment. And what face should one display to this assembly of inquisitors? Aren't we liable to merge with the appearance that others propose for us, even as we strive to defend ourselves from it? Isn't this the equivalent of setting ourselves up as a target for misunderstandings and mockery, of offering a grotesque view of ourselves? (Unlike Chateaubriand, who carved a marble statue of himself, a marvelous paper mausoleum, in his *Memoirs from beyond the Tomb*, Rousseau inaugurates the deeply modern figure of the ridiculous man, disarmed, faltering, full of a stupid sentimentality, happy over something of no consequence, at the mercy of the freakish quirks of his moods and the infantile whims of his heart.) Thus, no one is sovereign of himself, no one survives but in fragments: where Jean-Jacques clears a new field compared to Pascal and Montaigne is in presenting *the individual. . . born in persecution, prey to the other.*

Rarely have we seen liberation erupt amidst so many sighs and tears. But the features are set and will not change henceforth: Rousseau the autobiographer remains our brother in emotion and pain. Like him, we are continually disappointed in our expectations and our hopes: affirming oneself as a free and autonomous person is so costly an ideal that it is connected with suffering, above all, and supposes the enormous pressure of the others' judgment on us. And with Rousseau, the plot is always the same: delirious objectivization, the notion that we do not belong to ourselves. In his mad misanthropy, Rousseau has a presentiment of the diseases of the modern individual; he outlines the contours of a space where we can recognize ourselves today. (He will achieve his quest for serenity, for a magical world in which the whole universe does not have carte blanche, by expelling his contemporaries, whom he describes en masse as a single and dreadful villain: there is no just person on earth, he says in his *Reveries* — "the league is universal," mankind is only "a society of the malicious" and salvation, if it must come, will come from posterity, from some others who do not yet exist. They alone will avenge him for human ingratitude, will comfort him; and he sees his last writings as "a deposit left with Providence." What is amazing is the accumulation, from one book to another, of the arguments he reiterates as he tries to convince himself of his goodness and of the world's deceit. As though, delivered from others, he remained embarrassed at the memory of them, and never managed to coincide with himself, to close up the wound in his heart.)[6]

A PYRRHIC VICTORY

The constraints that weigh on each of us have only continued to intensify since Jean-Jacques Rousseau, and in proportion to our liberation, at that. In the 19th and early 20th centuries the individual was still somewhat bound by constraints; as he gradually got rid of the obstacles that obstructed his acquisition of new rights, paradoxically his concern only grew. Let us forget for a moment the determinations of class and culture, and concentrate on the abstract person. At least Rousseau, when he was unhappy, could also accuse the obscurantism of his era, the arbitrary nature of the royal and the ecclesiastical, and the cabals of his philosophical friends (indeed, like Voltaire and Diderot, he was harassed for his writings, arrested, and exiled — even if he did amplify his misfortunes by morbid suspicion). At least he could point to the powerful men of his time as tormenters who were looking to destroy him. But today? What authority can I accuse of causing my woes? For in the long battle between the individual and society, since the end of the *Ancien Régime*, it is society that has receded and has stopped interfering in our lives and dictating our behavior to us.

Certainly it is always possible to up the ante, to indulge in paranoia and to accuse an obscure system of all the evils that overwhelm us, to cite a worldwide conspiracy that is all the more pernicious since it is invisible. As we will see later on, the victim ideology is only the inversion of the theory of the Invisible Hand: behind the chaos of the facts and events a malevolent destiny is working for our misfortune, and seeking to harm and humiliate each of us individually. The more the modern subject thinks he is free, deriving his *raisons d'etre* and his values only from himself, the more he will be inclined (to relieve his doubt and anguish) to invoke some cruel *fatum*, a premeditated disorder that holds him under a microscope and destroys him by some occult means. This trick of malicious reason, this obsession with machinations, can only grow with the progress of independence, always demanded but such a burden, so painful that one seeks loopholes, either magic or insane.

It is clear that the individual's victory over society is an ambiguous victory and that the freedoms we have attained — freedom of thought, of conscience, of choice, of action — are a poisoned gift and the counterpart of a terrible commandment. *Now it is up to every one of us to construct himself and find meaning in his existence.* Yesterday, our beliefs, prejudices, and customs were not only odious guides to conduct; they protected us from chance and from risk, in exchange for obedience to the laws of the group or the community; they guaranteed a certain peace. In days of yore, man could indeed subject himself to all kinds of mortification, to sacrifices that seem unthinkable to us today, but they ensured him a place, they inserted him into an immemorial order where he was linked to the others through all kinds of obligations. Thus, he was recognized and invested with a limited responsibility — whereas modern man, theoretically freed of any obligation that he did not take on himself, slumps under the weight of a responsibility that is virtually without limits. That is individualism: the displacement of the center of gravity from society to the particular person, on whose shoulders now rest all the constraints of freedom. By sweeping aside revealed truths and dogmas, the private person may have gained; but first, he has been weakened, and cut off from any form of support. Ejected from the protective shell of tradition, customs, observances, he finds himself more vulnerable than ever.

We can no longer join Aristotle in saying that "All beings are basically marked by nature, from the first moment of their birth: some to rule, others to obey." But we must admit that the individual is both undefined and unfinished. He is not predestined, he is not yet all that he should be. His future is unforeseeable, it is open and waiting to be formed. Being capable of "perfectibility" (Rousseau), he can also abdicate, vegetate, sink into mediocrity. His existence is not written in advance, it is full of surprise; he must forge it himself, vaguely and gropingly. It will have no other significance than that which he wishes to give it. Any society is individualistic where not only the subject is the fundamental unit of value but where the possibility of conducting one's life in one's own way is open to everyone, without distinction of status, sex, race or birth. And it is the sum of the individual wills freely associated inside a public space that forms the heart of the political and democratic system.

From now on my fate depends only on me: I can't blame any external authority for my failures or my errors. The flip side of my sovereignty: if I am my own master, I am also my own obstacle, and I alone am accountable for the failures or successes I experience. Such is the unhappy awareness of contemporary man: any failure, any disappointment, leads to self-criticism, an examination of conscience, a list of flaws and mistakes that all lead to one conclusion: it is my fault!

Christianity already had made life on earth the scene of a merciless confrontation between salvation and damnation, the antechamber of either paradise or hell (with a kind of posthumous correction system that is purgatory, a belated creation in the history of the Church). Our lives as nonreligious men are no less torn between the possibility of succeeding or of failing — with these aggravating differences: for us, everything is played out down here, in a brief flash of time; and whereas religion posits in advance the values to be honored, we come up with our own criteria of success or failure ourselves, at the risk of not having them recognized by the others (some strive for material enrichment, others for the ideal of the honest man, still others for internal serenity). Freudianism certainly dethroned the subject, removing him from the pedestal upon which the 19th century had placed him; it humiliated man and took away from the self its prerogatives as absolute monarch, opening gaping holes in his reign. Perhaps it has also offered each of us an inexhaustible battery of excuses and subterfuges (my unhappy childhood, my lousy mother) to explain our actions. But by no means has it exonerated the individual, who may have lost some of his powers but did not lose any of his duties. After Freud, while man is no longer sovereign of himself, he is still responsible for himself and cannot blame his errors on a rebellious subconscious or a tyrannical super-ego. Before confronting the world, he butts heads with himself, with that core of complexes and neuroses that he will have to disentangle in order to progress. A strange paradox: the more conscious we become of our infirmity, the more a responsibility accumulates on our shoulders that nothing can remove and that makes each one of us the source of actions whose repercussion are incalculable. The convergence of these two phenomena is unique, and the awareness of our ever-increasing weakness goes hand in hand with a burden that is increasingly heavier. (Just think of all those trades — airplane pilot, train conductor, truck driver, laboratory assistant, doctor — where the slightest mistake threatens disproportionate damage.)

ALL EQUAL, ALL ENEMIES

Another burden comes on top of that one: the competition of all against all, a consequence of equalized conditions. We used to make fun of the absurd obligation to believe in God or to bow down before a being of high rank; we complained about the undue privileges of birth and fortune, the oppression of a caste or a class.

But those were no worse than that which individuals in competition inflict upon themselves when they collectively aspire to the same goals. Envy, resentment, jealousy and impotent hatred are not just unpleasant defects of human nature, they are the direct consequences of the democratic revolution. It is that revolution which, by legitimating ambition and success, and the legal possibility for each one to embrace the career of his choice, also legitimated the covert war that men wage upon each other, by turn vexatious or happy, according to their fortune. It is that which, while promising everyone wealth, happiness, and plenitude, feeds our frustration and encourages us never to be satisfied with our lot.

Combine that with the poison of comparison, with the resentment that is born from some people's spectacular success and other people's stagnation, and each one of us becomes engaged in an endless cycle of appetites and disappointments. We are all looking to make it to the top but there isn't much room up there, and the losers have to put up with the winners of the moment, while they wait for a chance to start over, to shake up the hierarchy. In an egalitarian society, the success of a minority and the stagnation of the others are intolerable. Since we are similar, this superiority is a scandal.

In modern times, Tocqueville tells us, men are easily agitated, anxious: "They destroyed the privileges of some and now they must compete with all. The boundaries have changed form rather than place."[7] And it is clearly in the cities that the talk of competition, of challenge, is harshest. The ecology fad may be related to this fatigue, to the immense lassitude that regularly grips us in a large city. Walking through the public spaces, mingling

with the crowd, facing hundreds and thousands of faces, we confirm our weakness at every moment and we envy, by contrast, the
famous personalities that are met with immediate recognition
everywhere they go. Tossed onto the pavement, the individual
feels himself expropriated from himself. Overcome by the fear of
passing by unperceived, he contradictorily aspires to becoming
everyone. We can all agree with the epigraph of the movie, *Taxi
Driver.* "In every street, there is a nobody who dreams of being
somebody. A man who is alone, abandoned by everyone, and who
is desperately seeking to prove that he exists." At least outside the
city, near the fields and forests, I am not called to account. For the
man of the cities, nature, as Goethe recognized, is "the great balm
to the modern heart," because it embodies regularity and harmony
that slice through the chaos and the arbitrariness of the metropo-
lis. The inconceivable, alarming energy of a city confronts me
with a higher power that stimulates me as much as it oppresses
me. In the recreated nature that is ours, a nature that resembles
brutality, the townsman will seek a haven of peace, a brief suspension of worries and sorrows: there, no one will provoke him, no
one will bother him, no one will try his integrity. Everything
there is in its place, and unfolds according to a predictable
rhythm. In these landscapes worked by the hand of man, I relax, I
recover, I am "wrapped up in myself" (Rousseau). But unless I
choose the life of a hermit, the sovereignty that I taste in these moments of solitude is a gratuitous sovereignty, since it is not enriched and is not disputed by others. And some day I will have to
leave the shelter where I have withdrawn from the world, and return to my century to face my contemporaries.

For before selling his labor on the market, before handling

EVERYMAN'S LAMENTATIONS

What is a complaint? The degraded version of a revolt, the essence of democratic talk in a society that allows us to us foresee the impossible (fortune, fulfillment, happiness) and invites us never to be satisfied with our lot. Complaining is a reticent way of living, taking advantage of our troubles, our dejection, and never coming to terms with everything in existence that is repetitive, machine-like. "I know an Englishman," said Goethe, "who hanged himself rather than having to get dressed every morning." In the jeremiad, the creature is nothing more than a reproach incarnate, a living No: it exudes its misfortune, takes the sky as witness, and abhors its stay on earth. This "dolorism" on principle becomes almost a convention, it is a way of stressing that we are not easily deceived, we know what is destroying us (the passage of time, frail health, the hazards of fate). But a complaint is also a discreet call for help: to keep a minor problem from degenerating into suffering, sometimes all we need is someone's ear.

On the whole, this refractory word is so widespread, from the top to the bottom of the social scale, that it exhausts itself in itself; it dissolves into superficial turbulence. "It can't go on like this!" How often do we say that, precisely so that it will go on as before? For certain people, complaining is a way of life and true old age, that of the spirit, starts (whether at the age of 20 or 80) when one is no longer able to communicate with others except by complaints and grumbling — when deploring one's life, defaming it, lingers on as the best means of doing nothing to change it. "I could not have any profession in this world unless I was paid for my dissatisfaction," (Joseph Roth). If we get upset with ourselves for sometimes giving into complaining, it is because it can quickly degrade into complacency with our little miseries. This means of resisting the order of things then becomes just a chatty form of giving up.

any social or political challenge, everyone must sell himself as a person, in order to be accepted, to win a place that no one would accord him freely in a world that does not belong to him. Our suffering, we other Westerners, is based on relating everything to that negligible unit, that tiny social atom — the individual —

armed with only one torch, his freedom, and possessing only one ambition: himself. Lack of self-confidence is not just a characteristic of a weak or neurotic personality, it is the symptom of a state where people are constantly fluctuating, like stock quotes, according to the higher or lower esteem allotted to them by public opinion — the ficklest court there is. One day up, one day down, the only thing we are sure about is the instability of our situation. And the misfortune of the "has been," the person who has had his chance and lost it, is in seeing his destiny sealed once and for all. (This gives rise to that very special form of worship that we devote to stars — the revocable divinities of egalitarian societies whom we adore and whom we shamelessly throw away, and who offer the illusion of being sufficient unto themselves, of embodying a promise of worldly redemption.)

THE CLONE SYNDROME

Another disappointment awaits modern man: believing himself to be unique, and finding out he is absolutely commonplace. In a world of orders and hierarchies, individualism was a pioneering experiment conducted by exceptional personalities who dared to emancipate themselves from prevailing dogmas and practices, to advance alone into the unknown. Da Vinci, Erasmus, Galileo, Descartes, Newton blazed their trails through the wilderness, setting aside the generally accepted ideas, opposing the prejudices of their times with the fundamental audacity of a rupture. And thus individualism was born as the tradition of rejecting tradition. These great reformers sketched the outlines of a different type of humanity, suggested a different relationship to the law, to the past, to transcendence. But while it became the norm, individual-ism itself was banalized and merged with the ambient ordinary. The private person undoubtedly triumphs but is lost in the multi-tude, shrinks, and as Benjamin Constant* noted, loses influence when he enjoys his independence in peace. He is only a fragment who takes himself for a whole alongside other wholes that are, themselves, nothing but fragments. Each one believes himself to be irreplaceable and sees the others as an indistinct crowd, but this belief is immediately swept away by everyone else's equal claim. Me and me: we are all made up of ego, whose vanity is al-ways keen.

The result of this adventure is that now men resemble each other in the ways that they try to set themselves apart. This de-sire to dissociate ourselves is precisely what brings us closer, and it is this distance that confirms our conformity. Romantic fasci-nation with exceptional beings — with the insane, the criminal, the genius, the artist, the pervert — stems from our fear of becom-ing lost in the flock, in the stereotype of the petit-bourgeois man. "I am different from the rest." That is the motto of the man of the herd. For the punishment that most hurts the contemporary indi-vidual is indifference, rather than imprisonment or repression: counting for nothing, existing only for oneself, to remain eternally a "pre-someone" (Evelyne Kestenberg) whom the others see as a presence, not as an interlocutor. (Ralph Ellison's book *The Invisible Man*, published in 1952, pointed out that his black compatriots in the United States were effectively transparent, their skin color having made them interchangeable and without identity. This

---

*For an overview of Constant's life and work, see Tzvetan Todorov's *A Passion for Democracy: Benjamin Constant*, Algora Publishing, 1999.

state of social death, to varying degrees, is the nightmare that haunts virtually every one of us.) This leads to "narcissism over small differences" (Freud), cultivated with ever more maniacal care as we all lead more or less the same existence, giving rise to the battle for our peers' attention, the rage to get people to talk about us, even by the most extravagant means. That is the experience of massification in a society where the private individuals are nothing, because individualism is everything.

What could be more symptomatic, in this respect, than the depression generated by sociology? This discipline engenders humility in that it shines upon each of us the spotlight of the majority, and reduces our most intimate gestures to statistics. With sociology I become predictable, my actions are written in advance, any spontaneity is a lie by the order that is written through me. It flagrantly contradicts the dream of freedom that supposedly unfolds in sync with my own initiatives. What good is it to invent myself, since a "science" tells me what I am and what I will be, no matter what I do? (Sociology is prescriptive as much as descriptive.) Sociology rejects my claim to novelty, to innovation. For example, you may believe yourself to be a refined lover whose heart beats only for exceptional women; you learn from a survey that you share the same tastes with 75% of the men of your professional background. You thought you transcended any particular definition, any precise determinism — but your romantic choices only underscore your class membership. With sociology, you are free only to act like the others, to be both equivalent and in conformity.

Finally, the royal privilege of doing things only your way, the will for personal realization, runs into a contradiction: I con-

struct myself beside the others, but also *with* them. I cannot construct myself without the support of examples, close or distant
models that help me but also enmesh me in a dangerous dispossession. All men claim to be self-made, without anyone's assistance, but they all plunder and steal shamelessly: lifestyles, ways
of dressing and speaking, behavior in love, cultural tastes — one
never invents oneself without affiliating with standards from
which one can only extract oneself little by little, as from quick-
sand. To create is to copy, first and foremost: with each of my
thoughts, each of my gestures, I experience the imprint of others
on me. I am made up of all these others, as they are made up of me.
Everyone dreams of being novel and finds out he is a follower, an
imitator. Never mind those marginal zones where the ego disappears in the anonymous haze, the lack of differentiation of Mr.
Everybody, Luther's "Herr Omnes." Our societies are obsessed
with conformity because they are made up of individuals who
pride themselves on singularity but align their behavior on everyone else's.

Contemporary individualism thus swings like a metronome
between two tendencies: a proclamation of self-sufficiency (Jerry
Rubin summarized it stunningly: "I have to love myself enough
not to need anyone else in order to be happy")[8] and the giddiness
of total plagiarism that makes each person into a weather vane
(like Woody Allen's *Zelig*, a glutton of imitation left exposed to
the chaos of the outside world, captured by images that he mim-
ics, always hopelessly being some other since he isn't anything
himself). We know that Barrès, for example, considered individualism to be as great a catastrophe at the level of the person as cosmopolitanism is at the level of the nation: the risk of fragmenta-

tion, disorder, and uprooting). This leads to the aberrant behaviors, the mixture of the pathetic and the ridiculous, that forms the backdrop of our existences: the apparent contempt for others and the panicky quest for their approval, the rejection of the norm and the anguish of being different, the aspiration to distinguish oneself tied to the happiness that comes from being part of the crowd, the assertion the we don't need anybody and the bitter comment that nobody needs us, misanthropy accompanied by shameful begging for others' approval, etc.. And let's not forget the *ostentatious strategies of dissimulation,* which consist in hiding in order to be visible, keeping quiet to make a deafening noise, making our presence felt by our absence. To conclude, everyone discovers he is a foreigner at home, filled with intruders who speak in his place, dispossessed of himself at the very moment when he thought he was expressing something in his own name. " 'I don't know which way to turn, I am everything that cannot find any way out,' groans the modern man," (Nietzsche, *The Antichrist*).

TIRED OF BEING OURSELVES

Those who wished to claim the grand title of free men and women used to face a two-fold task: they had to isolate themselves from the mass of sheep and work at becoming what they wanted to be. Leaving the well-charted territories behind, they turned full bore against the established powers and exposed themselves to their reprisals, they shaped themselves by fighting against the prevailing way of life, the prevailing faith, the prevailing values. It's not like that today: the state of the individual in the West is not only a collective phenomenon but it is granted to every one even before his life begins. I am made an individual to some extent before I have done anything at all, and I share this privilege equally with millions of others. This freedom, granted rather than achieved, falls on us like a cold shower: we are condemned to be individuals, as Sartre said that we are condemned to be free. And since this status is a right as much as a duty, the individual will tend to forget his duties and insist upon his rights, he will constantly trample his freedom, which delights him no more than it encumbers him. Vain, vague and vulnerable: that is how he turns out to be, just when everyone is assuring him that he is the new monarch for the new millennium. And his discomfort with being becomes an integral part of his own ideals.

The ultimate reversal: the triumphant subject, having swept past every obstacle in his path, becomes the victim of his own success. This valiant knight who had risen up against the standing powers and proclaimed, loudly and proudly, that he would conduct his life only as he sees fit, finds himself desperate at having won. He had denounced the intolerable encroachments of social control; now he accuses society of abandoning him to his fate. What a shock — his victory looks more like a defeat. The Unique One's rebellion against the crowd, against the masses, against the philistines turns out to have ironic consequences. Those shameful collectives also conferred on him, through their oppression, a certain weight. The prohibitions were a stimulant, the obstacles were a source of strength, an incentive to resistance. Now, the Unique One is upset with the whole world for allowing him to be himself, for not interfering more in his decisions; he pines for a few interdictions, a few taboos.

Once again it is Rousseau who, in his genius, recognized this tendency. Having arrived at an advanced age, he regretted not having tasted all the pleasures that his heart longed for, and said: "It seemed to me that destiny owed me something that it had not given me. What good was it to have been born with exquisite faculties, only to leave them unused until the end? The sense of my inner worth, by engendering this sense of injustice, compensated me to some extent and made me weep, filled me with tears that I enjoyed pouring out."[9] The aspiration to be oneself comes with such an appetite for happiness and fulfillment that existence inevitably generates disappointment. *Life is always structured as a promise*: the "promise of the dawn," Romain Gary called it; it cannot be fulfilled, the thousand wonders that it dangles before us are delivered only in droplets. Ultimately, we are always "rooked" and our existence appears to us as a succession of disasters, of missed opportunities. "I was born to live, and I will die without having lived."[10] Thus, we are all prone to muttering to ourselves: I deserve better than this, they owe me! What federates people now is the same feeling of nervousness about their identity, the same complaint about the injustices of fate since they can only blame themselves for their misfortune. Even when he triumphs, the individual likes to think of himself as having been defeated. In his victory, he suspects that something essential has been lost, the warmth and grounding of tradition, the protective supervision of the community. His distress is the result of a victory, not a defeat, yet he would like to continue to be seen as a victim of persecution.

It's understandable. Individualism is a fiction, unattainable, impossible. Even if it sounds attractive to become transparent to oneself, and the concept of the ego a white lie, it seems to be hard to back out of that and return to an organic concept of the social state, to a vision of society as a great collective soul that would relieve us of the need to construct our selves. It's useless to humiliate the subject, to abase it in every way possible. It remains, with all its ridiculous miseries, our only instrument of measurement, our central value; and, as Habermas suggests, while modernity may not be fully achieved, we do not consider it to be bankrupt. The desire to be one's own master and leader, to be "somebody not a nobody" (Isaiah Berlin) remains fundamental. This ideal must be constantly held up to the various counterfeits that circulate today under the name of individualism and that signal the diminishing, not the flourishing, of the subject.[11] It's still no less true that the life of any free man or woman is only a series of lapses, of escapes into cowardice, routine, and subservience.

We can answer Stendhal's famous question: "Why aren't people happy in the modern world?," by saying: because they were freed from everything and now they see that freedom is unbearable. While liberation takes on a kind of epic and poetic grandeur when it means deliverance from oppression, liberty, because it brings commitments and obligations, tyrannizes us with its demands. This gift is also a curse, and that is why so many men and women seek solace in neo-tribalism, drugs, political extremism, and cheap mysticism. That is why the modern individual, torn between the need to believe and the need to justify his beliefs, is also a professional apostate, a nomad wandering from one disavowal to another, in the course of just one lifetime embracing and then casting aside a multitude of beliefs and ideas, taking up one faith after another in a transitory and intransigent fashion. The history of the individual is only the history of his successive abdications, of the thousand tricks by which he tries to escape the assigned task of being himself. "Perpetually and irremediably haunted by his opposite,"[12] he is the sum of the resignations and new starts that mark his career.

Fortunately, there is a magic universe to alleviate our wounds, a delicious cocoon where we can derive comfort and relief. We know, since Max Weber (and Marcel Gauchet) that we are living in a universe that is no longer enchanted. It was Judaism that first broke with the pagan divinities to impose a single god; this was reinforced by Christianity and prolonged by the Galilean revolution that used mathematics to decipher nature. This disenchantment allowed the birth of instrumental reason, and modern technology and science. Thanks to this, we stopped looking for a malignant or beneficial force behind every phenomenon and instead look for facts that can be calculated and thus controlled. It is this disenchantment, again, that since the Romantic Age has fed a wave of criticism against the industrial society, which we see as guilty of profaning what was once sacred: of subjecting feelings, values, the land, and natural resources to the cold blade of profit and exploitation.

Capitalist progress thus comes at the cost of a terrible depoetizing and every protest movement in the past two centuries has waved the banner of passion and emotion against impoverishing rationality. And rightly so. It deserves to be moderated on one point: the liberal system has responded to the harshness of conditions, the coldness, with a completely original invention — consumerism. Leisure, entertainment, and material abundance constitute on their level a pathetic attempt to re-enchant the world; this is one of the answers that modernity brings to the suffering over being free, the immense fatigue of being oneself.

Footnotes

1. Jean-Jacques Rousseau, *Les Confessions*, Livre dixième, Folio, Gallimard, volume II, p. 281.
2. Jean-Jacques Rousseau, *Les Rêveries du promeneur solitaire*, Troisième Promenade, Garnier-Flammarion, p. 58.
3. Saint-Augustine, Les Confessions, livre X-5(7), Seuil, translated from Latin by Louis de Mondalon, p. 253.
4. Jean-Jacques Rousseau, *Rousseau, Juge de Jean-Jacques*, Deuxième Dialogue, in *Oeuvres complètes*, Pléiade, Gallimard, 1959, p. 813.
5. *Les Rêveries du promeneur solitaire, op. cit.*, p. 66.
6. Jean Starobinski masterfully analyzed these themes in *Jean-Jacques Rousseau, La Transparence et l'Obstacle*, Gallimard, 1971; see also Tzvetan Todorov in *Le Frêle Bonheur*, Hachette, 1985.
7. On the mimetic competition affecting peers and siblings, René Girard made an extraordinary commentary in *Mensonge romantique et vérité romanesque*, Grasset, 1961. On the suffering caused by the meritocratic ethos, see also a disciple of Girard, Jean-Pierre Dupuy, *Le Sacrifice et l'Envie*, Calmann-Lévy, 1992.
8. In his *Rêveries*, Rousseau has this terrible sentence: "I love myself too much to be able to hate anyone" (*op. cit.*), a kind of acknowledgement that he may never have loved. The dream of the insularity of the ego, for which every other is a parasite intruding in the delicious private conversation between oneself with oneself, dates from Rousseau.
9. *Les Confessions*, Livre neuvième, *op. cit.*, volume II, p. 179.
10. *Rêveries*, Deuxième Promenade, *op. cit.*, p. 47.
11. "How can the idea of the subject seem to be both a potential center of possibly dangerous illusions and an indisputable value?," asks Alain Renaut, in *L'Ère de l'individu*, Gallimard, 1989, pp. 18-19.
12. Louis Dumont, *Essais sur l'individualisme*, Seuil, 1983, p. 28.

CHAPTER 2

RE-ENCHANTING THE WORLD

> "The American approach is enchanting for simple beings and it delights children. All the children I know reason like Americans whenever it comes to money, pleasure, glory, power and work."
>
> George Duhamel, *Scènes de la vie future*.

> "The beautiful mechanical toys that tempt the eternal puerility of adults. . ."
>
> E. Levinas, *Difficile liberté*

When Emile Zola describes provincial young Denise's first sight of the great Parisian store *Le Bonheur des Dames* ("Ladies' Delight"), a century ago, he spontaneously picks up the vocabulary of passionate love. "This enormous building filled her heart, moved her, transfixed her, so that she lost sight of everything else,"[1] (p. 42). "She had never seen such a thing; she stood riveted to the sidewalk in admiration," (p. 44). Stunned by the cleverness of the window dressing, the displays of silks, satins, and delicate-hued velvets, "the volcano of fabrics," the young woman is literally possessed, body and soul. "At that hour of the night, glaring like a furnace, *Le Bonheur des Dames* won her over completely. In the great, black, and silent city, the Paris that was so unfamiliar to her, it blazed like a beacon, it seemed to her to be the light of life and the light of the city itself," (p. 65). In this novel that claims to be "the poem of modern activity" and that is primarily the story of the war between small and big business, Zola intuitively understood that industrial development not only exploits and destroys nature but also, and what is more important, it produces marvels. He showed that the profusion of goods in Europe was opening up unlimited terrain to desire. For it is temptation and only temptation that draws women toward "these hearths of shining light," to "delight their eyes," to dazzle themselves, to disturb themselves, to drive themselves to ruin, in rags.

IRREFUTABLE ABUNDANCE

Walk into a supermarket or a department store, drive through the commercial arteries of a city: you immediately know that you have entered the Garden of Earthly Delights, a terrestrial Paradise. All the dreams of the Golden Age that mankind cherished over the centuries are assembled here. The vastness of the space, the extraordinary variety of the wares on display, the light streaming down, the miles of shelf space, and the ingeniousness of the window displays create a living Utopia. If ever a prophecy came true, this is it. (South of the Sahara, legend long held that the streets of Europe were paved in gold). These temples of the market celebrate modern capitalist society's victory over scarcity. Here is the result of the legendary post-war boom, the Glorious Thirty Years[2] (Jean Fourastié), that freed the Western masses from misery and need, and put within everyone's reach an opulence worthy of Sardanapalus.

In the famous print *Luikkerland*, the Flemish land of plenty, Brueghel the Elder represents three well-fed characters, relaxing under a tree with an expression of absolute bliss. Not far away, a pig is wandering about, a knife stuck in her rind, ready to be cut up and eaten; a goose is stretched out on a silver platter waiting to be served; the gates in the fence are made of sausages; and a shelled egg, walking on two legs, with a place setting laid out on its collar, saunters between the sleepers. A mountain of pudding separates Luikkerland from the real world. This entire pastoral scene breathes satiety, satisfaction, and the generosity of a nature that provides for all of man's needs and relieves them of all effort. Let us imagine our three sleepers shaken out of their slumber and brutally transplanted into our era, in the midst of any food aisle in a supermarket: they probably would be suffocated by the diversity; they would fearfully recognize that men from societies with food shortages can have only poor dreams, pitiful dreams. What social reformer, in his wildest reveries, could have imagined such profusion?

There is too much of everything in the accumulation of riches in these big stores, and the surplus is overwhelming. The distracted eye is guided by a luxuriance of lighting that seems to come from everywhere at once, yet cannot embrace all the splendors laid out before our covetous gaze. Before we select one item or another, before we allow ourselves to be made giddy by the symphony of colors and brands — for everything in this spectacle is organized, ordered, arranged according to the strategy of absolute visibility — we are intoxicated by those wares that we have no intention of taking and that we cherish only with our eyes. Being a consumer means knowing that there will always be more in the windows and in the shops than one can ever have. No one dominates this jungle of treasures that suggests monstrous expense, a gigantic production and organization machine, and infinite possibilities (in the United States, a million products are available for every individual, on average). In these cathedrals of superfluity, our fault is not in wishing for too much but, as Fourier said, of wishing for too little. If poverty, according to St. Thomas, is the lack of the superfluous whereas misery is lack of the necessary, we are all poor in the consumer society: we are inevitably short of everything, since everything is available in excess.

What is magical about the big stores is that they deliver us from the constraints of immediate needs while suggesting to us a multitude of others: the only pleasure is in wanting something that we do not need. The gems that accumulate here have nothing to do with any logic of utility but relate to the miracle of endless fecundity. (And that is precisely the role of the buffet, in the big hotels and resorts, which are founded on the principle of waste: to ward off a feeling of shortage through signs of prodigality.) We step into this pandemonium not only to make purchases but to see that everything is there with hand's reach. We go there to verify that the god of wealth exists, that we can touch it with a finger, we can go right up close to it, sniff it. It is this immediate intimacy with luxury that is astonishing, that throws us for a loop from the time we learn to walk. We inhale the perfume of a promised land, where milk and honey flow in abundance, where humanity is finally redeemed of its weaknesses.

This marvel has all become banal, you say? The spectacle of the shopping malls and the rows of elegant boutiques in our cities no longer kindles any sparks in us? That is true: but just as there are both routine purchases and sumptuous expenditures that give us a strong surge of pleasure, all it takes is the threatening specter of a recession (or a visit to poorer countries) to remind ourselves of the outrageous privilege that we enjoy. *There is no great beyond,*

beyond abundance; it is irrefutable. Now the world can be divided between nations where the windows are full and nations where they are empty. The first are inherently welcoming, friendly; the others seem cold and hostile. How hypocritical were certain West German intellectuals, shortly after the Wall came down in 1989, in deploring their compatriots from the East for advancing "in a furious horde. . . closed ranks, on the clinking trinkets" of Western supermarkets (Stefan Heym) and to call it regrettable that the civic uprising was drowned out by a vote in favor of bananas and chocolate (Otto Schilly).[3] Mussolini defined Fascism as the horror of convenient life. But even among the prophets of the new frugality, who would like to exchange our current prosperity for the relative scarcity that used to be part of our everyday life? For without these marvelous artifacts such as bathtubs, refrigerators, and upholstered furniture that spare us effort and soften our condition, we would go to pieces. The best proof is that people from the southern hemisphere and from the East envy us only one thing: not our human rights, our democracy and even less our cultural refinements, but only our material plenitude and our technological prowess. The tepid hell of our countries that are "infected with well-being" is a heavenly dream for millions. Because our way of life could not likely be extended to include all of humanity, as it is, without major damage to the environment, and because it may all disappear one day following a crash, it remains an extraordinary (and highly expensive) exception. During the Gulf War, in Saudi Arabia, the American troops guarded the approach to the oil wells, while the Arab forces (Egyptians, Saudis, Moroccans) guarded the access to Mecca. To each his own holy places!

PERPETUAL EASTER

It has been said that consumerism is the ownership instinct pushed to its extreme, the subjugation of men to things. However, we are not living in a culture of possession so much as of circulation: goods must expire, their destruction is planned, their obsolescence programmed (Vance Packard). Whereas possession supposes permanence, our objects have only the seduction of the transitory, of the mini-series; they soon go out of style, and are immediately supplanted by new ones that scintillate for a moment before being carted away in their turn. We only buy them to use them and then buy others of them. The depreciation has to be fast, and general, for our wealth is tied to dilapidation not to conservation. Doesn't the wild looting by urban rioters, and the pleasure they take in plundering stores and setting fire to cars, conform profoundly to the logic of the system? This wreckage is involuntary homage paid to our society, for the goods are intended to be removed and replaced. The vandals are consumers in a hurry, they are just cutting corners and going from the first to the last step of the cycle all at once: devastation. Our world may be materialist but it has a strange way of denying that, since it impels us to demolish what belongs to us, to intoxicate ourselves with demolition as much as with the acquisition of objects. The only thing that really lasts is waste, which seem to be promised a grotesque kind of eternity: they say that the life expectancy of a baby's diaper is about 72 years, and they've opened a trash museum in San Jose, California!

Disappearance is euphoric because it announces the dawn of a revival. What is so extraordinary, in fact, is that things die only to reappear. Their disintegration is technically calculated, their durability would afflict us — it would deprive us of the insane pleasure of a world that changes so that we need not change ourselves. Consumption is a degraded religion, *the belief in the infinite resurrection of things, wherein the supermarket is the Church and advertising is the Gospels.* Everything becomes obsolete except obsolescence, which never ends. And indeed, fashion serves to parody modernity: a break with the past, and innovation. But the break is soft and the innovation tiny: it is practically the same thing that keeps coming back under different masks. We need something new that resembles the old, and astonishes us without actually being a surprise. And innovation is going on principally at the level of accessories, of minor modifications (the variety of which is sometimes paradoxically an obstacle to purchasing). This agitation ends up being equivalent to a quasi-immobility; the faster the rate at which these styles and gadgets replace each other, the more static the ensemble appears. We are basing a pretence of perenniality on perishability; and this superficial tumult serves to weave a seamless continuity, to clog every hole in our history, to sew together the disparate pieces of time, to distract us so that we don't feel disoriented.

There is one crowning moment in this cycle: when the celebrated object appears, every week, every day on television and in the papers. A new quartz watch that is so waterproof it can withstand a run through the wash, new musical slippers for baby, new speakers that highlight certain sounds: again and again we celebrate surprise — simultaneously with déja-vu. When the object appears, and that is its day of glory, its state of grace, a holy moment full of promise, and it gleams gloriously before fading. This is where the techno-scientific genius of our society finds its calling. Hour after hour, the god Innovation adds curios to the immense bazaar of existing things, odds and ends of limited originality in general but with the addition of a detail that is supposed to make all the difference. It is a never-ending process that consists in blending the novel with the known, an inexhaustible providence casts up a profusion of images in catalogues, those miniature storefronts that so amuse us and reassure us. The festival of progress never stops, it saves us from the double dead end of anguish — there is no vacuum — and saturation: desire is always reinvigorated again.

The crowd goes to the shops, stuffed to the gills with packages and gifts, to dress itself, feed itself, furnish itself, and warm itself, and it goes there to taste happiness, to assuage its concern. This world that, in its eccentricity, sometimes attains a kind of paradoxical beauty, does not ask us any question, it only brings answers and reaches out to us with full hands. These hubs of rapture, the malls, the megamarts of suburbia, testify to a duration that goes beyond ordinary life and suggests a perpetuity of resources, an inexhaustible fountain of provisions and benefits (the largest shopping center in the United States is in Minneapolis, and covers the equivalent of 88 soccer fields).[5] And if many people are depressed on Sundays, it is because so many stores are closed that day, at least in certain states and most of Europe, and activity is suspended. With the curtain down, we find ourselves left to our own devices, to our "feeling of insufficiency,"[6] wandering about the deserted streets, bored. And while respecting the Sabbath may divert our minds from material things, as Tocqueville thought, perhaps it also stokes our appetites and makes the rest of the week more delectable, since then we can spend and buy at our leisure.

SUBLIME STUPIDITIIES

In a small principality with a pleasant climate, E. T. Hoffmann tells us, lived many fairies who worked "the pleasantest wonders" in the villages and the forests. One day the new sovereign decides to institute the Enlightenment, and orders the people to "cut down the forests, make the river navigable, cultivate potatoes, have roadways built and get everyone vaccinated against variola." To go along with these measures, his Prime Minister advises him to remove from the State "all people" who "turn a deaf ear to the voice of reason," and in particular the fairies, "enemies of the Enlightenment" who propagate "under the name of poetry" a secret venom that makes people unsuitable for implementing inapt service of the reforms. The police attack the fairy palace, haul them all to prison, confiscate their winged horses and transform them into useful animals by cutting off their wings. But the fairies, of course, continue to haunt the principality and to offer their charm and their imagination in opposition to the heavy state administration.[6]

If only Hoffmann had lived to see our world! He would have seen what seemed to him inconceivable in his own era: the reconciliation of the quantifiable with the marvelous, of the Enlightenment with the Age of Romanticism. This is a far cry from the spirit of rational computation that, according to Max Weber, was the original basis of the capitalism ethos: commercial production put to the service of a universal fairyhood, consumerism culminating in the *animism of objects*. Opulence and its corollaries (leisure and entertainment) place a kind of cheap enchantment within everyone's reach. The products exhibited for sale in our commercial temples, according an erudite art of presentation where everything is calibrated to the millimeter, are not inert: they are alive, they breathe and, like spirits, they have a heart and a name. Advertising gives them a personality through a brand name, and confers upon them the *gift of tongues*, transforming them into talkative, insipid or merry little people who generally promise a great happiness. No item is too banal — from a whisk-broom to a paper towel or an electrical gadget — to make us laugh, cry, or groan; it transfigures everything that comes into contact with it. It is no surprise that on both TV and radio, advertising spots strike like a trumpet blast, the volume goes up, and the tone goes from serious to euphoric; it's no surprise that from morning to night every media channel is flooded with factitious courtesies. All these splendors that they want to sell us are presented like so many little servants, ready to help us, to relieve us from effort, to reduce our concern. Mr. Clean, like the legendary *djinn*, comes out of his bottle and cleans the household from top to bottom; *Belin's* Chipsters beg us to crunch them; *Elle et Vire* butter challenges us — "to keep me fresh, put me back in the refrigerator immediately after use;" and *Sansonette*, a deodorant, makes your garbage chute sigh with pleasure, while your electric furnace whines and begs you to clean it with *Décapfour*, and a whole chorus of men and women of all ages, with a roll of *Clover* toilet paper in hand, sings of the pleasures of a world scented with vanilla, with lavender, with menthol.

In the 16th and 17th centuries, historians tell us, everyone was convinced that calamities, deaths and especially diseases were the work of occult powers that acted on the elements, conferring health or infirmity — in short, that the world was not so much magical as possessed. Conduct was regulated by the certainty "that nature does not obey laws, that everything in it is animate, liable to unexpected volitions and especially to worrisome manipulation by men and women who had ties with the mysterious beings that govern the sublunary space and consequently are able to cause madness, disease and storms."[7] We have by no means left behind this "pre-logical" thought that governs our relation to everyday objects. Sometimes people are surprised, when traveling in Asia, to see truck drivers giving flowers to their vehicle, or addressing them with the signs of deference and respect that we usually reserve for a divinity. Treating a machine as a sort of extension of oneself or ascribing to it "a beneficent or malevolent emanation," as the Indian psychoanalyst Sudhir Kakar says,[8] is not specific to people of the Orient; we too give the least carbonated beverage or piece of candy a voice and a life. All the tools that surround us are fetishes, objects equipped with forces that we have to know how to control. While the user remains passive and has only to let things take their course, the product is active, convivial, cordial: the "smart" house, the intuitive telephone, talking watches, cars that say "seat belt" when we forget to use one, appliances that start up when we clap our hands, voice-activated alarm clocks — these objects are nothing more or less than friends to us. "Eat me," "drink me," "rent me," they whisper; they order us to consume them with the impatience of a partner who has abandoned all self-restraint. They are at our disposal, they ardently desire us. Acquiring is a means of improving our existence, of acting upon the world. All these products that do good while doing us good are actually more alive than we are. While Galileo saw the language of nature as having been written in mathematical form, the language of consumption is written in magic spells: it builds itself through wild syncretism, and welcomes into its pantheon the residues of myths, legends, religions and ideologies, which it arranges to suit itself. Our entire technological universe is haunted by the occult, by insane or fabulous causalities. Advertising is also a smiling form of sorcery. It constantly shows things conspiring for our satisfaction and elevates each of us to the rank of a monarch who deserves perfect service. "Nobody takes care such good care of me," as the Calor epilator says. And that is why the woman and the baby are two of the most frequently used advertising images: our appetite for purchasing is copied on insatiable Eros, and the invitation to happiness is embodied in ecstatic babes-in-arms. A BMW ad shows the most inseparable pair, admirably joined together: an infant trying to grasp a beautiful inflated bosom with this caption: Remember your first airbag.

THE ASCETICISM OF LEISURE

In earlier times, a loafer would aim to distance himself from the petty universe of work and material enrichment. His ostentatious inaction was a very aristocratic revolt against the regularity of days and the reduction of the human being to a paid worker. He wasn't so much denouncing bourgeois morals as dropping out from them, and he distinguished himself from the busy crowd by doing nothing. In our day, when labor and leisure start to look the same, we see a new human type appearing: the hyperactive loafer, always in overdrive, attacking the Babylon of entertainment. "Learning vacations," a dynamic *far niente*, applied hedonism, constant mobilization — this breaks with the traditional alternation of frenzy and monotony, festival and work. And just as work is likely to become the last refuge of the elite — the patrician's contempt of tasks reversing itself into an exaltation of work — it is possible that time off will soon be the curse of the poor, the destiny of the plebes condemned to cakes and games.

There is a rigor and almost an asceticism in our all-consuming quest for every occasion to have fun, a false indolence that reconciles two antagonistic morals: that of absolute uselessness and that of stress. These days, having fun is a duty: not only an intermission that breaks up the painfulness of work but potentially the only reference points in time that model the rhythm of our existences (and fun has its own tribes, rites, newspapers and even metropolises).[9] Pascal gently scoffed at the nobles who were anxious to escape from themselves and threw themselves into hunting, war, the pleasures, for "a king without entertainment is a man full of misery," (*Pensées*, Brunschvicg edition, 142). Nowadays we all have access to the royal dignity of boredom; as it was for the princes of yesteryear, absolute repose is a torment to us. What better evidence than the retirees who continue to get up at 6:00 or 7:00 in the morning, adhering to the wake-up time inculcated by a life of office or factory work. Leisure is not idleness and even less is it that "essential peace at the profound depths of our beings" exalted by Valéry; it makes it impossible to do nothing. Everywhere haste, speed, and alarm in the service of the greatest futilities: on TV, the tyranny of the schedule (governed by advertising requirements) gives the program sequence an air of absolute emergency. Ludic behavior and silliness meet with the ethics of forcing.

Existence, said St. Augustine, is a combat between the essential and "a rush of frivolous thoughts." We have reversed this proposition twice: we toss out the essential in the name of the insignificant, and we take the insignificant very seriously indeed. Even in his moments of relaxation, modern man remains "a worker without work" (Hannah Arendt), and forms a paradoxical hybrid: an anxious idler, a Stakhanovite sensualist, an overwhelmed epicurean. Modern leisure? It's the art of doing nothing, disguised as overwork.

EVERYTHING, AND RIGHT AWAY!

Clearly, this consumerist logic is above all an infantile logic which, in addition to lending vitality to things, appears in four forms: the urgency of pleasure, habituation to gifts, the dream of absolute power, and a thirst for amusement.[10] The first of these culminates in the invention of credit which has, as we know, upset our relations with time and short-circuited our sense of duration. It allows us to borrow from the future, which becomes our new partner; it is a gracefully anticipated pleasure in the desired object. Saving, says Daniel Bell, was the dominant characteristic of the original capitalism; with the advent of credit, the puritan morality has been replaced with a militant hedonism where the incentive to have things, without down time or delay, has become legitimate and even recommended. As in the famous tale, credit acts to remove all interval between a wish being stated and being fulfilled: what matters is not what I can have but what I want to have, "Where you want it, when you want it," as one French bank's ATMs proclaim.

By abolishing everything in life that has to do with waiting, maturation, and restraint, credit has made the generations of the latter half of the 20th century terribly impatient. The extraordinary carefree feeling that was released retrospectively for us in the 1960's and 1970's comes from crossing the dream of liberation with the advertising dream: the liberation of all impulses plus the profusion of goods. A whole age group was accustomed to see its least imaginations appeased without delay, the pleasure principle triumphed over a world that not only yields to our every whim but strives by every means to multiply them. We are no longer oriented toward economizing, calculating, and doing without, like our fathers, but to take and to demand. What is a customer? In the world of services, he is analogous with the pampered child in his family, a little king who proclaims: I want and I demand. Everything has to be accessible immediately. As in Lewis Carroll's tale where a character shouts before being pricked with a needle and heals before he has bled, we reap before we have sown. Credit takes away the pain of having to pay in order to get something; and the smart card, by liquidating the materiality of money, gives the illusion of exemption from payment. The pains of accounting are over: our gluttony is not spoiled by any inopportune disbursement. Mortgaging the future is nothing compared to the irresistible joy of immediately having what one covets. The effective payment — and it does come one day, and even cruelly, in the form of repossessions, penalties, the bailiff, and frozen accounts — is deferred to that formless and faceless distance that is called tomorrow and which the passion of the moment completely effaces. We enter into Faustian mini-pacts with our banks, where we are entreated as by Mephistopheles: sign here, and everything is yours!

HAPPINESS IS A GOOD INHERITANCE

The revolution of well-being gives us the delightful ambiance of Christmas every day. We find a small child's joy at the foot of the tree when Santa has come: gifts and goods proliferate around us, given by a hand that is benevolent and invisible. (And the Christmas festivities themselves result in buying sprees, a unique commercial licentiousness each year to which everyone succumbs.) But the offerings granted by our societies come to us impersonally, and this anonymous gift spares us any humiliating need to thank anyone. The established order exudes devotion and generosity from all its pores and it exaggerates its kindness to the point of exempting us from feeling that we are in debt with respect to it.

In this respect the work that we do is completely out of proportion with the goods that we receive in exchange. Progress does indeed mean a chronological injustice, as Herzen said, "since the last-come benefit from being able to take advantage of the labor achieved by their predecessors."[11] Our current prosperity in the West is built on the sacrifice of former generations that could not enjoy the same standard of living nor an equal stage of technical improvements. In terms of what each of us finds at birth: extensive infrastructures, urban transportation networks, modern hospital complexes — not to mention the redistributions of all kinds that the Welfare State has given — we are the spoiled children of history, and all we have to do to earn this is to come into this world. We are not so much founders as recipients, who got their start with an enormous inheritance. Even for the poorest, if we compare our situation with that of the previous centuries (or the countries of the southern hemisphere), there is no relation between what we produce by our labor and what we receive in the form of public gratifications, care, education, transport, leisure pursuits. (We are speaking only historically or geographically, here; the comparison doesn't work socially: the have-nots of the developed countries take no comfort in knowing that a peasant in the Sahara is poorer than they, or that their fate is overall preferable to that of men of the 17th century. They can only be compared to the happy and the elite of their own society.) The great achievements of modernity (higher productivity of labor, reduction of infant mortality, extended life expectancy, diminished physical effort) are now regarded not as extraordinary prophecies but as attainments. "An American schoolboy," said Henry Ford, "is surrounded by a greater number of useful objects than you'll find in an entire Eskimo village. A list of our kitchen utensils, dishes, and furniture would have astounded the most luxurious potentate of 500 years ago!"[12]

And the funny thing is that what our society honors through its generosity and its munificence is the simple fact that we exist. As in the television game shows where you always win a prize even if you lose the game, we live in a universe of constant reward without reciprocity. Not only are all the exchanges in the commercial galaxy accompanied by gifts, discounts, and concessions, but we are also constantly congratulated, thanked for having had kindness to be born. Our appearance on earth is a wonder that justifies the mobilization of an army of inventors, engineers leaning over us in the cradle and cajoling us as future customers. "Rhône-Poulenc welcomes you to a better world." A logical consequence: we should be paid for living, existence should be remunerated. (In the 1960's, Marcuse demanded a stipend, a prerequisite, according to him, to the integral self-determination of human beings.) The notion is being studied and in France it has already been proposed that the State should provide everyone with a kind of minimal allowance — which would complete our transformation into perpetual welfare clients.

INSATIABLE DEMAND

What is technical progress itself, as a will to dominate nature, but the realization of our childhood fantasies when — in reaction to our being so dependent and fragile, we dreamed of being omnipotent? (A television reporter questioned a bunch of little boys and girls after a screening of the movie, *Honey, I Grew the Baby*[13], in which an absent-minded scientist has an accident in the laboratory and sees his two-year-old son grow enormous and sow terror in the neighborhood; the kids acknowledged that they wanted to grow like that so that they could correct their teachers, beat up their pals and [for some] even kill all the authority figures, parents and teachers. The contrast was striking between the candor of the faces and the horror of the remarks. The innocence of children, as St. Augustine said, lies in the weakness of their members, not in their intentions.) What's great about technology is that it makes it possible to escape the constraints of space and time, to enjoy an illusion of quasi-ubiquity. From the airplane that, with a buzz of propellers or turbines, transports us to other skies and makes the traveler a weightlessness particle above the globe, to driving a car, which puts us in control of a speeding pile of metal, technology extends our limited capacities and underscores the gulf that separates a man's real strength from the dizzying possibilities that his tools give him.

It invests us with absolute sovereignty, the epitome of which is those chiefs of state who can cause a nuclear apocalypse with a flick of their fingers. A gesture alone can ignite a general flashover, releasing fantastic energies. In the same way the *vade mecum* of the new planetary nomad, the cell phone, notebook computer, and fax, makes it possible to contract the earth like a shrunken head and to call anybody, anywhere, any time. We use these apparatuses, which are themselves miniaturized and that may soon be reduced to tiny receptors inserted in the body, to miniaturize the globe, which we reduce at will to the size of a little toy. Reality seems like clay to be modeled as we like. The triumph of the micro: by reducing everything, it elevates us to the size of a Titan.

You would think it was a fairytale, Freud exclaimed, talking about the invention of eyeglasses, the telescope, the camera, and the gramophone.[14] For, these inventions give everyone powers that used to be ascribed only to magicians or wizards. All the delusions of grandeur, of being able to act upon the world remotely, of overcoming gravity, and of experiencing the all-powerfulness of thought, can be satisfied by pressing a button, by crossing a photocell. Even doors open automatically before us, as though our consciousness controlled objects. What does the consumer see as progress? A higher form of magic. These fabulous prostheses that we have are not only beautiful and ingenious; their sophistication is such that we do not understand how they operation and have no choice but to have faith in them. Taking a plane, a car, a drug, means believing in their solidity, their effectiveness, their reliability. If credit had not been granted to all these auxiliaries and consolidated by usage, we would never have dared to adopt them. Technology is thus an act of faith. For the layman, a television set or a transistor is no less mysterious than the pronouncements of a fortune-teller (the computer and electronics industries are rife with cabalistic jargon, in any case, to explain the unexplainable). The complexity of the mental operations that it takes to manufacture a simple computer chip renders these instruments impenetrable to their users. That explains why we relate to them in rage, in worship, or as a game, why we pray to them, and why we scream at them and hit them when they have the nerve to break down. These little mechanical slaves throw us into a fury when they go wrong: we expect flawless devotion from them. We see any failure as an act of malice directed against us; it means that we are not Masters of the instruments we control. But we have a means of avenging ourselves for their failings, their stupid and stubborn secrets: replacement. Since the industrial object can be reproduced *en masse*, it may represent an obscure magical formula but it is not sacred (price is the only obstacle to acquisition). Its destiny is to pass out of fashion and to be changed. Technology fascinates us so much that it has come to seem banal. And we do not show any gratitude for the amazing progress being made in speed or in medicine. A train that is ten minutes late scandalizes us, a slow elevator or ATM makes us scream. As for science's inability to cure every disease, it shocks us beyond all: 'incurable' is the only obscene word in today's vocabulary. We no longer see the incredible improvements that have been made in the last century, we only see the deficiencies. The miracle of perpetual invention has become routine. Progress only stokes our fever: every day, in every field, we expect quick improvements. Technology keeps us in the religion of greed: with it, the possible becomes desirable, the desirable becomes necessary. The best is our due. Industry and science have accustomed us to such fruitfulness that we curse when we run short of lucky finds, when we have to postpone satisfaction. "It's unbearable," we exclaim, with the huge anger of capricious child who stamps his feet in front of a toy and screams: I want it![15]

LIFE IS A PARTY

"What can I do? I don't know what to do." This famous apostrophe of *Anna Karenina*, in Jean-Luc Godard's *Pierrot the Mad*, testified to a France that was bored under de Gaulle and that would awake with a start in May 1968. The 20th century invented two major figures of mobilization: professional revolutionaries and professional organizers. The first category doesn't move crowds easily anymore, since its promise of justice turned into a nightmare; but the second seems to have endless potential. From planners of insurrections to organizes of entertainment: the history of the century lies in the continuum between these two poles. The democratic fable suggests that when the poor grow rich and form a middle class, they don't devote their time off to politics or to culture but above all to entertainment. The French Republic assigned itself noble objectives: to free the people from the vice of need and to elevate it to the dignity of a political subject through good citizenship and education. Relief from misery and coarseness was supposed to coincide with the each person's regaining his full humanity. This hope was not borne out: for most people, the delicious dumbing-down of leisure activities takes precedence over the many forms of commitment and personal fulfillment that are available. And in this regard, we probably haven't seen anything yet. People used to look for rest from exhausting labor; now they want to escape the annoyance of free time with which they don't know what to do. How should we handle the problems in the slums, for example? The immediate worry is to keep the young people busy by any means possible to divert them from violence and self-destruction. The agitated, worried masses have to be kept busy, their empty hours filled, to drive out the monotony. And since in a few decades we may have as many workers as we have unemployeds today (since the economy keeps on producing more with fewer producers), it seems likely that the unlimited expansion of leisure activities will be the only means of maintaining a certain social cohesion.

Modern man has at least two ways of escaping the weight of the daily grind: war and entertainment. War is a dreadful butchery but it can also become recreation, distracting people from the routine, a setting aside of marital and family dullness, a great vacation from order and legality. It exalts as much as it frightens, promises ongoing excitation and a certain form of impunity since it authorizes one to kill. But for we other Westerners who no longer believe in sacrifice and who do not hold anything higher than life, the military career attracts only a few hard-heads, and the price of a conflict seems too expensive for an altogether tiny surprise (even our soldiers are no longer willing to die under fire and the Pentagon has adopted the zero-dead option in combat). Our civic ideal is no longer that recommended by young Hegel, of the soldier who works and the worker who makes war. Bellicose passions have been diverted into a taste for comfort and rather than the gruesome atrocity of battles, we prefer the combination of comfort and recreation. And how dizzying is the range of pastimes that our societies offer to their members!

Take the TV: could there be any more fabulous tool for re-enchanting the world? We may all still be virgins when it comes to television, it may be that its relative novelty as a technology explains our inadequate or misguided use of it. And we might yet dream of television being used as a tool for mental development and combining its immense power of attraction with a genuine pedagogical purpose. Still, today, with rare and remarkable exceptions, television is primarily in the business of entertainment. And it is unbeatable. Given that it's available 24 hours a day, refracts its message across a spectrum of channels, in every language, and presents fiction series, sports, movies, documentaries, floor shows, games, and shopping advice, it has become the entertainment medium *par excellence*. Soon, thanks to digital compression and the "information highways," we will soon be able to receive 500 channels at home, and watching the box will become a full-time job. And future generations will have to ask computers to help them find their way through this maze. Television requires of the witness only one act of courage — but one that is superhuman — that is, to turn it off. Anyone who has not experienced the atrocious, the irresistible temptation to spend the whole night frantically surfing from one channel to another, without being able to tear himself away from the ribbon of images, does not understand how strong is the magic in this little window. There is always something more interesting going on at the station than in our life. Television's hypnotic power lies in the fact that it roasts us with its light like butterflies around a lamp: it produces continuous jets of flowing colors and impressions that we suck down with a never-ending thirst. Television is an animated piece of furniture and it speaks, it serves the function of making dullness bearable. It does not extract us from the overwhelming pressures, or from habit, but makes them pleasantly tepid; TV is the continuation of apathy by other means, and as a fundamental element it blends into the immense panoply of banality.

A SEDATIVE FOR THE EYES

Aside from the utopias and the terrors that it evokes, what is so compelling about television is that it is the simplest way to fulfill and appease our thirst for adventure and easy derivatives. Combining maximum escape with a minimum of constraints, this medium has the immense virtue of being practically a way of life. It keeps us home, exerts boundless ingenuity to catch our attention, invites the whole world into our living room: since the universe comes to us, why bother going out to meet it? While going to a movie still means displacement, waiting, and being restricted by fixed time schedules and the need to keep quiet, sitting with strangers in a room — in short a whole ritual, I can catch the television whenever I want, without moving, at home; I can watch it lying on the sofa, sprawled on the floor, standing up, while eating, working, chatting, or drowsing. The Americans invented the term "couch potato" to denote this new mutant lounging on its sofa and devouring chips, a big baby stuffing its eyes and its mouth. The junior version of the couch potato is the child glued to the screen, put into orbit by the video games that have become a kind of electronic of babysitter, the child himself absent and virtualized; his final achievement will be to disappear in turn into the images and become a character in the game. The screen is a "permanent promise of fun"[16] that supplants everything else. It neither prohibits nor limits anything but renders everything else useless, tedious. It doesn't control thought, nor reading; it just makes them superfluous.

One of TV's charms is that you can pay attention to it intermittently: you can leave it on while doing something else, and many an apartment has a TV running day and night without anyone paying attention to it at all. In extreme cases, it becomes the god of the household, an everyday companion. Kant said that school is mainly the place where we learn to remain seated; television keeps us home but without making any demands, and tends to dilute us progressively with its images. And for those very many people whose live revolve around that little planet, who have re-organized their day around the TV schedule, it may be a tyrannical mistress but it is also a very accommodating one, who requires only the most nonchalant, the most relaxed worship from her admirers. The mind sails from one subject to another, attracted by a thousand events that it picks up without retaining, the eye is caught by some nothing, until another nothing distracts it; a delicious circular surfing that transforms us into vagrants, into fleas hopping from one channel to another. That is the spontaneous pathology of television: we watch it because it is there and it is on, and it has a power of leveling that ends up making us willing, once we are hooked, to watch just about anything with an unbounded indulgence.

Television distracts us from everything, including itself. Far from founding the dictatorship of the image, it impoverishes our perception, and we lose our ability to look at the world. Because it means to be immediately accessible to everyone, that kind of visual is dedicated to the extenuation of vision (whereas a pictorial work, as J.-F. Lyotard says, tells the person who contemplates it: "You will not soon understand me.")[17] Its form devours its contents, liquefies its contrasts, and makes all the movies, shows and advertising equal; it's often hard to tell an advertisement apart from the sit-com or series that it interrupts (Nestlés launched an advertising soap opera in America and Great Britain that was an enormous success). All this leads to a feeling of nausea that we experience after several hours of uninterrupted listening, the head stuffed with stupidities, nonsensical intrigues, and disparate impressions; as from a concussion, it takes time to recover from this slow hemorrhaging of oneself through one's eyes. You thought you were opening up to the vastness of the universe, but you wash up, stupefied, in a vacuum. And full-time TV is the lot of very young children or retirees and convalescents. Their watching only increases with age, that is, with sedentariness and the progressive loss of autonomy. Having begun as noise and drama, television ends up as herbal tea for the eyes, a sedative for boarders in old people's homes, a fetish for those sectors of humanity that are dying out slowly (and there cannot be good television 24 hours a day, since quality always occurs within a context of imperfection; therefore television broadcasting that lives up to its potential is, as all parents of schoolchildren know, a rarity).

Addiction to music programs now plays the role of lady's companion in the West, drowning out any possibility of silence in urban spaces. Music while you're on hold on the telephone and background music on the answering machine, music in parking lots, elevators, the subway and even the cable cars, music in local parks, and on the street during festivals, "muzak" in the supermarket, chatty videos that add further to the hubbub of shops and restaurants, re-mixes that render innocuous and inane the most sublime airs, everywhere we go a wall-to-wall carpet of music dulls the hard edges of the world, smoothes transitions, softens contacts. Saturating the space with noises, images, and colors (not to mention the imminent advent of telebracelets and pocket TVs that will enable us to never be alone with ourselves), assures us that we have not been abandoned, that they are thinking of us; this sound syrup is a sign of interest and almost of affection. This is not Big Brother any more, it's Big Mother. It adds up to an unbearable din, to be sure; but as in those ceremonies where demons are driven out by shouting, this continuous noise is supposed to obviate our melancholy, to dissipate our bleakness, to break our isolation.

UNIVERSAL CONSOLATION

Whatever else we make of it, we have to admit that consumerism and the entertainment industry represent an extraordinary collective creation unlike anything else in history. For the first time, men have erased the barriers of class, race, and gender to blend into a foolish crowd endlessly looking for fun, looking for surprises. It is easy to see why the stores full of treasures (that are as extraordinary as they are vain), the myriad media networks, and the intelligent machines that assist us, exert such an attraction on the other people of the planet. In these cathedrals of *la vita allegra*, the human being is distracted from the nightmare of history (and his own history), forgets the storms outside, and finds an essential simplicity. The universe of competition and uncertainty in which we are immersed would be intolerable if it were not moderated by this life jacket, these little islands of bliss that protect us from fear and hostility. Shopping, entertainment, mental vagrancy in virtual space dim everything with a shadow that may be stultifying but is so soft, so pleasant that we mistake it for the brightest of lights.

"I shop, therefore I am," such is the cogito of the consumer, always ready to retreat to that "hedonistic trap" to drive away the blues or world-weariness, the "mal de l'être."[18] In cruising the shopping centers, submerging oneself in the soft radiation of these paradise-like caverns, allowing oneself to be soothed by the soft voices and the intoxicating goods, we enroll ourselves among the present but absent, we relieve ourselves of ourselves, we enjoy the happiness of being undifferentiated. Then I become a being without specific qualities, open to every suggestion, "an industrially-produced personality" (David Riesman), a patchwork of disparate influences.

There are two misconceptions that obscure our interpretation of commercial societies: one that denounces them as a new Inquisition that approaches totalitarian hell, and another that glorifies them as an infallible means of educating people in freedom and good citizenship. This double, symmetrical misunderstanding ascribes to the system the worst defects or the noblest virtues.

The first, critical, view, now a minority viewpoint, survives in a routine anti-Americanism,[19] while the second school (which dominated the 1990's) still has many partisans. For the latter, consumerism admirably exploits the crudest and simplest side of mankind to put it to the service of the highest goals. The buyer's fantastic freedom of choice supposedly encourages each of us to take ourselves in hand, to be responsible, to diversify our conduct and our tastes and most important, supposedly protects us forever from fanaticism and from being taken in. In other words, four centuries of emancipation from dogmas, gods and tyrants has led to nothing more nor less than to the marvelous possibility of choosing between several brands of dish detergent, TV channels or styles of jeans. Pushing our cart down the aisle in a supermarket or frantically wielding our remote control, these are supposed to be ways of unconsciously working for harmony and democracy. One could hardly come up with a more masterful misinterpretation: for we consume in order to stop being individuals and citizens, rather, to escape for a moment from the heavy burden of having to make fundamental choices. Contrary to the person who forges his own life, making decisions that commit him and accepting the consequences that cannot fully be foreseen, the consumer only decides between already existing products, options that have already been formulated by others and that he is satisfied to combine or cross in new ways, at most.

Abundance to what end? asked David Riesman. To drive away concern, to personalize ourselves at little expense by pledging our allegiance to standard mass-produced items that clothe, feed, and amuse a million people along with us. "I'm more myself, wearing Duvernois," says an ad. What a delicious relief: being oneself requires nothing more than putting on a jacket, a shirt, a suit that everyone can also get. I am invited to the great festival of spending money only insofar as I resemble all the others, only insofar as my quest for authenticity coincides with the commercial requirements of such and such company.

But this herd mentality is happy and voluntary: there is a real pleasure in conformity, a pleasure in being one of a crowd, in joining the mass of others. Wound up into a ball in his society of birth, Western man dons a carapace that protects him from his own inventions. This is why consumerism does not have a civilizing effect; its only virtue (immense as it may be) is that it relaxes us, it's a remedy for stress and loneliness. How pleasant it is to allow ourselves to be led by the nose, to be the puppet of marketing strategies, how restful is this abandonment, what happiness this passivity brings! Without these niches of pleasure, we would have no way to recover from the violence, the vexations, the wearing effort of contemporary life. Consumption is consolation, a truce in the competition, a bandage for the wounds inflicted by the world. At least in these radiant moments, I do not have to answer any more for myself, to prove that I exist; I have gotten out of the "ontological insecurity" (Eugen Drewermann) which is the fate of the individual in the West.

THE ROUTINE AS A ROUTE TO RE-ENCHANTMENT

Of course, abundance and entertainment don't really give us a sense of fulfillment: they liven up the banality without actually freeing us from it. You can listen ad infinitum to the chatty little gods of advertising that suffuse our daily life, you can fill your ears with the breathless messages from the media, surf all the Internet and television networks in the world, and in the end all this profusion only seems to add up to more junk, more primitive garbage. This re-enchantment is a parody, this romanticism reeks of the kitsch and the fake. Consumerism can only be disappointing, in the end, since it invites us to expect everything from a purchase or a spectacle, excluding any internal experience, any personal growth or lasting relationship with others, which are the only generators of real joy. The person whose wish has been granted always wants something different from what he got, because what he really wants, no one can give him. Imagine a being living under

the exclusive influence of advertising, television, and video apparatuses, whose brain, whose life would be imbued with thousands
of images and anecdotes from current events (like the "Otakus" of
Japan, photographed and filmed by Jean-Jacques Beineix: young
people who communicate only by computers, screens, and comic
strips, forsaking any other way of relating to others). He would
be retired from both spiritual life and powerful passions, he would
be protected from the élan of a more intense existence. He would
be a sponge soaked in a perpetual present, dripping with the slogans, sound bites, and anecdotes swallowed from evening to
morning. He would be "poor in the world," to use Heidegger's
expression, from living day to day in a stultifying effort to avoid
building himself. However, even in the grip of this stupor, of this
vegetative state, such a being would still remain capable of
change, of improvement.

*Television's real crime, like that of advertising, is that it never succeeds
in completely transforming us into zombies!* Even the compulsive viewer,
the profoundest fool can still tell the difference between his TV
set and the external world. There is always life after the supermarket and television, and that is the drama. It's not its weakness
or superficiality that we hold against consumerism, but its inability to keep its promises, to take care of us completely. And the
omnipresent smile in our society is not friendship or sympathy: it
is a tonic, a medicine stuck on people's faces to ward off depression. We always need to be comforted, to be reassured. The
manic-depressive structure may be the true structure of Western
man, engaged in a thousand endeavors the vanity of which he is
always afraid he will perceive too brutally: phases of enthusiasm
followed of phases of melancholy. The medical-commercial gim-

mickry only outlines a holy mirage: it cannot form the basis of that which remains the prerogative of religions, the space for transcendence. In spite of its commitment to redeem us all collectively and personally, it is never enough and we need other crutches, other, stronger, opiates: tranquillizers, psychotropics, mood enhancers that erase our discomfort and our suffering — that play the part of social worker. Once we get what we want, we want that which no object can give us: secular salvation, transformation; and we waver between the overwhelming pressure to have too much and the fear that we are missing the essential.

But it doesn't matter that the idea that happiness can be bought and that it lies in appeasing tensions is false and generates disappointment; we keep going back to it as to the easiest approach. Do we get tired of the ineptitude of the audio-visual shows, tired of the hype, the trash? Perhaps. But it is only a short respite before we start a new race toward other acquisitions, other opportunities to have fun. The survivors of abundance suffer from never being completely redeemed by their purchases but they keep going back, unable to disengage themselves. And it is enough for the risk of poverty or scarcity to re-surface in Europe to find an insane appeal in the glittering shop windows and luxury boutiques. This is why "disillusions of progress" (Raymond Aron) are purely romantic and never inspired anybody to turn off the television, or to stay away from the supermarkets. And that is why we don't revolt so much against the society as against the misfortune of not being able to take full advantage of it, and why its benefits still remain out of reach for too many people. Consumerism is undoubtedly "a miserable miracle" (Henri Michaux) that turns us into brutes, and dispossesses us of ourselves; we dive into it like a fountain of youth, we are willing and fascinated prey to the commercial fairyland. Thus our paradoxical relationship with it: we neither fully subscribe nor reject, but waver in the impossibility of giving up anything — neither our criticism of this world nor the advantages that it provides. Thus our oscillation between denigrating and praising modernity, and the impossibility of finding one's place between those who despise it and those who adore it.

CONSUMERS ARE NOT THE SAME AS CITIZENS

But can it be said that the "media maniacs" fed on sound bites and ads have evolved into demanding and critical purchasers, that consumer movements, demanding quality and honesty in addition to opulence, have pushed consumerist intoxication into adulthood? That's the truth, and we can't congratulate ourselves enough on this objective progress in the defense of our rights. But it still remains true that an educated consumer is not the same as a citizen, and that finding discounts, getting bargains, and evading the traps of the fine print may be very convenient but by no means do they teach us to step back and look at our society objectively. Like entertainment, consumption educates us only as to itself; its moral value, its teaching value is scant. In the same way mass culture entertains us but it does not emancipate us, even if it echoes or condenses great works of culture. And that is why commercial bliss is compatible with every form of political regime including dictatorships (from Saudi Arabia to Singapore). To be a user is to concern oneself solely with the defense of one's own interests, to remain tied to one's own specific background (even to form a lobby), whereas to be a citizen means trying to transcend one's own private interests, to abstract oneself from one's conditions to band with others in managing public life, to share with them as co-participants in power. Citizenship exists as soon as the individual agrees to suspend his private point of view to take into account the common good, to enter the public space where men speak to each other in equality and act in concert. Liberation from material need is only one of the conditions of freedom, it is not its synonym. And consumer defense magazines and associations share the tendency of ordinary newspapers and magazines to obsess us with objects, with their qualities and their defects, instead of freeing us from them. There has indeed been a revolution but it took place within the world of merchandise: the countervailing power of purchasers simply means that the rules of the game are better controlled, not hat we have ceased playing.

We are inhabitants of the supermarkets as much as of the city, and our attachment to democracy is above all an attachment to the immoderate advantages of prosperity. Consumption is not responsible for the political disaffection that pre-existed it and that has other causes, but it is an aggravating factor. In the developed countries, the democratic spirit is entirely subjugated to the market and worships only economic growth and rationality. For our governments, whether right or left, a good policy means maintaining abundance, and the citizens' freedom mostly means the freedom to grow rich (in a crisis, keeping up a high rate of consumption is almost a national duty, an elementary gesture of patriotism). We have only one definition of happiness, these days: personal well-being; and we've forgotten the French and American revolutionaries' passion and taste for what Hannah Arendt called "the public thing," the joy they took in emulating and competing in excellence for the development of political freedoms.[20]

We know that many immigrants already regard their origins in a poor nation as a form of discrimination and persecution; and their choice to emigrate to such and such country in Europe or to the United States is dictated less by the nature of the governments than by the range of social services and the advantages they are likely to receive there.

It is true that our democratic ideal results from irreconcilable requirements: the free realization of the individual and cooperation in the life of the city, success and solidarity. Montesquieu hoped that the Republic would be run according to the sole principle of virtue — and especially virtue as selflessness; but our regimes are not like that. For us, it's wealth and the triumph of the private life that accompany the expansion of political and social rights. And it is hard to see how a system that encourages abundance and personal fulfillment can at the same time develop the instincts of participation and fraternity. (How is the West getting Russia to go the way of democracy and pluralism? By buying it with dollars and loans. Lures, bait and bonuses become the conditions of the State of Law and parliamentarianism.) Honored guests at the banquet of history, we want to win across the board, we want to square the circle: complacent citizens, made drowsy by conveniences, and active, concerned citizens. According to Aristotle, in ancient Greece opulence was the precondition to citizenship — only a man without material concern could devote himself to the *polis* — whereas for us, ease seems acquired in exchange for good citizenship. Comfort remains the noblest invention of Western man and the fight for purchasing power is the last taboo; no one dares touch it. Even so, comfort, however imposing it is, tends to relegate all the other ideals to lower status and to narrow considerably the circle of our concerns. Claude Lefort made the point that we are supposed to be at the same time citizens, patriots, private persons and consumers, in short to serve several incompatible masters; but the current eclipse of the patriot and the citizen, at least in Western Europe, leaves the person and the consumer face to face, a confrontation where the latter usually wins. Our passions have stopped being republican or national, they are cultural, commercial or private. And civic disaffection is not the only effect of the spectacle or of the degradation of the public debate, it is grounded in law like the universal vote or social security. A government is democratic if it authorizes its citizens to not take an interest in the fate of the democracy. In other words, our societies are constantly put in the position of preferring well-being over freedom: as if we had too much to lose to defend our independence in the event of danger. Because we have never lived better on the material level, we have never been so loathe to die for a cause, however just it may be. It is time to recognize this — the democratic individual can talk all he wants in the language of the heart and of feeling; he still prefers himself above anything else. No ideal seems worth sacrificing ourselves, anymore; nothing is worth more than our life (even humanitarian action is devotion to other people's survival, not to their freedom).

CANNIBAL LOGIC

The major risk of consumerism is not waste so much as gluttony, the fact that it grabs everything that it touches and destroys it, reduces everything to its mercy. It is no longer discussed only in terms of pleasure but borrows the language of value, health, humanitarian concerns, and ecology to advance its pawns. Advertising has taken over politics, which now uses sound-bites and slogans; television claims to salve our broken hearts, to render justice, to supplement the police force, and to make school redundant. Consumerism itself long since escaped from the supermarket to become part of a media-commercial logic that is presented as a universal solution to every problem. It makes its fortune by suggesting to us that everything we found difficult yesterday will soon be accomplished in the blink of an eye, that "fun" can take the place of study — in short, it develops our taste for immediate and easy pleasures.

In short, it shows an unparalleled talent for taking over the sectors in crisis (culture, education, political representation), embracing them and finally distorting them, emptying them of their substance. It's the triumph of the chameleon society that can pick up every line of talk, including criticism of itself, and replacing all the ideologies because it believes in none, and replaying all the great political and religious passions as farce. Everything that is not it (history, ethics, rites, beliefs) it voraciously swallows up. It is a stomach that can digest anything. And it is in revolting against its contents that we obey it best. The supreme irony of consumerism is that it allows us to believe that it has gone away, while in fact there isn't a single domain left in which it does not rule.

Thus we have to rein in this commercial logic, limit it, protect those pockets of preserved space where it is still trying to consolidate its monopoly. But this system thrives on having its parapets weakened or breached. And the day when television takes take the place of the court, the classroom, and the couch, the day when college students read a commercial instead of Balzac or *Madame Bovary*, when Schubert will be nothing but the background sound for food commercials and Verdi will be nothing but the sound track for sanitary napkins, that will be the day when the helot will have triumphed and Western civilization will be finished. This is why the crisis today may also have positive effects, by exerting a moderating virtue on our intemperance, our frivolity; we must avoid this trap. "Where the danger is growing, there also grows the possibility of that which will save us" (Hölderlin).

THE PUERILE LAND OF PLENTY

Consumerism's wildest bet is in seeking "to turn man's greatest defects to the public advantage" (Mandeville), in trying to transform cupidity, voracity, and egoism into means of reinforcing civilization. Perhaps for the first time in history, a society has authorized its members to forget some of the constraints that it imposes on them in order to use that energy to build themselves. And the danger, of course, lies in taking as a model that which must remain an exception, to make leisure the real life, to make

---

PORTRAIT OF THE IDIOT AS A MILITANT

In the 18th century, people distinguished two forms of foolishness. The first had to do with prejudices, that is, with all that is inherited without examination; it was supposed to be the target of progressive thought (before that too, in turn, sank into a more opaque form of stupidity — that which has to do with idolizing History, Science and Technology). But the Enlightenment, as the continuation of a certain conservative form of Christianity, went along parallel to this and under cover of praising the natural state, praised the happy ignoramus who retained his morality and virtue by remaining humble. The lowly, the peasants, the poor have no need for instruction, which should be reserved to the enlightened classes.[21]

Some vestige of this apologia for the rudimentary found its way into the following century in the figure of the Idiot. In a positivist era devoted to knowledge, to schooling, to industry, he represents far more than a holdover or a failure of the intellect. He may not have the nimble mind of the learned ones but in his primitiveness he speaks in a language more original than that of reason, the language of the heart and even of the soul. The Idiot is a hero of authentic feeling against perverted civilization. Dostoyevsky would anoint this character by making Prince Muishkin an extraordinary being, almost an avatar of Christ returned to earth: an adult inhabited by the soul of a child. Epilepsy made him simpleminded, as if the disease were the intermediary of a celestial word.

For this ingénue fells the others with his acuity, he unleashes storms that make it both hateful and spellbinding. "Ah, prince! you testify to an ingenuity and an innocence that even the Golden Age did not know; and suddenly your profound psychological penetration slashes through a man like an arrow," one of the novel's protagonists tells him. Through him, a primordial, almost divine wisdom speaks, which makes a scandal, smashing to pieces the worldly agitations of the people. A romantic inversion of values: now it's not the powerful and the scholars who hold the truth, but the outcasts. The naive one, the half-wit join all the heroes of antimodernity: the child, the madman, the artist, the rebel, the savage, all those who still remain inhabited by something fundamental.

Our epoch no longer reveres study and instruction. Its idols are elsewhere and include everything that glitters, and corrupt politics, and fakery. Television, the most popular of our media, succeeds in pushing this to such an extreme, on some channels, that one can only watch openmouthed in amazement. While those who fear drivel, fatuous arrogance and mindlessness are still obsessed with stupidities, there is not much left of the shame that used to keep the dunce and the ignoramus quiet. On the contrary, in the media they reign supreme, lazy new kings who, far from blushing at not knowing, actually take pleasure in it. Worse yet: they are the spokesmen for a militant, aggressive stupidity that exudes hatred for everything that smacks of mental discipline. At the word "culture," they brandish the TV rating charts and make the public howl at all the snobs, the pedants, the kill-joys who fail to appreciate the great media/advertising Barnum and Bailey. Not content with ridiculing school and the university, they intend to take their places, and to prove by their own example that these temples of knowledge are no longer the route to success and money. Their obstinate stupidity will not suffer to see its empire disputed, nothing must resist their arrogant foolishness that deploys all the weapons of spinelessness, coarseness, and baseness. And their debility is irrefutable because it excludes any idea of distance and irony. The triumphal return of the illiterate to the boob-tube is carried out under the twin signs of pride and combat: this is no longer the mediocre mind, conscious of his inferiority, but a big mouth who barks and makes his detractors run for cover. If the aggressive imbecile comes to reign single-handedly in our society one day, then it will be the cultivated person who will be taken for an idiot, a strange specimen of a tribe on the verge of extinction that still reveres books, rigor and reflection.

the interchangeable, the transitory and the spectacular into absolute values. When he defined the Enlightenment as mankind's exit from the state of minority, could Kant have foreseen that the spiritual and moral adulthood would go hand-in-hand with a puerility so persistent that one can no longer think of the one without the other? For it is impossible to be master and leader of oneself full-time: there comes a time to pay down one's arms, to give oneself up to the little artificial Edens that help us to live. And in some respects we remain hopelessly pre-modern, unable to attain that wisdom that the 18th century praised as the loftiest goal of mankind. It is because it does not "civilize" us, does not entail any improvement of man, that material progress in some sense is essential to us. The state of childhood for everyone, at any moment and at will: such is modernity's response to the pains that it causes. This infantile-future is not an accident, a little slip in the over-riding dynamics that inclines everything to move toward measure and reason, it is embedded in the very heart of the system, it is consubstantial to the individual tempted by capitulation in proportion to how much he has to build himself. *The empire of consumerism and entertainment have added the right to regress to the general inventory of human rights*: an exquisite forfeiture, a delectable facility, undoubtedly. But beyond a certain degree, the antidote is liable to transform into poison, to degenerate into a new disease. How far can this divine levity go without doing away with our taste for reflection and reason? The triumph of the pleasure principle was the great Utopia of the Sixties and we still live in that dream. How can we limit or moderate the puerile phantasmagoria that proclaims, "Everything goes"?

Footnotes

1.   *Au bonheur des dames*, Garnier-Flammarion, 1971, chronology and preface by Colette Becker.
2.   Jean Fourastié, *Les Trente Glorieuses*, Pluriel, 1979.
3.   Quotes taken from an article by Tzvetan Todorov, *Lettre Internationale*, June 1990.
4.   According to Pascal Dupont, *La Bannière étiolée*, Seuil, 1993, p. 220.
5.   Karl Abraham, "Les Névroses du dimanche," in *OEuvres complètes*, Payot, 1989, Book II, pp. 70-71.
6.   "Le Petit Zacharie," a story that is cited and retold by Michael Lowy and Robert Sayre, *Révolte et Mélancolie*, Payot, 1992, pp. 48-49.
7.   Jean Delumeau, *La Peur en Occident*, Pluriel, Fayard, 1978, p. 86.
8.   Sudhir Kakar, *Enfance et société en Inde*, Les Belles Lettres, 1985, p. 86.
9.   Marc Fumaroli wrote a superb passage on the American Mecca of games and kitsch, "Las Vegas," in *L'Etat culturel*, Bernard de Fallois, 1991, pp. 214 sqq.
10. Georges Duhamel, in his book on America (*Scènes de la vie future*, 1930), Erich Fromm, Jean Fourastié, Edgar Morin and especially Jean Baudrillard have emphasized the close correlation between childhood and consumption. However, no one has systematized this intuition, or positioned it within a general history of the individual. The majority prefer to see the consumer society as a vast system of social distinction, a strategy for elevating people, if not a new, subtle but tenacious, order of repression.
11. Cited by Hannah Arendt, *Du mensonge à la violence*, Presses Pocket, p. 130.
12. Henry Ford, *My Life and My Work*, quoted by Peter Sloterdijk, *Critique de la raison cynique*, Christian Bourgois, 1987, p. 540.
13. Antenne 2, January 1993.
14. Sigmund Freud, *Malaise dans la civilisation*, PUF, 1971, pp. 38-39.
15. "Today so much has changed that it is astonishing that everything hasn't changed," Jean Fourastié wrote in *Les Trente Glorieuses* (*op. cit.*, p. 241). "Every new achievement very soon comes to be seen as natural, indispensable, and living without it seems unthinkable."
16. Neil Postman, *Se distraire à en mourir*, Flammarion, 1986, p. 161. Television transforms everything into spectacle even when it claims to be serious. It can become a formidable instrument for vulgarization unless appropriate guidelines are established. The best cultural programming serves as an appetizer, to paraphrase Pascal: it doesn't replace reading or watching a film, but better than any other medium it can awaken our interest (provided we have the strength to turn it off, some time, and read the book or get out to the cinema).
17. Jean-François Lyotard, *Que peindre?* La Différence, 1988, p. 110.
18. Dominique Roux, author of a study by the same title, tells us that in the United States, in 1987, people were spending an average of six hours a week cruising the malls, and one hour reading or gardening. Most of the purchases were acts of impulse buying intended to mitigate people's

loneliness and to fight boredom. Clearly, hedonism is a trap that has its therapeutic effects.

19. As a founder of mass culture and entertainment, the original paradise of modernity, America has become the focal point for part of our hatred of our civilization. Since George Duhamel's 1930 criticism of the "fake culture of America" (which, in his eyes, was worse "than the fascist and Soviet dictatorships") to the authors of the Frankfurt School and Guy Debord, not to mention Heidegger denouncing in Russia and America "the same sinister frenzy of unleashed technology and the rootless organization of standardized man" (*Introduction à la métaphysique*, Gallimard, pp. 48-49), Americanism has become synonymous with all the evils of our era. In our rejection of the New World, it is hard to disentangle that part that is due to objective political factors — the insolent success of this kid from Europe that has put its parent in the shade — and that which has more to do with an aversion for the present time whose every shortcoming America exemplifies. The vituperative diatribes against American society are a function of its immense seductive power over us. America has achieved the wonder of flooding the entire planet with its own images, and for that very reason remains largely unknown, all the more secret since it displays itself. America obviously is not the same as Americanism, even if, like all other cultures, she is threatened by this creation that emanates from her own territory.

20. Hannah Arendt, *Essai sur la Révolution*, Gallimard, p. 166 sq.

21. On this subject, see Philippe Sassier, *Du Bon usage des pauvres*, Fayard, 1990, pp. 139-140, wherein he analyzes this idea in particular with regard to Mandeville.

CHAPTER 3

TINY LITTLE GROWNUPS

"I have the right to answer all your complaints by an eternal me. I am separate from everyone and do not accept anybody's conditions. You must give in to all your fantasies and quite simply accept that I allow myself similar distractions." — Napoleon, to his wife.
(Nietzsche, *Le Gai Savoir*).

"It is only by using adequate personnel that we will be able to bring down the whole world into childhood."
W. Gombrowicz, Ferdydurke.

In the 17th century, if we take Victor Hugo's word for it, secret brotherhoods called the *comprachicos* were trading all over Europe in children for the use of kings, popes and sultans. They bought the little ones from their families, which were generally poor, and using a dreadful orthopedic science, locked them up in urns to stunt their growth, to deform them, to turn them into monsters, eunuchs or buffoons to amuse the crowd.[1]

Our era has repudiated this type of "villainous industry" and, at least in the democratic countries, has surrounded youth with a series of rights and protections. Still, one might wonder whether we don't promote some other, less overt, metamorphoses quite as amazing, whether we are not experiencing a mutation that affects our very definition of the human being. In other words, whether we are not all acting under the pressure of a constant invitation to immaturity, a way of infantilizing adults and imprisoning children in childhood, to prevent them from growing up.

THE GOOD SAVAGE IN RESIDENCE

Childhood, like the family, is a recent notion in Europe, Philippe Ariès says in a famous study.[2] Regarded in medieval times as a fragile little thing with neither heart nor face, a *res nullius* — the infant mortality rate was very high in those days — the child attained humanity only very lately. He lived there right in the middle of his elders in a state of total promiscuity that would scandalize us today, and his contact with them was his apprenticeship in existence. It wasn't until the 17th century, in the more well-to-do classes, that the religious orders inaugurated a school movement and children began to be set apart and the family was conceived as the locus of intimacy and private affections. Credited with innocence, after the image of the Christ child — until the Renaissance, babies had been depicted as miniature grownups — the little child was then supposed to be preserved from any noxious influence, he was isolated and placed under the control of pedagogues who would endeavor to prepare him for the adult state. The educational effort brought to bear a procession of attentions, specialists, and appropriate methodologies, and had its apogee in the 19th century.

We have rejected this heritage or, rather, we have reorganized it along different lines. Another tradition inherited from Rousseau and Freud has refashioned our vision of childhood; it has not only become the key to the development of the adult, a key that has been forever lost (according to psychoanalysis), but it is a treasure that we have squandered and that it is important to recover by any means possible. The alliance between the child and the savage dates from Rousseau, since one and the other live in an immediate communion with things, in the limpid apprehension of truth, a purity that civilization and society have not yet contaminated.[3] From Freud, we retain above all the emphasis placed on the first years of life — and childhood has all the beauty of a foundation that haunts us to our last breath. In this strange coalition, it is Rousseau (but a reinterpreted and distorted Rousseau, since for him the happy state of nature has been irremediably abolished) that leads the dance. Anticipating our interest in primitive people, he announced, in his usual fulgurating manner, two of the most intense intellectual obsessions of modernity: ethnology and pedagogy. After him, something would develop in the 19th century that would place the madman, the artist, the rebel, the child and the savage all on the same plane, all impervious to the civilized order, all making signs toward an origin that has been lost under the clusters of conventions and the constraints of the system. "I am two things that cannot be ridiculous: a savage and a child," said Gauguin during his voluntary exile in the islands of Oceania; he was tilting with the bourgeoisie that he execrated (yet whose recognition he craved).[4] The historian Michelet, as a good post-romantic, would see the People as a composite substance mixing genius, insanity and childhood,[5] and Claudel would celebrate Rimbaud as "a mystic in a wild state" who by virtue of his youth was capable of capturing in his verse a dash of the divine.[6] The child has been colonized the family, as the primitive is the child of humanity, the madman the pariah of reason and the poet the savage of developed society, all carriers of a flame that disturbs the established order. And since age is a descent into the lies of appearances and the industrial world is a deterioration of natural equilibrium, we must rely on these fiery characters, we must drink from these fresh sources to rediscover the truth.

I have indicated elsewhere how the ideology of colonialism, the ultimate product of pedagogical optimism, was based on the metaphor of the master and the pupil. It was up to the "higher races" to civilize the "lower races" (Jules Ferry); Europeans had the mission of guiding toward the Enlightenment the indolent, cruel or spontaneous native,[7] mired in his emotions and his ignorance. Anti-colonialism and its prolongation, pro-Third World activism, would be satisfied to reverse this metaphor without changing it: they would entrust the young nations of the South with the task of saving the metropolises of the North; they would make the former colonies the only spiritual future of the former colonizers. By gaining their independence, the first offered to their former rulers the chance to redeem their souls. It was thus in the interest of the materialist West to become prisoner of its own barbarians, to regenerate itself in the cradle of the cultures that it had oppressed.

But in both cases, it is the reference to the infantile that triumphs. It is because they are said to be under-developed that the African, Indian, and Chinese are better than us, they are not "backward" but premature; their backwardness is really an advance, for they are still in touch with the origins of the world at a time when we are already in the twilight. Thus the worn-out civilizations create oases of retrospective youth. And just as our fascination for tanned skin comes from our certainty that the native lifestyle is healthier than ours, the child is now our "good savage in residence" (Peter Sloterdijk), who blurts out profound words and leads us toward the enchanting edge of frankness. In spite (or rather because) of his weakness, he knows everything better than we do; he is almost entitled to become his parents' parent. In our day, when "pedagogy has become a theology,"[8] we give him the responsibility of teaching the adult; we confer so much value onto his puerility that it reverses itself into superiority. He is both our past and our future, *the Golden Age in short pants.*

He not only awakens our nostalgia for an abolished Eden, he invites us through his example to rediscover that disappeared splendor. Since growing up means losing one's privileges and betraying the promises of youth, we venerate the eternal child sleeping within ourselves and waiting to re-emerge. The more the individual becomes conscious of his responsibility and his burdens, the more he projects his lost ease and unconcern onto the little one he once was. This magical state is an absolute from which he is excluded: maturing means, in a sense, gradually dying, becoming an orphan of one's origins. Oscar Wilde's *The Portrait of Dorian Gray,* from the end of the 19th century, is a fantastic illustration: aging is a sin, even a crime. The deterioration of the face reflects that of the soul.

Yesterday we isolated youth to protect it from the stains of age; today, we would rather try to preserve it from the pains of maturity that we see as a form of punishment. Thus we have gone from a time when childhood was seen as imbecility and fragility, when it was necessary to relentlessly polish one's manners, to form one's character, to contain one's excesses; no one would dare, nowadays (especially at school) to say of our little creatures that they are badly behaved. Their least silliness is venerated like a profound treasure, a well of spontaneous poetry; their scribblings are worshiped like masterpieces. (And how about the thousands of pedagogical reforms intended not to educate the child, Oh, sacrilege!, and even less to guide him, but to promote his free expression, his "genius.") These Vandals in ankle socks can teach us everything, because they live under the great light of beginnings. Such is the belief of the Children's Liberationists, who invite the ingenuous tribe of children to free themselves from adult domination, to assert its self-determination in the name of "children's rights,"[9] or those, more radical still, who decry the family and the school and plead for a mobile, fluid childhood that would dislocate the egöisms and thwart the despotic machines of the powers that be.[10]

HIS MAJESTY THE BABY

We are still seeing the consequences of this revolution that is disrupting the borders between age groups (as in medieval days, but in the opposite direction). Our solicitude for the child is partly an obvious will for mastery, a desire to create a perfect lineage, to control the formation — from the uterine stage onward — of small wonders to suit our likings. But what we love most about our little blond or brown heads are their levity and capriciousness. It is the prerogative of this stage in life to be carefree, to have nothing to answer for since a guardian authority takes us under its wing and protects us. And above all, the child is free of the curse of having to make choices. A purely virtual being, he bathes in the marvelous pool of possibilities. This state of perfect availability, of exciting anticipation does not last long; growth is already taking place, and by emphasizing certain pathways one inevitably begins to exclude some of the other possibilities. But for a few years (at least in our retrospective illusion) the child appears to be a bouquet of potentialities, a first morning of the world, carrying within himself every conceivable destiny. Compared to us, who are already "made," he seems to be outstanding, an undefined form embodying the hope of a new departure for humanity (which is why so many parents hope to correct their own failings through their offspring).

Finally, we cherish our small young imps' sacred and remorseless selfishness, the feeling that they are the creditors of the adults whom they did not ask to give them birth. Tightly controlled by the others due to his very constitution, the little fauna is in fact a lord to whom all is due. "Disease, death, the renunciation of pleasures, the enforced limits to one's own will should not be counted with regard to the child," notes Freud; "the laws of nature and of society should stop before him, he must again be the center and the core of creation, His Majesty The Baby as he used to be considered."[11] In short, by liberating the Child King who survives behind the wrinkles of the mature man, I crown myself monarch, and all my desires are legitimate since they come from me; I confer absolute sovereignty on my narcissism.

Thus one grasps the ambiguity of this over-valuation of one's first years: we are not celebrating the rights of children so much as the right to childhood for all. The real child is that which signals to us our mortality. The birth of children, said Hegel, is the death of the parents; they are the ones who someday will take our places and through whom we contemplate our future disappearance. But to venerate childhood as such is, on the contrary, to claim that everyone from the age of 7 to 107 has the right to be irresponsible, to settle into a delicious quarantine never to join the unpleasant planet of the Grownups.

Just to be sure we all understand: nobody actually wants to become a small child or baby again. We want, rather, to collect the privileges of all the ages, the pleasant frivolity of youth plus the autonomy of maturity. We want the best of both worlds. (And neither do we want to return to adolescence, which is a model of breakdowns, of identity crises, whereas the baby exudes fulfillment and equilibrium.) Thus it is not so much the childish that we exalt but the infantile; we look on a lifestyle of regression as compensation for the harsh reality of fate.[12] And since childhood exists only in the unconsciousness of oneself, the "nonconsciousness" or *nescience*,[13] playing at being a child when one is grownup can only amount to antics and grimaces in big people who wish they could combine knowledge and naivety, strength and thoughtlessness. We no longer join Dostoyevsky in saying that children without sin "exist to touch our hearts, to purify them," but that they show us the way, that they are our guides to carefree behavior, caprice, and fantasy. All of humanity is summarized in this primordial rapture: and coming down from it is like being in exile, far from real life. We are survivors of our early youth; we mourn the little child that we were, and we age without growing up.

FROM CHILD-CITIZEN TO CITIZEN-CHILD

The ultimate sign of this evolution is to declare, as the UN did on November 20, 1989, that the child is already a full human person, a full citizen with all the rights appertaining thereto, and that confining him to the status of a minor because of his age is as discriminatory as it would be to treat Blacks, Jews or women that way. In this campaign, everything possible has been said: that despite the legislators' goodwill, this was a poisoned gift to childhood, delivering it bound hand and foot to all forms of manipulation; that it's sheer demagogy to declare the state of the minor compatible with the full exercise of rights, since the latter supposes legal capacity; and finally that this new approach is once again likely to undermine the duties of the teachers and of the parents.[14]

In our view, the UN convention is also revealing as to the way in which adults project themselves onto children. To say, as it does, that kids are already big people, that only size separates them from their elders, is to imply that nothing prevents the elders from being kids gone to seed, that the reversibility can be total. It implies according the child a wisdom, a rationality that one no longer wishes any more for oneself, swamping him with an overwhelming responsibility — for obviously he cannot answer for himself — the better to let us off the hook. In infantile regression, there is always one character too many, and it is the child himself, titular of prerogatives that we seek for our own and that he seems to usurp at our expense, the child is guilty of monopolizing childhood instead of letting us have it. What we are calling for, in fact, is less the recognition of the little guy as a subject and more the right for all of us to mix up our ages.[15] From the child as citizen to the citizen as child: this backing-and-forthing could contain the entire destiny of the contemporary individual. While attributing sapience, discernment and measure to our cherubim, we abdicate our responsibilities towards them.

This mentality is admittedly the counterpart of one of the real luxuries of the rich countries: age has ceased being a verdict. There is no clear boundary anymore, demarcating the point beyond which a human being is out of the game; today one can start his life over at the age of 50 or 60, modifying his destiny until the final moments, counterbalancing the disgrace of retirement that tosses out people who are still intellectually and physically capable. "To age is to retire gradually in appearance," said Goethe. He is quite positive that men and women in great number nowadays wish to *persist in appearance*, in a state of relative good health and without suffering discrimination.

This broadening of possibilities has taken place in a society where, by the year 2010, the over-60's will represent more than 27% of the population in France. The oldies (who have formidable purchasing power) band together in senior citizen movements and protest against discrimination and the progressive dispossession their physical means and for the right to pleasure. This is immense progress since the desire to live full lives is getting stronger as the threshold of entry into old age moves back (two centuries ago it began at the age of 35!). It will be fascinating to see whether, in the years to come, this movement will follow the infantile model of complaints and recrimination, whether the sexagenerians will form the ultimate category of spoiled children in our society or whether, on the contrary, on the strength of their legitimate will for recognition, they will try to create a different model based on dignity, serenity and the transmission of memory.[16]

Now, the first right that children should have is to be protected from violence, from arbitrary and sometimes cruel treatment by his elders. But there is also the contradictory right both to be respected in their spontaneous and carefree nature and to be equipped with the means of gradually evolving out of that condition as they grow. If one wishes "to mature them for freedom," as Kant said, concerning people in general, we must enlighten them and inform them, and not abandon them to a splendid indolence. It is thus dangerous to destroy the shelters (school, family, institutions) through which they slowly learn to manage the chaos of life[17] and which are essential in taming them to responsibility by offering them tasks suited to their age, by giving them gradual control over broader and broader spheres. (And not by asking them to parody adults, for example by meeting in a conclave to mimic parliamentary life, or by disguising themselves as journalists to interview a personality. Our era prefers just one relation between the age groups: reciprocal pastiche. We copy our children, who are copying us.) Clearly, the prepubescent should be put in a position to answer for his actions, himself, whenever possible, on the condition that a precise field had been defined that is within his range, and responses should be offered that mark either progress or failure.[18] Such is the paradox of education: to predispose man's offspring toward freedom through obedience to adults, who help him get to the point where he no longer needs assistance, and to accompany him in his progressive emancipation. In education, the authority is the ground on which the child stands and buttresses himself and from which he will gradually detach himself; and the ideal teacher is the one who learns how to kill the teacher (whereas many teachers are tempted by the abuse of power, the pleasure of reigning over malleable souls that they decree inapt for maturity, so that they can dominate them more). Childhood is a complete world, a state of perfection that is not lacking in anything, which sometimes moves us to the depths of our hearts. We cry in admiration and tenderness in front of these little people and we are reluctant to diminish, through our lessons and our commands, this living wonder. Great people often appear awkward, ugly, defective next to the perfection of children. But since "innocence is made to be lost" (V. Jankélévitch), it is also important to respect in every child the human that he is to become, whom we must strengthen by developing his character and reason. Thus, constraints are not oppressive if they sharpen the mind and oblige it to grow within certain boundaries; or, to be more precise, constraint is the very condition of freedom.

Not being able to speak for himself, the child is the eternal prey of those who speak in his place: in his mysterious limpidity, he legitimates the most radical and the most conservative Utopias, he represents purity as well as evil, subversion as well as docility. The child is a mystery in plain view, and we build altars to him while we burn him at the stake, we dress him as an angel or a demon. And our society oscillates between laxity and authoritarianism, laissez-faire and reform school, the toy and the whip. It idealizes the child exactly in proportion to how it demonizes him and vice versa. And what better exemplifies the fusion of the infantile and the victim than the recent promotion of the fetus to the rank of subject of law, a new alibi of the American and European conservatives as well as of the Vatican? The fetus: absolute innocence paired with the most extreme destitution, the prototype of precariousness and weakness joined together, a soul that could have been denied the privilege of incarnation. Rather than being someone who, by dint of his birth, brings something new into the world and offers humanity a chance to start over, in the idyllic image that we give the newborn he has no other job than to confirm childhood as a legend, as Hanna Arendt said. And in truth, through this legend, we are mainly painting the portrait of what we would like to be: adults who are physically able but who enjoy on top of that all the privileges of a minor. Someone who has all the rights but none of the duties or responsibilities.

IT'S SO HARD BEING AN ADULT!

Our societies show many and blatant signs of a will to return to our youth, a collective drift toward the cradle and the pacifier. There have been so many hit movies where the heroes are still in diapers, virtuosos before they have their baby teeth, toddlers as models, multimillionaire idols by the age of 7, as imaginative at hamming it up for the camera as any veteran star. (And look how popular knee-high superstars have always been in American movies, from Shirley Temple to Judy Foster; they parade on the screen at an age when others are sucking lollipops). And in France, we have a miniature 4-year-old singer, a hoarse little squirt who sends the crowd into stitches by whining about her weariness with life: "It's sooooo hard being a baby."[19] This childish invasion of the rock scene, variety shows, and movies, reserved until now to the adolescent — this flood of micro actors and crooners touches the public deeply. Kids are on the preciousness attack everywhere, moving us all to tears. Babies are the scaled-down gods of our universe and they have already unseated the teenagers, who'd better be ready for retirement. Baby imperialism is now boundless, the little lords and ladies dominate us in their bibs and diapers!

The grownups are not waiting idly by; they are making every effort to get back into childhood, to reverse the arrow of time, to bend it back like the fingers of a glove. Just look at Michael Jackson, one of our contemporary myths, who by fulfilling his own aspiration to become an angel, a man from before the Fall, has thwarted the double curse of age and race (to the point that he now resembles a cross between Bambi and Count Dracula). In his mad attempt, this Faustian singer testifies to the contemporary passion for eternal youth, the desire for immortality. "Aging will be over soon," proclaims the cover of a magazine.[20] Incredible news! If old age is already just a question of time, if it is possible not only to erase our wrinkles, to fill in our creases, to correct our figures, to re-implant our hair, to delay our senescence, but above all to turn back our biological clocks, then the ultimate enemy, death, should soon be felled. In fact, the definitions of "normal" and "pathological" are being upset: not getting sick is the least of our accomplishments. First of all, we have to be cured of that fatal disease that is called life, since that is what comes to a halt some day. We don't distinguish anymore between fates that can be modified (the physical dilapidation that can be slowed, existence that can be prolonged) and inexorable fates (finitude and death). Death is no longer the normal terminus of a life, the condition to some extent of its sudden appearance, but a failure on the part of therapy to correct everything that leads to the end. We think that machines and science are releasing us from need and effort; now, it's from the future that we aspire to be freed. Modernity dangles before us the gleaming possibility of controlling life and producing the "second creation," which would no longer be constrained by the vagaries of nature. By now, it's not this ambition that seems insane but the delay and the roadblocks that stand in its way.

From a more prosaic point of view, this furious aspiration to irresponsibility means that, on television and the radio, the "excrement" level prevails (organic or scatological jokes, schoolboys' jokes, not to mention certain programs featuring characters disguised as high-school students, pupils, or babies, or those who dispense erotic advice while sucking breasts and baby-bottles, etc.). As if the witnesses galvanized by hyperactive clowns were invited to unwind collectively, to forget accepted practices and conventions for a few hours, to give themselves up to long stretches of happy stupidity. As in the aforementioned movie, where a two-year-old zapped with electricity becomes a giant who steps over houses and buildings, crushes cars and buses with his feet and terrorizes the whole city, we have all grown up while disregarding moral development, and we do not miss any opportunity to prolong the childhood that is still superimposed upon us. And since real life is still ahead of us, we make ourselves into a *distorted version of the grownup*, always heading toward the land of eternal youth.

One might say that this eccentricity is too blatant to be significant. But for these oddities to be accepted, we must already be so impregnated with childishness that it bathes our entire environment and is offered up to us so openly that we don't see it any more. It's as though having the audacity to speak in the first person came at the cost of a terrible punishment; the West's new Adam regresses, and sinks deliciously into silliness, spoiled behavior, and picaresque tomfooleries, provided that he can take advantage of the privileges of that age group without any of the constraints that go with them. The "puerilism" in our societies is not the same as that of the traditional worlds; it is based on mimicry and parody, an evasion of an accepted standard of wisdom and experience. This tendency to regress is not related to what Sudhir Kakar, speaking about India, calls the "underdeveloped ego." He describes a psychological structure in India, where the fusional relationship between the mother and the child, and then that of each one with his caste and his gods, may be followed by difficulty in acting as an autonomous person, able to adapt to new situations and extract himself from the universe of hierarchy and subservience. Let us repeat: infantilism in the West has nothing to do with the love of childhood; it's a quest to return to the timeless state, and we dangle all the symbols of that age before our eyes, dazzling ourselves with fantasy. It is a counterfeit childhood, a grinning usurpation, and it discredits childhood as much as it denigrates maturity; and it maintains a prejudicial confusion between the childish and the child. The baby becomes the future of man when man is no longer willing to answer anymore for the world nor for himself.

THE TWO IMMATURITIES

Contrary to a heroic idea that is too widely shared, no humanity is possible without regression, without senility and babbling, without exquisite relapses into silliness. To be bearable, the dull grind of life must also be accompanied by a relentless puerility that rebels against order and gravity. But there is a good way to use immaturity, a way of staying closer to the enchantment of childhood that gives us an energizing dash of life to counter the sclerotic and the routine. At every stage of life we are hounded by two risks: that of resignation, which is sometimes touted as a form of wisdom but is often just the other face of fear; and that of caricature, which encourages us to feign youth, to simulate an eternally youthful enthusiasm. How can we mature without becoming resigned, how can we keep a freshness of spirit without falling into adolescent over-simplification?

Now, what we learn from these moments of grace, these marvelous moments when we are submerged in ecstasy, is that there are two possible childhoods in a life: the first, which leaves us at puberty, and another childhood of mature age that comes in flashes, blazing visitations that escape us as soon as we try to capture them. Childhood is the second candor that one finds after having lost it, a beneficial rupture that instills new blood in our veins and breaks the straightjacket of habit. So there is a way of taking on a childish posture as a commitment to renewal against the petrified and fossil life: a capacity to reconcile the intellectual and the emotional, to step outside the long-term, to welcome the unknown, to be astonished by the obvious. Making the most of all our childhoods, as St. Francis de Sales suggested, is to stay in touch with the creativity of our first years, to break the limitations of the old me by dunking it in a lustral bath.

Perhaps that is what a successful life is: a life that is constantly in a state of rebirth, of continually rebounding where the faculty to start again overrides the acquired characteristics and the concern of preserving itself — a life where nothing is fixed and irreversible and that grants some play, some freedom of motion to even the most rigid-seeming destiny. Then childhood is no longer a pathetic refuge, an unacceptable travesty into which the faded old adult may fall, but a supplement to an already flourishing existence, a merry excess of that which, having achieved its goal, can be re-tempered in the spontaneity and the charm of one's earliest days. Then childhood as a quasi-divine grace can touch the face of the old man as much as early senility can be imprinted on the face of the young man. "Being born twice is no more surprising than being born the first time." (Princess Bibesco).

TOO MUCH OF TOYLAND

This wrong-headed pedagogy has a natural environment that is like a digest of all our era's mythologies: Disneyland, the promised land of insipidity, Babylon of the syrupy. Disneyland was originally conceived by its founder in 1955 as "a magical park where adults and children can amuse themselves together;" we sail to this land of wonders to wash ourselves free of our worries. This phalanstery is a protected enclave in the interior of the world, and to enter there we use a passport that symbolizes that we are crossing a border. Everything has been calculated so as to take our mind off the ordinary nature of things: the staff are called Cast Members, as if they were actors in a play that is being performed with our participation; they only use first names and they are compelled to smile, with permanent good humor — basic conditions in this fortress of obligatory happiness. Here nobody has marital status, that unpleasant practice of societies that belong to history; we are in the Land of Nowhere, in the interstices of the century when all are equal in rapture.

Planet Disney has replicated all the world's continents, climates and landscapes in miniature (although the dominant style is still clearly American). Here, you can pass from prehistory to space flight without any transition, from the land of Indians and fur trappers to the Castle of Sleeping Beauty, from Pirate Island to the Futuristic City, all on a backdrop of palace turrets, minarets, roofs, domes and pinnacles. It is a happy combination of the centuries, beliefs and manners where everything that has artificially divided mankind has been obscured. With a consummate art of reconstitution, Disneyland gives the world a conglomeration of epochs and cultures that coexist with cheery intelligence in this benevolent space. And the Red-Skin's teepees, like Cinderella's tavern, are colored in the same shades of ochre, rose and pastel, giving all the recreated regions the same calm and soothing patina, manufacturing a harmony between the disparate elements. In this puerile encyclopedia of world history (where even nature has been re-worked), the centuries and the remote nations come to us, but stripped of their worrying aspect: this happy potpourri has been crafted antiseptically. It offers only the adulterated aroma of times past, not their truth.

This effort to sugarcoat everything culminates in *Fantasyland* in the attraction "It's a Small World," a hymn to the tenderness of the planet's children. Here, you take a cruise, on flat boats, down an underground river and on each side of the river dolls dressed in national costumes dance and sing exasperating songs against backdrops designed to represent their native countries. Thus we go past the savannas of Africa, the Eiffel Tower, Big Ben, and Taj Mahal, in an elementary school cosmopolitanism that is as appealing as a cheap tourist brochure. Never mind that it is just a collection of stereotypes; what matters is that all abrasive edges have been removed from any potentially threatening aspect of remote customs; what matters is to celebrate the foreign without allowing it to appear strange. (In the United States, *niceness* is the obligatory counterpoint to the orgy of brutality and bloodshed that explodes at all hours on the television. Sentimentality goes hand-in-hand with brutality in daily life.) Thus the pirates (animated figures, ingenious automats, that look like humans, animals or plants, as the story requires) from the Caribbean Islands can get drunk on rum, howl, eat like pigs, and clash their sabers, their cries sound like they are playing, and it is difficult to take them seriously. Disney suggests evil only in order to neutralize it, reducing it to the dimension of a fabulous toy, stripping it of any hint of real concern or danger. Races, civilizations, beliefs, tribes can be mixed together without risk since they have been vitiated to begin with, cleansed of any asperities, reduced to their folksy aspect. Differences, sources of disagreement, are irrelevant and do not hinder the sweeping wave of good feelings and ardent kindliness that circulate here. Mercilessly reduced by the theme park, the external world is nothing but a trivial impurity, a wasteland, since it now has a double where death, disease, and spite do not exist.

THE SEDUCTION OF KITSCH

The enchanted kingdom seemingly marks the apotheosis of the fairytale: all our familiar characters mingle here with those of Walt Disney. It is as if they had all just stepped out of the pages of a book or an animated movie. They come forward to greet us, and we can dance a step or two with them, we can laugh with Bambi, Jumbo the flying Elephant or the Seven Dwarves, and we can even dress like them, wearing a pair of Mouse ears or masquerading for a few hours as one of the heroes of the fables. But this familiarity is misleading and the ensemble is as far from the traditional European tale as from the early Walt Disney, which was far more corrosive and caustic. While phantoms, cruel queens, and skull-and-crossbones are present, that is just a concession to the universe of our legends: they never threaten the good humor. The sense of the happy ending prevails: Pinocchio, Snow White, Captain Hook, the Mad Hatter, the Cheshire Cat all file by, but steeped in their stereotypes, detached from the stories by Grimm, Carroll, Perrault, or Collodi that gave them depth and meaning. The fairytale, as Bruno Bettelheim remarked, is the passage from anguish experienced to anguish overcome, through a narrative that speaks to the child of his own inadmissible complexes and impulses.[21] It is a subtle guide that directs fantasies and ambivalences toward a coherent outcome. In this sense it has an important educational function, it disciplines the internal chaos notwithstanding the violence it deploys and that has put off so many teachers.

There's nothing like that in the magical domain of Mickey: everything is smooth, clean, impeccable, and any narrative connection is forgotten, history is disarticulated until it is nothing but a continuous series of attractions that breaks up into playlets, story-boards, episodes sprinkled about at random. Fiction can only be consumed and contemplated, it cannot be recounted, here. Disney's success is that, through this presentation, it is able to recycle all mythologies of childhood in just one, Disney's own, from the Thousand and One Arabian Nights to Lancelot of the Lake. And this melting-pot of European and Oriental imaginations, by eluding their ambiguity, likewise eludes their power of enchantment.

So it turns out that it's not childhood that this vast closed empire exalts so much as the ensemble of symbols and representations that have been imposed upon it: not so much the childish as the puerile. This entire pharaonic construction is dedicated to the great modern divinity: "transcendental goofiness" (Witold Gombrowicz), sweet and dopey, with every element of ambiguity removed. A distortion of Freudianism: childhood, here, is not polymorphic but asexual, oozing with sweetness the way adults like to represent it, as a mirror of their own dreams. The child finds himself in an idealized version of his universe thanks to a fantastic labor of expurgation: it is a synthetic childhood, frozen and fixed. It takes on the tones of an initiatory course, but an initiation to nothing but complacency, to the pleasant affability of the world and all things, serving to keep at a distance the cruel universe of men and their passions. The instructive novel comes up short.

And yet the magic works: despite everything, one is filled with wonder at these singing dolls, these animated mannequins, these pasteboard decorations, these insipid melodies that end up being permanently engraved on the memory. It's not only the innumerable little wonders of invention (for example, the ghosts' ball, created by hologram, in the Haunted House), the architectural exploits, and the multitude of special effects that place the Disney company well ahead of its competitors. Kitsch has a terrible seductive power when it is coupled with childhood; they reinforce each other to a dizzying degree, making the mushy and simple-minded compellingly attractive when they occur in the setting of a vast nursery. Flaubert pointed out that stupidity is one form of the infinite; and that bad taste can become mystical if it is associated with the saccharine, the "nice." This soft sentimentality brings together all the ages: it reassures, relieves, and builds a powerful rampart against the attacks of reality. "Disneylandizing" the world and history means sweetening them in order to disarm them.

Of course this excess of attention and of preciousness ends up making you uncomfortable; you start to feel a compensatory longing for the unforeseen, for hardness and confrontation. And in the end you suffocate under the despotism of softness that overwhelms you with smiles and benevolence. You leave there reeling with insipidity, high on false friendship. For the dream to be perfect, we would have to we leave the place metamorphosed in our turn into comic strip characters, smaller and younger, cast as Pluto, Merlin, Alice or Donald. At least, for a few hours, we have tasted the elixir of innocence that transforms us all into stereotypes of little boys and small girls. And in this honeyed Arcadia where no one is ever malicious, everything ends for the best in the eternal smile of Mickey, the fixed grin of insipidness.

BE YOURSELF

What does it mean to be an adult, ideally speaking? It means agreeing to certain sacrifices, giving up exorbitant claims, learning that it is "better to vanquish one's desires rather than the world order" (Descartes). It means discovering that obstacles are not the negation but the necessary condition of freedom which, if it never encounters any hindrance, is only a phantom, a vain whim since it exists as such only through the equal freedom of the others founded in the law. It means recognizing that one is never entirely one's own man, that we owe something to the others —

which shakes our claim to hegemony. Finally, it means under-standing that we have to form ourselves by changing ourselves, that we are always manufacturing ourselves in spite of ourselves, at the expense of the child that we were and thus, that all educa-tion, even the most tolerant, is a challenge that we undertake in order to haul ourselves out of immediacy and ignorance. In a word, becoming adult — if anyone ever makes it that far — means training oneself about limits, it means reining in our insane hopes and working to be autonomous, capable of inventing oneself as much as of stepping outside of oneself.

However, infantile individualism, on the contrary, is the Utopia of the *renunciation of renunciation*. It has only one watch-word: be what you are, for all of eternity. Don't hamper yourself with any tutor, any obstacle; avoid any useless effort that does not confirm your identity as you see it; listen only to your uniqueness. Don't worry about reform or progress or improvement: cultivate your subjectivity, which is perfect just because it is yours. Don't resist any inclination, for your desire is sovereign. Everyone is re-sponsible, except for you.

Such is the ambivalence of the phrase, "Be Yourself": in order to be oneself, it is still necessary that the being unfold, that possi-bilities to be brought to fruition, that one realize that he is not yet that which he will one day become. However, we are being in-vited to develop ourselves without reflection or work, and the idea of paying with one's person for the right to existence has lost currency. Left to myself, I have nothing to do but to exalt myself without reservation: the supreme value is no longer that which transcends me but that which I perceive within myself. I do not "become," any more, I am all that I must be at every moment, I can stand by my emotions, desires, and fantasies, without second thought. Whereas freedom is the faculty of breaking free from determinisms I, on the contrary, intend to wed them. I will not erect any barrier to my appetites, I do not have to build myself any more — that is, I do not have to introduce any distance between me and me; I have only to follow my inclinations, to become one with myself. This gives rise to an ambiguous use of the term "authenticity": it can mean that each is his own law (Luc Ferry);[22] but it can also be understood to legitimate the simple fact of existing, asserting oneself as the absolute model — that being is such a miracle that it spares us from any duty or requirement. Certain contemporary philosophies of the individual can be reproached for failing to exalt the individual sufficiently, for proposing a reduced version of it, for taking its degeneration as a proof of health; finally, for forgetting that the idea of subject supposes a constitutive tension, an ideal to be reached, and that imposture starts when one takes the individual for a given when in fact it remains to be created.

I DESERVE IT

No concept is richer and more likely to get us on our feet than the "right to" something. By allowing criticism of what is in the name of what should be, it impels us to demand an incalculable number of privileges from the State and from various institutions, without having to justify ourselves. This careless attitude takes the consumer society literally and conceives it as a gigantic horn of plenty, at the risk that soon we may see it crumble away, bit by bit. In the Welfare State, welfare has devoured and devalued the majesty of the State, which has become nothing more than a donor and redistributive authority from which we extract countless concessions, one by one. Initially set up to distribute over the entire nation the tasks of national solidarity, it wound up encouraging a taste for public assistance on everyone's part, and has encouraged endless complaints. This fundamental factor of social peace invites us to see our needs as always well-founded and our deprivations as intolerable. The triumph of the "I deserve it" generation is that now we feel we are entitled to everything, in exchange for nothing, as Michael Josephson said. And that is the state of mind of a broad faction of American youth, which feels entitled to reject any type of standards or obligations that could impede their quest for success or comfort.[23] The union of the Right, the Welfare State and consumerism thus contributes to the creation of a voracious being, impatient to be happy immediately and who, if that happiness is delayed, feels that he has been cheated, that he is entitled to compensation for his imperfect dream. The relationship between infantilism and victimization resides in this: both are founded on the same ideas of *rejecting obligation*, denying duty, and feeling certain of having infinite credit with one's contemporaries. They are two different ways (one laughable, the other less so) of removing oneself from the real world by abdicating responsibility, two ways of isolating oneself from the combat of life, since victimization is nothing but a dramatized form of infantilism.

We want everything and its opposite: for society to protect us without prohibiting anything to us, for it to shelter us without limiting us, help us without bothering us, leave us alone while supporting us with a thousand strands of affectionate care, in short for it *to be there for us without our being there for it.* "Leave me alone, take care of me." The self-sufficiency on which we pride ourselves is like the self-sufficiency of the child who plays about under the supervision of an omnipresent mother and nurturer, whom he no longer sees because he is so entirely surrounded by her. Here we are, among all the others, feeling and behaving as though we were on our own; and we live in the fiction of a world wherein others exist only to help us without our having any obligations whatsoever. We take what we like from the collective, and we refuse to participate when it comes to the rest. Held as an absolute value, the pleasure principle, that is the will to do only as we wish, weakens us and degenerates into a poor hedonism, into fatalism. Then it conflicts less with the principle of reality than with the principle of freedom, with the ability to avoid submitting, caving in to the order of things. The sovereignty of whim, when it is carried to the extreme, pulverizes not only the principle of otherness; it weakens the foundations of the subject. Or, to put it differently, a certain unbridled individualism is even self-contradictory in principle and draws up the conditions of its own defeat.

FROM OLD REBELLIOUS TEENS TO YOUNG OLD FARTS

What was the generation of the Sixties? The one that exalted youth so much that its watchword was "Never trust anyone over thirty." It developed the theory of rejecting authority and devoted itself to ending paternal power. It's the one that swept away all rules and taboos in the name of the absolute power of desire, convinced that our passions, even the most incongruous, are innocent and that to continually multiply them, to deny anguish and guilt, is to get closer to happiness, to great joy.

We cannot emphasize enough the extent to which these years, in spite of the terrorism of pleasure (that was sometimes as stifling as Puritanism), were a time of euphoria and irresponsibility. No disease was incurable, no confusion of the senses or erotic combination was dangerous, and one only invoked the Revolution in order to spend long nights locked in an impassioned embrace. The wealth from the post-war boom plus a protective State ensured young people the double status of respected protestors and spoiled rebels giving their least whims a subversive hue. It was intoxicating to overthrow the old authoritative order, the more so since the walls of the interdicts, already quite worm-eaten, caved in almost without combat. A happy time when one could maintain, without blushing, "The more I make love, the more I'm making revolution!" Even Leftism, with few exceptions, was only a spontaneous way of supporting pure ideas without worrying about people or causes. Spouting extreme doctrines and radical slogans, and convening in Paris, Berlin or San Francisco with those phantoms called the Proletariat, the Third World, and the Revolution — most of the time this was just a game without gravity nor tragedy, an epic way of splicing one's own small history into the bigger one. And the transition from the radical Left to the conformity of the Eighties was less a disavowal that a profound continuity: nobody really mourned the death of those ideals that had been constantly on his lips. Under the leaden language of ideology, another music could be heard: the thundering emergence of the individual in the democratic universe. The "*tout politique*" was only a rhetorical trick that allowed one to talk about oneself. Is it surprising that in this climate of rapture, there was an incredible artistic fecundity (especially on the musical level) that today's youth is often satisfied to repeat or to plagiarize?

But this indulgent generation did not want to transmit anything to its children but the rejection of authority as an arbitrary restraint. And the kids of the baby-boomers have made their deficiency a dogma, their indifference a virtue, their resignation the last word in liberal pedagogy. Now we have the supremacy of dads as pals, moms as girlfriends, denying any difference between them and their kids and offering the youngsters only an ultra-permissive creed: do as you like! And these "youthful adults" (Edgar Morin) — by failing to arm their offspring for the tasks that awaited them, in the belief that they were giving birth to a new humanity — manufactured anxious, disabled beings who are often tempted by conservatism in order to compensate for having been abandoned. Thus their offspring's call for order, for tighter morals (often superficial), the need to establish boundaries at all costs. And thus again we see these aging adolescents who mooch off their parents until the age of thirty, crowding the parental nest while sometimes begging their elders to help them rebel against them (a pathetic demand that recalls Marcuse's indignation against bourgeois society, guilty of not being more repressive). Today's young men and women have been deprived of the experience that is summarized in the saying that "every age group rises up on the symbolic murder of the preceding one." For them, everything was a gift, not a conquest. And the drama of the too-liberal upbringing, without interdict or standards, is that this is not an upbringing.

What a strange mix-up are today's sundered families where the young old folks demand that their Peter Pan fathers and mothers finally act their age and shoulder their responsibilities. But beer-bellied, balding and near-sighted, the children of the baby-boom, often having become well-established and cleaned up, remain riveted to their dreams; little hellions until the day they die, side by side with decrepit young people who age prematurely, aware that their parents, by refusing to grow up, stole their youth from them.

Footnotes

1. As Victor Hugo recounts in his extraordinary novel, *L'homme qui rit*, Paris, Nelson, 1952.

2. Philippe Ariès, *L'Enfant et la vie familiale sous l'Ancien Régime*, Seuil, 1973.

3. Once again, I must refer to Jean Starobinski's fine writing in *J. J. Rousseau, La Transparence et l'Obstacle*, *op. cit.*, pp. 40 and 319, as well as to Peter Sloterdijk, *Critique de la raison cynique*, *op. cit.*, pp. 85-86.

4. His account, a mixture of crucifixion and exaltation, can be read in the collection *Oviri, écrits d'un sauvage*, Folio, Gallimard, 1972, texts verified and annotated by Daniel Guérin.

5. On Michelet, see Roland Barthes, *OEuvres complètes*, Seuil, 1993, book I, p. 459.

6. Paul Claudel, *Préface aux Poésies complètes*, Livre de Poche, 1960.

7. Pascal Bruckner, *Le Sanglot de l'homme blanc*, *op. cit.*, pp. 223 sqq.

8. Jean-Baptiste Pontalis, "L'Enfance," *Nouvelle Revue de Psychanalyse*, Gallimard, 1979.

9. On this topic, see Irène Théry's chapter by on the new rights of children in *Le Démariage*, Odile Jacob, 1993, especially pp. 342-343.

10. René Scherer and Guy Hocquenghem defend this thesis in a strange and beautiful book that combines a clear Fouriérist inspiration with an elegy to pedophilia, *Co-Ire*, Recherches, 1976.

11. Sigmund Freud, "Pour introduire au narcissisme," in *La Vie sexuelle*, PUF, 1969, p. 96. Here, Freud is speaking from the viewpoint of parents who project their narcissism onto their child.

12. On the distress of the ego and infantile temptation, read Conrad Stein's, "Majesté et Détresse," in *Pédiatrie et Psychanalyse*, edited by Danielle Brun, PAU, 1992.

13. "It's the common fate of childhood and innocence to exist only retrospectively: at the moment, youth is substantially and ontically youthful; it is by this lack of self-awareness that we recognize authentic youth." (Vladimir Jankélévitch, *Traité des vertus*, "L'Innocence et la Méchanceté," Flammarion, 1972, book III, p. 1196.)

14. Irène Théry showed the danger and the demagoguery inherent in such a convention (*Le Démariage*, *op. cit.*, last chapter). On the same subject, see also Alain Finkielkraut's and André Comte-Sponville's very enlightening comments in *Autrement*, September 1991, no. 123.

15. As psychoanalyst Liliane Lurçat puts it: "Children are now committing adult crimes: the things they see on the screen. They say that the 20th century the children's century, but that's wrong. It was the century of

the fusion of age groups." (*Le Nouvel Observateur*, December 2, 1993.)

16. On this topic, see Jean-François Collanges's excellent article in *Réforme*, June 6, 1993.

17. See Hannah Arendt, *La Crise de la culture*, Idées, Gallimard, 1972, chap. V., and Jean-François Lyotard's comments on it, *Lectures d'Enfance*, Galilée, 1991, pp. 82-83.

18. See Alain Etchegoyen, *Le Temps des responsables*, Julliard, 1993, pp. 192 and 208.

19. *Little Jordy*, 4 years old in 1993, produced and directed by her parents; the songs and the video were a hit in France and abroad.

20. *Le Figaro-Magazine*, November 14, 1992.

21. Bruno Bettelheim, *Psychanalyse des contes de fées*, Pluriel Poches, P. 191.

22. Luc Ferry, *Le Nouvel Ordre écologique*, Grasset, 1992, p. 265. On the same topic, see also Alain Renaut's article, "Politesse et Sincérité," in *Faut-il être ce que l'on est?*, Éditions Esprit, 1994, pp. 135 sqq.

23. William Raspberry, "En Amérique enseigner l'éthique," *Libération*, November 12, 1990.

SECOND PART

A THIRST FOR PERSECUTION

CHAPTER 4

JOINING THE ELECT, BY SUFFERING

> "God is just: he knows that I suffer and that I am innocent."
>
> Rousseau, *Les Rêveries du promeneur solitaire.*

> "So many people have believed they were persecuted and have written a literature of persecution, without any persecution taking place."
>
> Jean Genet.

> "You would think that people envied one's misfortunes."
>
> Christine Villernin.

In one chapter in his *Essays on Applied Psychoanalysis,*[1] Sigmund Freud examines the nature of certain people who, having suffered diseases or setbacks during their childhood, believe themselves exempt from the sacrifices that apply to humanity as a whole. They have endured enough to never have to accept any further deprivation, and their behavior, notes Freud, is analogous to that of "a whole people burdened with a past that is heavy with misfortunes." They can commit injustices since they have suffered injustices themselves: they are exceptions, and life owes them reparations. "We all believe," concludes Freud, "that we have the right to resent nature and destiny because of congenital and infantile damage done to us; we all claim compensation for early mortifications of our narcissism, of our vanity. Why didn't nature grant us the high forehead of the genius, the noble features of the aristocrat? Why were we born into bourgeois apartments and not in a royal palace?"

THE MARKETING OF AFFLICTION

What Freud outlines here, picking up on Rousseau's intuitions, is a phenomenon that is on its way to joining infantilism as the determining pathology of the contemporary individual: the tendency to cry over one's own fate. But why should mankind be more unhappy today than before? We in Europe, yesterday, in particular those of us on the left, took a positive stance on being a victim. What was socialism if not the temporal version of Christianity, swearing to the exploited that a more just world was at hand, where they would finally come first? *Siding with the poor* meant waging a common fight against an oppressive system, and private grievances, seen in the context of this battle, cleared a way in a cause that transcended them and came back to each one in the form of various benefits and advantages. Collective and personal emancipation were one.

But since the great historical excuses that enabled us to blame our miseries on capitalism and imperialism have disappeared, since the East-West divide has disappeared and since we no longer have one identifiable adversary, our enemies are proliferating, scattering like a swarm of little Satans that may be hiding behind any face we see. What made us free for the last 50 years was the coincidence of material prosperity, social redistribution, medical progress and peace ensured by nuclear deterrence; in the shelter of these four pillars we could talk about "me" without any concern. Now that these pillars are shaking, and unemployment strikes, and the thin net of social security is disintegrating — with war returning to Europe, and finally with AIDS embodying the old alliance of sex and death — now the individual, having been hit where it hurts, is shifting from complacency to panic. We are hardly out of the delicious cocoon of the post-war boom and we are already on the brink of a stormy period, with a mindset forged during an era of opulence, and imbued with reflexes that are no longer in synch with reality. And since the ultimate redemptive class, the working class, has lost its Messianic role and no longer represents the oppressed, everyone is free to claim that quality for himself: the new downtrodden, that's me! Thus, having outlived the revolutionary doctrines, victimization is thriving on their corpses, it is flourishing, going berserk, veering off in a new direction, and metastasizing throughout the social body.

It's taking on the dimension of a contemporary market of the "emancipation of the judiciary" in our societies.[2] This elevation of the law as the preferred means for regulating conflicts also results in a political crisis: it has weakened the apparatuses of the traditional mediators (the left, and the trade unions), which used to make it possible to act jointly and to lighten the tax burden; the end of the workers' culture and its capacity to integrate, the suffocation of the republican pact founded on school and the army, and finally the increasing lack of distinction between the right and the left sap our governments' credibility. The middle classes, who are closely watched by the poorer classes, are becoming the "anxious classes" (Robert Reich), and so many people feel at a loss because the traditional shock absorbers and cushions are worn out, leaving everyone facing heavier and heavier problems. There doesn't seem to be anything left in place to attenuate the brutality of the economic and social system, especially since the welfare state, the "reducer of uncertainties" (Pierre Rosanvallon), faces new upheavals. Then all the conditions come together to favor the victim's stance, which has a powerful ally, besides: the lawyer. He is now the third party that steps in between the individual and his malaise, as an essential ally but who can, calculatingly and self-interestedly, lead to the proliferation of undue subjective rights to the detriment of the common good.

America leads the field, exemplifying the traps to avoid (since victimology is becoming a national plague).[3] The legal annals abound with anecdotes that are grotesque and hard to believe. How does a serial killer answer for his crimes? He pleads over-exposure to television and its relentless sequences of violent images. A father kills his little daughter? She was asking for it: in fact, it was she who was killing him with her nasty personality. A woman develops lung cancer after forty years of avid nicotinism? She hits three cigarette companies with lawsuits for not publicizing information on the dangers of tobacco. Another accidentally puts her dog in the microwave to dry? She holds the manufacturers guilty for not having specified in the instruction manual that the apparatus is not a drier. The murderer of the mayor of San Francisco wants to explain his act? He'd eaten too much junk food and it temporarily made him unstable. A mother kills her baby? Her lawyer talks about a hormonal imbalance and demands an immediate acquittal. A fortuneteller loses her divinatory talents? She accuses her hairdresser of using a shampoo that caused the gift to disappear. A university president is caught making obscene telephone calls to young women? Alas, he suffers from abnormal amounts of ADN in his chromosomes, which causes these acts of uncommon turpitude. Not to mention the killers with multiple personalities who never recognize themselves as the ones who delivered the blows, or those criminals who complain about their arrest as if it were a particularly underhanded form of discrimination: why me and not the others?

In every case, the extenuating circumstances (perfectly legitimate in a State of Law) have become exculpatory circumstances that are intended to clear the accused before the case is tried. The rights industry is proliferating,[4] with everyone standing up for his own characteristic, right down to the individual, the *smallest minority there is*, and assuming the permission to prosecute the others if they so much as cast a shadow on him. "If you can establish a right and prove that you have been deprived of it, then you acquire the status of a victim" (John Taylor). The phenomenon is growing, and groups and communities are springing up everywhere, defending their images, up in arms against any pejorative allusion to them. "Dieters United," an association for the large and the obese, organized a picket line in San Francisco to protest in front of the cinemas where Walt Disney's *Fantasia* was playing. Why? The dance of the hippopotami in tutus ridiculed fat people. Any cause, even the most eccentric, becomes pleadable, and the legal universe is degraded into a vast fair where lawyers solicit customers, persuade them of their misfortune, make up cases of litigation and promise a big payoff if they find a third party to pay.

WE ARE ALL CURSED

Are these purely American extravagances, excesses of a system where the defense has more weapons than in other countries?

Probably. France, for example, would appear to be secure from such exaggerations insofar as it remains a political democracy centered around the State, whereas America is a legal democracy where the law limits and circumscribes the State. And France enjoys a degree of social protection, an array of welfare provisions that the U.S. is missing and that it tries to compensate with an explosion of legal provisions.[5] But America stands as a great challenge to Europe, which usually responds with either complete rejection or servile imitation. America is fascinating in that it anticipates the ills of modernity and, like a magnifying glass, reveals pathologies that are not yet discernable elsewhere. Because she was in the vanguard in the fight against discrimination, she is a model and, at the same time, repulsive. By revealing what works and doesn't work, she enables other countries to avoid certain errors. But it would be misleading to claim that distance or a difference in traditions would protect Europe from developing such bizarre conditions.

For in the last thirty years or so, a fundamental mutation, very similar to the evolution in American, has affected France. As a side-effect of all the new technological and therapeutic breakthroughs, which have led to serious accidents on a scale that had been unknown up to now, we have gone from a system of responsibility centered on fault, that is, on the designation of a responsible party, to a system of compensation centered on the risk and where the chief concern is to compensate the victims, to restore equilibrium. And since, in the name of solidarity, French law consistently evolves toward guaranteeing reparation for any damages (especially for the consumer and the user), there is less emphasis on seeking to prove an infraction or a serious error and more on finding solvent entities, however remotely they may be implicated in the litigation. In short, just as in civil law one can be "responsible without having responsibility" (François Ewald) — it is enough to be covered, that is, insured, even if it means disqualifying any form of sanction.[6] The legislators have given the status of victim a special dignity, and rightly so, in fact.[7]

France's 1985 law on traffic accidents already automatically lays the blame on the driver, discharging the pedestrian from any responsibility for his own imprudence (in consideration of the disproportion between the vehicle and the human being). In the same way the Council of State, in keeping with the proverb that "tears don't come from the blue sky," now allows that mental anguish and various emotional disorders can be taken into account. And for certain crimes the statute of limitations goes well beyond the ten years established by the law; the judges already can modify the clauses of a contract in order to find a legal alibi to provide compensation, at all costs. And everywhere, under the pressure of morality, belated lawsuits are being heard,[8] the lawyers are being called in, and cases are reopened, due to a growing ambition to repair emotional damage, even several decades later. "The law," said Kant, "does not come into existence by means of the law alone," and major changes in legislation result mostly from the pressure of public opinion.

However, on this point attitudes are fairly similar on both sides of the Atlantic. We in France have a political class that, whenever there is the least whiff of suspicion of corruption, howls about outraged innocence, media plots, and the tyranny of the judges. We have our trade unionists and especially our farmers who allow themselves to hold protests, occupying and trashing public buildings, burning files and archives, polluting the streets by spreading liquid manure (and fruit and vegetables), and wildly attacking the police without worrying about the consequences, in the belief that the crisis in farming — or if it comes to that, in fishing, mining, or freight haulage — justifies their depredations *a priori*. And the same ones rise up, outraged and threatening, if by chance someone calls them before a court to answer for their actions. France may find itself with a return of the old labor mentality, excusing in advance any attack against the capitalist and the employers, combining with the new legal trend imported from the Anglo-Saxon world and triumphing in the proliferation of lobbies, each socio-professional category establishing a monopoly in a certain sector and striving to extort the maximum benefit without concern for the collective interest. And it will be far worse if, as in America, the division between right and left gives way to an aggregate of communities and special interest groups, if ethnic, religious, tribal and regional divisions override the spirit of citizenship, if each minority, to defend itself, poses as having been martyred by the collective.

"Halt the genocide," the farmers and fishermen shout in concert. The former have had continuous State subsidies for many years, the latter protest against the declining price of fish. Survivors of the Holocaust or of Rwanda will appreciate this extensive use of the word. Businessman and politico Bernard Tapie exclaimed, during the summer of 1993: "I feel like a Jew being hounded by the Gestapo," when he was put under investigation by the magistrates of Valenciennes (he later apologized for making this comparison); and at the same time the Socialist Bettino Craxi, pursued by justice as part of the Clean Hands operation in

Italy, used the same metaphor. Young Moslems in Grenoble, in February 1994, protested the prohibition on wearing the Islamic scarf at school by wearing arm-bands with the crescent of Islam, in yellow, on a black background, together with the inscription, "When is our turn?", an obvious allusion to the yellow star that the Jews were made to wear under the Occupation. And when militant Islamists, suspected of sympathizing with the Algerian FIS during the summer of 1994, were placed in detention in a barracks in northern France, they immediately hoisted a banner calling it a "Concentration Camp."

Why does everyone want to be a "Jew" today — and especially the anti-Semites? It is a fantastical means of attaining the status of the oppressed, because in Europe we have a Christian vision of the Jews as the crucified people *par excellence*. And to elevate the tiniest conflict to the level of the fight against Nazism. The far right in France, the United States and Russia are also adopting this victim-rhetoric, and their flamboyant tirades on white supremacy, the superiority of the blonde brute, are receding to the background. Their approach, defensive now, is that of the subjugated, the slave fighting for his survival: we're the real Jews (implied: the others are usurpers). And from what are the French suffering, for example? From ethnic purification, of course, on the part of the immigrants who spread crime and insecurity.[9] And all of France is victim of a genocide, according to Jean-Marie Le Pen, since under the leftists the State "imposed a socialist art of conformity worthy of Doctor Goebbels."[10] All you have to do is pick up the vocabulary of the Second World War and reverse it. They preach "resistance to the invasion," but it is the invasion of wops and immigrants they are talking about; they condemn the "FLN collaborationists," i.e. the various rightist and leftist governments that brought Algerians into France, they call for a "second purge" but what they want is to try the traitors to the fatherland (the last presidents of the Republic) who opened the doors of our beautiful country to the invaders.[11]

The process is not new and the winner is always the one who sounds the most pitiful. The expert in *victimist inversion* was the great Céline, the exaggerated anti-Semite, the anarchist collaborator. In the tradition of the extreme right lampoonists, he deplored his condition in 1957, vomiting with the arrogance of the winners, a self-designated lost soul, crushed, demolished, making much of his kindness for the elderly and the beasts and calling the tribulations of the Jews mere trifles compared to the martyrdom that he was enduring (thanks to which he could continue to execrate them, in all good conscience). The proscribed writer gave in to today's most widespread pastime: weeping for oneself. If he did not receive the Nobel Prize, it is because he was a true Frenchman, not one of those foreigners who were taking over the whole country. "I should have been named Vlazine . . . Vlazine Progrogrof. . . If I had been born in Tarnopol on the Don, . . . but Courbevoie, the Seine! Tarnopol on the Don and I would have had the Nobel long ago . . . but me, I'm from here, and not even Sephardic . . . they don't know what the hell to do with me . . . Naturalized Mongolian . . . or a fellagha like Mauriac, I'd be driving a big car, I could do anything I want . . . I would have been secure in my old age . . . cherished, pampered, I swear to you . . ."

Generally speaking, for a cause to catch on with the public opinion, it has to seem to be an underdog; it has to present a miserable vision of itself just to win our sympathies: and to that end, nothing is excessive. Extreme vocabulary is recommended, the least affront must be elevated to the supreme insult. Under these conditions is it any surprise that more and more of those in French prisons, far from sympathizing with the misfortunes of those whom they have wounded, robbed or killed, fob off all the blame onto society? Why should delinquents feel accountable for their offences when the whole nation rejects any idea of fault and offers only models of blazing irresponsibility? How can one believe in punishment — when no one has a sense of infraction anymore; and why practice virtue when the majority ridicules it?[12] And let's not forget that when laws were established limiting the right to smoke in public spaces or making it obligatory to wear seat belts (or helmets, for motorcyclists), so many good souls screamed about the return of moral order, about insidious totalitarianism, Communism no less! How many then, calling themselves enemies of the new police state, draped in the mantle of the damned, of the cursed, called for the right to smoke where they want, and to drive at whatever speed they wish, ready to be mowed down in the street to defend these basic freedoms? Such measures, modest and useful as they are — since they moderate the conflicts and the boorishness that govern relations among motorists, or between smokers and nonsmokers, and limit the rule of the most powerful — were met with a range of reactions from reluctant consent to vociferous reprobation. But the same people who accused the State of infantilizing its citizens by controlling their morals fell, themselves, into the role of the crybaby, who wants do everything his own way and stamps his feet when he hears the word "No"! In any case, nothing — not even the hysteria of certain Americans when it comes to the fight against tobacco — justifies the over-reaction we hear sometimes in Europe, such as a note in *The Independent* (London), in August 1993, commenting on the death of a heavy smoker on whom a cardiologist had refused to operate before he stopped using tobacco entirely — "the twelve million British smokers are on the way to becoming social pariahs; they are already confined to certain zones, outlawed in most public places . . . Now, they no longer are offered first-rate care. . . This is medical fascism: the right to survival for the strongest, the elimination of the weakest." Fascism! The great word is dropped like a bomb. What is fascism in an age of infantile laxity? A totalitarian regime founded on conscripting the people and worshiping racial purity? Not at all: fascism means anything that opposes or challenges an individual's inclination, anything that restricts his whims. So then, who is not affected, who does not suffer and have a right to complain? Why do the citizens of democratic countries want to be absolutely convinced that they live in a totalitarian state, that corruption, advertising, and censure are the equivalent, here in the West, of assassinations or torture elsewhere, in short, that there is no difference between them and the martyrs of the rest of the planet? Isn't this a way of donning the guise of the resistance fighter, without running any risk? Isn't there any other way to repudiate the moralism (which is only very relative, at that) of our societies without invoking the two abominations of the 20th century, nazism and Stalinism? *Isn't it time we re-learned to weigh our words so that we can measure the world more accurately,* instead of elevating trifles to the rank of ignominies and insidiously corrupting the language?

Of course there is no direct relationship between the various examples stated above, between the panic of the wage-earners and workmen pushed to desperation by their precariousness and the rhetorical effects of a powerful orator or a demagogue, except that from the top to the bottom of the social scale (and especially among those at the fringes), everyone is desperately fighting for the "most desirable place," "the place of the victim."[13] Indeed, many of our habits and attitudes in France are heading us down the slope of generalized complaining. Thus we find one of the most common faces of the contemporary individual: a big, whining baby with a lawyer at his side. Senile infants allied with the clerical chicanery of these men of law: that seems to be our future.

DON'T JUDGE ME!

In the Fourth Promenade in his *Reveries*, Rousseau distinguishes the truth according to society from sincerity according to oneself. The first depends on public opinion, appearances, and the false values that are current in society, the second is based on one's inner voice and feeling. Now, the soul cannot lie, it is the seat of the Good and this is why Rousseau recognizes only one court: that of his own conscience. In the name of this good inner nature, he decides for himself for which faults he owes repentance and for which he can be exonerated: a lie he told a girl in his youth bothers him more than the fact that he abandoned his offspring, a fault for which the world and society castigate him. For he knows only one idol: "the holy truth which [my] heart adores," far more real than "the abstract concepts of the true and the false."[14] "One must be true to oneself, that is the homage which the honest man must pay to his own dignity." In the evening of his life, taking stock, Rousseau declares that he has paid for his sins and, taking posterity as witness, pronounces that he is free of blame. For he is basically good and whoever doubts him and thinks he is dishonest "deserves to be destroyed, himself."[15] His faults came to him from outside, he sometimes was mistaken but "the desire to harm never entered [his] heart."[16] (Rousseau's torment was that in seeking to embody, in his own existence, the Utopia of the natural man, he paid the price of being a great misanthrope. He who believed himself virtuous and blamed sin on others ended up in resentment and hatred of humanity.)

Here, the father of *Emile* inaugurates, with consummate sophistry, the entire modern movement of relativism. If only authenticity counts, then everyone is entitled, in the name of himself, to hold himself apart from the common laws that would deprive him of his fidelity to itself. Don't judge me: you would have to be me to understand me! Each one becomes an exception to which the code should adapt, each one deduces the right of its own existence. The law, instead of restraining the appetites of an immoderate ego, is required to fall in line with its vagaries. And the pain that we feel when it strikes us gives an objective base to this relativism: it purifies us and gives us an unhoped-for gift, a renewed sense of candor. And this candor is not only the absence of evil: it is the impossibility of spite, of being bad. It is not the relative innocence of man, who is fallible by nature, but absolute innocence as an ontological status, the innocence of the angel who can never sin. Any act emanating from me cannot be bad since I am the source and the source sanctifies it: I remain pure, even when I make a mistake out of carelessness. This means saying, like Rousseau, "In my situation, I have no other rules than to follow my inclinations without constraint. . . I have only innocent inclinations." In this sense, victimization is the complainers' version of privilege; it makes it possible to become innocent once again the way one can become a virgin again; it suggests that the law must apply to everyone except me, and suggests a society of castes behind which the fact of having suffered harm replaces the advantages of birth. Other people's misconduct toward me is a crime; my own failures are mere peccadillos, venal sins that it would be indelicate to emphasize. Democracy now boils down to the permission to do what one likes (provided one appears to have been hurt) and the weak one's right to protection disappears behind the clever one's — the ones who have the money and the connections to plead the most incredible causes — right to advantages.

The risk is that posing as a victim confines one to imposture, that the losers and the humble are dislodged in favor of the powerful, who are experts in the art of assuming the mask of the humiliated. The brutalities of arbitrary rule crop up in the State of Law in its most sophisticated forms, and efforts to give more opportunities to the disadvantaged turn into a perverse reinforcement of the powerful. Take, for example, the petition sent to the head of the French State in January 1994 by a hundred doctors, asking him to pardon two of their colleagues who were wrongfully condemned (according to them) in the contaminated blood scandal. The object of such a request is to affirm that Science, in the name of medical uncertainties, must remain above the law and that in the future no researcher or expert should be disturbed, even for grave errors. As though the risks of transfusion were nothing more than an inevitable tax that humanity must pay for the advancement of medical knowledge. The worst thing about this petition is that it tends to expel the affected patients and give their place to the accused doctors, who take on the privileged role of the victim.[17]

Those in positions of influence, using excellent arguments, are trying to ban restrictions on their own conduct and looking to leave to the lower ranks the unhappy privilege of answering for one's errors and being judged accordingly: an abdication that, if it were to spread throughout all of the middle classes, would mean the end of the democratic pact. All our acts disperse and are reflected on others in a multitude of resonances. We try to take advantage of this dilution by distinguishing ourselves from them and by saying, *it wasn't me!* But "the consequences of our actions grab us by the hair, indifferent to the possibility that in the meantime we have become better" (Nietzsche). When the elites want to set themselves beyond the judgment of good and evil and refuse any form of sanction, then the whole social body is invited to banish the very notion of responsibility (and that is the same risk of corruption: it makes a mockery of honesty, makes it the exception, both futile and obsolete).

The pathetic pleas referred to above — the pleas of all those who think they should be exempted from the rigors of the law — must be regarded in this light. There is no doubt that in France the police are still arbitrary and brutal, seeing the ordinary citizen as a potential suspect. There is no doubt that when someone is placed under investigation the accompanying publicity makes a mockery of the presumption of innocence. There is no doubt that we have seen terrible miscarriages of justices and that the legal machine — with its rigid pomp, its ceremoniousness, and its lan-

guage that is as incomprehensible as Church Latin — is intimidat-
ing to the layman. And finally, it is true that the judges' obligation
of reserve (which often hides a respect for affluent and a contempt
for the poor), the maze of procedures, the trap of interrogations
give this entire institution an appearance of inhumanity. But this
detachment, which is supposed to be immune to prejudice, to
feelings, to the intimate impulses of the heart, is precisely what
makes justice essential. It is the dispassionate third party that
introduces reason and arbitration and makes the judge, as we read
in *Ethika Nikomacheia*, the incarnation of the law: he weighs the
pros and cons at equal distance from partisan influence. The
natural fear that grips any man when he has to deal with the
courts (the fear that he will be crushed by a machine that is bigger
than he is), leads to a perverse syllogism: since the innocent sometimes are wrongly condemned, if I am accused, it must be that I
am innocent. Consequently all of justice is suspected of despotism, of being the embryo of a new Inquisition.

TOWARD A HOLY FAMILY OF VICTIMS?

While it is excellent that jurisprudence is evolving toward
better protection of those who have been harmed, those who are
at the bottom, the good intentions thus expressed are not without
ambiguity. In this respect the French law of 1985 on road accidents is an instructive example: a pedestrian can commit all sorts
of stupidities, cross the street against the light outside the designated crosswalks, or dash into the street, and he is assured of being covered (even when he commits "an inexcusable fault," a concept that is almost never retained by the courts). Such a law sup-

poses that only the motorized person (the powerful one) must be virtuous, for the weak one is always right; that in the confrontation between them, the first starts with a handicap, the second with an asset. Under such guidelines we are no longer assessing a precise damage but assigning statuses that take precedence over any other consideration. In other words, if this system were to spread to other spheres of endeavor, individuals would not be judged any more but would be prejudged, pardoned ahead of time, based not on what they did but on what they are: absolved before any inquiry, if they are on the right side of the divide, and condemned if they are not. In an effort to defend the weak, we are establishing certain categories that are outside the common law, and exempting them from the need to be prudent and cautious. Accordingly, justice is becoming a political means of repairing social inequalities and the judge is being used as a direct competitor of the legislator.[18]

It is true that the great adventure of modern times has been the emergence of the underdogs onto the public scene, and their gaining access to all the privileges of ordinary citizens. It is perfectly legitimate that more and more groups and various minorities (the handicapped, the disabled, the obese, the petite, homosexuals, lesbians, etc.) are becoming legal and political activists to fight against the ostracism to which they have been subjected. France, in this respect, unquestionably lags behind the New World (we all recognize, for example, how impossible it is for the handicapped to get around in our cities). But the war against discrimination must be waged under the principle that the law applies to everyone, with the same rights and the same restrictions. If it establishes as a precondition that certain groups, because they are disadvantaged, are entitled to special treatment, then everyone else will be tempted to band together in new feudalities of the oppressed.

If all it takes to win is to be recognized as a victim, then everyone will fight for this gratifying position. Being a victim will become a vocation, a full-time job. However, a former abused child who commits a homicide as an adult is no less a murderer even if he excuses his act because of his unhappy youth. Because historically certain communities were subjugated, the individuals who comprise them would thus enjoy a credit for misdeeds for eternity and would have a right to the jury's indulgence. Society's debt towards such and such of its constituents would automatically translate into leniency, into forbearance for any person belonging to one of these groups, even long after the time when they stopped being persecuted. What remains of legality if it recognizes the privilege of impunity for some, if it becomes synonymous with exemption and is transformed into a machine for endlessly multiplying rights and without anything in exchange?[19]

This could lead to an environment of civil war in the microcosm, setting child against parents, brother against sister, neighbor against neighbor, patient against doctor, weaving relations of mistrust between everyone. In the field of health care, for example, how much remains of the concept of risk — "the chance of incurring a harm, with the hope, if we escape it, of obtaining a good" (Condillac) — if all medical risk systematically confers the right to compensation? How can anyone provide a highly toxic treatment if the patient is going to bring a lawsuit over the least negative outcome or effect? How can we reconcile the questions of cost, proper patient care, and the possibility of innovation?

How can medicine avoid taking a defensive stance, in which the fear of litigation results in foregoing advanced techniques that imply particular dangers and certain vocations are losing their appeal (such as anesthesiologists and surgeons)? How, in a word, can we avoid the American situation where the very high cost of insurance for obstetricians (who are the target of innumerable lawsuits) renders the price of childbirth prohibitive and constrains many low-income people to settle for the services of a mid-wife?[20]

In short, if the dispute were to multiply *ad infinitum*, the common world would become the community of our dissensions, and the law would no longer be what unites men (as Montesquieu suggested), but on the contrary would be the agent of their separation. And politics, subordinated to the legal world, would devolve into simple arbitration between incompatible subjective rights.

Every type of damage, even the most eccentric, could be taken into account; in extreme cases, even a panic attack should have its price, a set value, and should justify searching for a culprit. We need a persecutor, and a wealthy one, since we are so lucky as to be living in an era when "the scapegoats are solvent" (Pierre Florin). The fear of harm would become a harm in itself, as it is now in the U.S..[21] Little everyday setbacks and misfortunes would no longer be seen as normal episodes in existence but scandals that open up the right to compensation. Boredom would have to be compensated. The reason why our era is overrun with pullulating victims of imaginary wrongs is because that is what they have to do in order to be able to take advantage of their woes. The table of penalties is arranged by dollar amount.

(This is one of Robert Nozik's favorite ideas: that every problem is a harm that can be compensated by a payment.) And this has the effect of creating a commercial vision of pain that is now thought of in terms of profit, of interests. Then the temptation is great for each one to invent parental abuse, an atrocious childhood (which one would rediscover, if need be, under intensive psychotherapy), to cultivate one's miseries like hothouse plants in order to derive benefit from them, to accumulate failures as others do nest eggs. From the fetus to the bald person, the thin, the fair, and the short-sighted, swaybacks and hunchbacks, smokers. . . the holy family of victims would expand to include all of mankind. While we are at it, why not apply the quality of victim to the inanimate world, to trees, stones, and land, as the radical environmentalists do, and proclaim ourselves their defenders?[22]

Here again the lawyers' influence will be decisive since in France there is an effort underway to increase their role in the course of lawsuits while avoiding the abuses that are found in the American system. (In America, lawyers set their fees according to the amount they win; thus they are tempted to exaggerate claims, systematically hustling the client. In France, their more limited role limits this propensity to file lawsuits wrongfully with the sole aim of extorting money. However the Sapin-Vauzelle law of 1992 allows lawyers to demand further investigations by the examining magistrates. It is a real, though tiny, progress and in France it is still the judges who control the lawsuit and not the parties: for example while it is common to cross-examine witnesses in the U.S., in France it is extremely rare.) As political agitators used to persuade workmen of their potentially subversive nature, the men of law can transform themselves into creators of artificial litigation, suggesting to each of us that we are unhappy, even if we are unaware of it, and canvassing clinics and hospitals to flush out possible plaintiffs. Such is the paradox of our situation: on one hand, the right to reparations is still in its infancy here; defense has very little room for maneuver, and the underprivileged have limited access to justice; the State, the administration, the hospitals form untouchable monsters against which the individual has practically no recourse; and more generally the legal order in France is still a second-rate authority and remains under the control of the executive even if the judges have already freed themselves from it mentally. On the other hand, the right to responsibility, which is jurisprudential and thus liable to evolution, could lead us toward certain of the excesses of American society while failing to provide us with any of the advantages. That will probably be one of the greatest challenges of the future: how to synthesize the republican spirit in France with Anglo-Saxon democracy, when the law is becoming more and more a complement of political actions to repair injustices that politics alone cannot resolve. It is not simply a matter of legal activism versus traditional representation, but of combining their reciprocal benefits to ensure better protection of the citizens. We face a twofold task that is delicate yet imperative: to lead the legal revolution that is underway to a proper conclusion, while setting up safeguards (for example, by enacting criteria of inadmissibility to discourage abusive suits), without which it would fall through even before being applied.[23]

DEMONOLOGIES OF ALL KINDS

The collapse of ideologies has deprived us of a convenient excuse: blaming our misfortune on imperialism, capitalism, communism. It's getting harder to say "it's X's fault" and make it stick. However, it would be a mistake to think that the disappearance of these bogeymen means our societies have become wiser. On the contrary — now that the big scapegoats have disappeared, we are tempted revive them in some abstract form, and to ascribe our fatigue, our discomfort to the treachery of some obscure entity that covertly bothers us. This kind of reasoning is well-known. Do we think we are free when it comes to sexuality? A more cunning censure still weighs upon our impulses and penalizes real libertines. Do we think we enjoy total freedom of movement? It's a Machiavellian stratagem of the powers that be, to control us all the better. And our wealth itself is only testimony to some kind of underhanded fascism, some covert totalitarian control.

Homo democraticus entertains an ambiguous relation with respect to despotism: he hates it but regrets also its disappearance. In extreme cases, he seems almost inconsolable at the loss of oppression. Now, for want of real enemies, he forges imaginary ones; he delights in the idea that he perhaps he really is living under a dictatorship, that fascism will fall on him from the sky, a prospect that fills him with hope as much as fear. Thus for William Burroughs and for Allen Ginsberg, "The first hallucinogenic drugs in America was not LSD or mescaline but *Time* magazine and television. There is indeed a 'plot,' but it is that of the ruling power, a monster that seizes you, a cancer whose metastases corrode you to the bone. One is all the more controlled by his torturer when one is grateful to him for not having resorted to violence." A well-disciplined State does not need police. "The conspiracy is everything that filters into your cranium and penetrates your knowledge through images, through the codes and messages of the language. 'My body is a soft machine' invaded by parasites."[24]

This kind of talk succeeds because it is unverifiable: nothing confirms it, and nothing contradicts it either. It mires those who go along with it in the dual role of watchman and warrior. He is not easily deceived: unlike all the naive ones, he combines clarity and intransigence. He knows that the system is all the more diabolical for appearing tolerant. But his war cry is, You are all slaves without realizing it. This reassures us; he thinks he is revealing to us the apocalypse, and he points out to us a vague cabal, evil and imperceptible, which embodies all that is negative, all that is incomprehensible. Invoking these shadowy forces relieves us: since a diabolic causality determines our destinies in spite of us, we do not have to answer any more for our actions: we are cleared, and the origins of our sorrows lie outside of us. It's better to invoke extravagant conspiracies based on subliminal images and invisible substances than to accept the sad, banal truth: that is, that we shape our own history even if, according to the sacred formula, we do not know the history that we shape. And so, by means of fantastic wild imaginings, we return to the candor of the seraph.

A THIRST FOR PERSECUTION

What is moral order today? Not so much the reign of right-thinking people as that of the right-suffering, the cult of everyday despair, the religion of obligatory whimpering, conformity in distress that so many authors make into a honey that is a little too adulterated. I suffer, therefore I am worthy. Instead of competing in excellence and enthusiasm, men and women compete in displaying their disgraces, and make it a point of honor to describe the particularly appalling torments to which they are subjected. But our idolatry of pain goes hand in hand with a terror of adversity; it is not endurance school but fear-of-pain school. And what are our reality-shows on television but an exhibition of pained hearts, the promotion of the victim as national hero, with whom we each should identify, and the idea that only those who have suffered attain dignity? Suffering is analogous to a baptism, a dubbing that inducts us into the order of a higher humanity, hoisting us above our peers. The stars of misfortune can then hold

up the patent of their curses like reverse lineage, an obscure royalty that makes them part of the majestic class of outcasts. The
thirst for persecution is a perverse desire to be distinguished, to
come out of anonymity and, in the shelter of the fortress of affliction, to take advantage of other people. "God is paying attention
to me," says a sentence painted on a wall in one of the old people's
homes in Beaune, "and I am being particularly tested only because
I am particularly well-loved." Misfortune is the equivalent of election, it ennobles those who endure it and assert it, it sets one
apart from the main flow of humanity and turns disaster into
glory. This only happens to me, says the one who is sorely
tried — in other words: I am the object of a persecution that is
tied specifically to my person and that means that I have been
chosen out of all the others (the inverse of that belief: thinking
that you are protected by your lucky star, that fortune smiles on
you). Thus the writer Knut Hamsun, starving in Norway in the
19th century, saw his misery as a divine sign. "Was this the finger
of God pointing to me? But why me? Why not just as easily some
man in South America? The more I thought about it, the more
inconceivable it seemed to me that the divine Grace had chosen
me arbitrarily as a guinea-pig to try out its whims. It was, rather,
a unique sign that out of everyone in the whole world, he had selected me. I found the most powerful objections against the notion of an arbitrary Lord who made me expiate the sins of all."[25]

As Aimé Césaire noticed in connection with slavery, there is
a special beauty in the degraded, the debased, the disparaged — a
grandeur in those who, being nothing, think that they will become everything and who read their misfortune as a promise of
the Kingdom to come. We are not talking about that secret pride

among the have-nots, here; but of the strange contemporary figure of the *professional pariah* who whines in rich countries and across all the social classes, including the highest. This is an elite that is ranked according to a strict hierarchy and to the traditional aspects of nobility they add the greatest of all: the aura of the rejected. By a curious reversal, the fortunate and the powerful also want to belong to the aristocracy of the margins. They take on a particular luster when they are seen as outcasts, and they talk not like the dominators but like the oppressed. Today, the real notable is the one who is posing as a dissident; the true master is the one who, in order to reign, invites everyone to trample the masters and who presents himself as if he were a slave. (It is easy to see, for example, how the society's denunciation of the spectacle on television — a way of slandering the media — makes it possible for the spectacle to acquire even more power.) I mentioned, above, the secret admiration for the figure of the Jew, a dubious philo-semitism that can shift so suddenly into its opposite. Other false façades are possible: history is a bottomless trunk and we can dig out, with both hands, a vast repertory, a theater where oppressed figures of all kinds are just waiting for us: we can don the guise of the dispossessed proletarians, the victims of colonization, the guerilla, the boat-people, or battered woman and children. But why do we want, at all costs, to resemble the exploited when we are in fact well-off? Do the well-off have such a bad conscience? Or, rather, do we want to have it all, both the ease of the middle-class and the sulfurous prestige that adheres to the damned, the distinction of erasing our banality by devising a tragic background? So many regular people, good parents and good spouses, absolutely make a point of pretending to be rebels and contrarians when in fact they lead a life of conformity that has not the least drama. They have not undergone any particular wrong but they cast themselves in the grandiose light of torment. If Christ, in our civilizations, is the incarnation of the victim, then in declaring ourselves to be plagued by problems, we suggest that we are ourselves of divine origin, we give the beauty of an epic to the inertia of our lives.

There is more to this. If pain lends value to those who suffer, then the ostentatious exaggeration of one's least concern makes it possible to exert a profound will for power over our close relations (as Nietzsche recognized in the Christian worship of the ascetic and of the penitent).[26] Then the least adversity is enlarged to the scale of a major event, transformed into a bastion where one settles in to make a lesson for others while placing oneself above criticism. It's a haughty way of holding oneself at the margin of the margins, absolutely outside the pale, where the claimed misfortune coincides with supreme arrogance and is transformed into strategy for domination. Claiming that we are persecuted becomes a subtle way of persecuting others.

Such is the message of modernity: you are all disinherited and have the right to cry over your fortune. You survived your birth, your puberty, you survived that vale of tears that we call existence (in the United States, a whole body of 'survival literature' has come together, where those who have experienced the least tribulation, however tiny it may be, describe it to everyone else). The victim market is open to all, provided that you can display a beautiful open wound; and *the supreme dream is to become a martyr without ever having suffered anything but the misfortune of having been born.* In our countries the individual thinks of himself by subtraction: the powers that be, churches, authorities, and traditions, until he is reduced to a tiny base, the ego, independent of everyone and everything, isolated, unburdened but also infinitely vulnerable. Alone vis-à-vis the power of the State, vis-à-vis that great Other that is the society, worrisome, immense, incomprehensible, he is frightened at being reduced to himself. Now he has only one recourse: to change direction and start from his wounds, which he amplifies and increases in the hope that they will confer on him a certain dimension and that finally someone will take care of him.

COMFORT IN DEFEAT

But it would be wrong to believe the current cliché that stigmatizes this attitude as the ultimate stage of individualism. It is exactly the opposite: of all his possible roles, the contemporary individual tends to retain just one of them: that of the plaintive, colicky, whining baby. But you can't play sickly child with impunity. There is a price to pay for the comedy of abuse and this price is reduced vitality, weakness, and a return to the state of voluntary destitution. And a new human model is indeed surfacing nowadays in the West, stunted, petty, and frail, defined by his own assent in his weakness and a penchant for disavowing himself and withdrawing from life. There are two ways of handling a setback in love, politics, or profession: to blame oneself and draw the necessary conclusions, or to accuse a third party, to point to some other person or event as responsible for our loss. "'I am suffering; certainly somebody must be the cause of it,' thus reason the morbid sheep," (Nietzsche, *Genealogy of Morals*, Third Essay). In the first case, we give ourselves a means of overcoming the failure,

of transforming it into a stage on the route to personal achievement, into a necessary detour that enriches the journey. In the
second case, we condemn ourselves to repeating it by blaming the
fault on the other and by refusing any introspection.

*Thus, the statement that one is never guilty comes at the cost of saying
that one is never capable.*[27] The goal of life is no longer to grow or to
surpass oneself but to adhere stingily to that which one already is.
Instead of exalting all that enhances man and especially the mastery of his own fears, we sink into a conformity of whining that
makes survival our sole concern, taking pleasure in our smallness,
defensive and uptight. Victimization is the choice of those who
are prey to their fears, who make themselves into objects of compassion rather than facing up to what frightens them. Trying to
eliminate suffering at all costs only worsens it; we become obsessed with an evil that expands all the faster as we focus on it.
Between being resigned to misfortune (which was the odious
message of the leading classes and the Church in the 19th century),
and our insane allergy to the least pain, there may be less difference than we think: in both cases, the same fatalism impels us to
give up, to give away our authority by calling on all kinds of inter-
mediaries (lawyers, doctors, experts) who are supposed to protect
us from harm. While it is wise to avoid suffering, some minimal
difficulty is inherent in our condition, some amount of irreducible
danger and harshness without which life cannot blossom. Refusing those risks means looking for a free ride from cradle to tomb.

How can we avoid seeing that our disappointments, our little catastrophes, even our worst enemies help us in their own
way, strengthening us, forcing us to discover unsuspected resources within ourselves, energy, tricks, dynamism and valor? A

person's strength of character is measured by the number of hurdles or affronts he can get past without falling; obstacles only fire him up, hostility encourages him, he rises above the others who are stopped by fear and pusillanimity. Oppression, as Solzhenitsyn likes to say, produces greater personalities than the insidious softness of liberalism. But without actually wishing for oppression, being overly tender is also dangerous; it locks people up in their role as victims and prevents their going further. Saying "I suffer atrociously," when one hardly suffers at all, means disarming oneself in advance, making oneself unable to face a real problem. (This gives rise to the propensity to treat everything as a medical problem, to eliminate all discomfort by taking pills, to promote tranquillization to a form of universal cure.)

Recognizing each one's fragility should not kill our spirit of resistance; and today we need thoughts that exalt energy, joy, light-heartedness. We need alacrity, cheerfulness, serenity. The victimary rhetoric that becomes exhausted in its own statement must be countered with a policy that directs complaints toward a reasonable goal and offers them a viable discharge system, allowing people to express their pain in measured terms in order to surmount it. Harping on our problems — mental Onanism — keeps us from distinguishing between what can be changed, what depends only on our will, and the immutable, which does not depend on us at all. Any bad luck is seen as an inescapable decree of fate. The individual is great only if he takes part in something bigger than himself — in particular, civic sovereignty — and does not remain immured in himself; but he capitulates to the attentions with which we surround him and, believing he is gaining additional protection, he actually becomes more precarious. Tocqueville pointed out that it is a mistake to confuse individualism and selfishness: the second is an eternal feature of human nature, the first is a recent formation in the history of cultures. May it please heaven to make the contemporary individual egoistic, at least, that he have at least a minimum of vitality, of the instinct of self-preservation. We are living in a paradox of selfishness that ends up killing the ego by trying to preserve it at all costs, to keep it safe from the least opposition.

The proof: the more secure we are, the more we feel a need to be protected against a polymorphic adversity that can come out of nowhere. The less exposed contemporary man is, the more he feels he is in danger. Fear of disease is keeping pace with the progress of science, and medical breakthroughs generate an irrational anguish over every type of pathology until we are "suffering from health," as George Duhamel already observed in 1930.[28] In short, imaginary dangers are proliferating even as we gain better control over the real dangers. Beyond a certain threshold, the instruments of our liberation thus transmute into auxiliaries of our debasement. And we are seeing the twilight of the great libertarian revolt of those heady years: our claims of autonomy are given up as we undertake a frantic search for assistance, and the courage of self-affirmation dissolves into a culture of small and wan pleasures based on the comfort of being protected. Those who declared they were sovereign over themselves and the world become slaves of their own fears and have no choice but to call for help and to struggle along, supported by all kinds of crutches.

But being free means, above all, enjoying the bonds of affection and reciprocity that tie us to our counterparts and make us people with responsibilities. We are burdened with all the obstacles that, by limiting our independence, renew it and enrich it. Being a subject means being subject to the others, never believing we have paid all our debts to them, participating in the network of gifts, exchanges, and obligations that constitute human commerce. But what remains of the individual and his responsibility when, relieved of all debt towards the others, he can no longer answer for himself? How can we ask to be protected by the others when we can no longer handle our own protection? "If I am not for me, who will be for me? But if I am only for me, am I still me?" (Hillel).

Footnotes

1. Folio, Gallimard, 1971, p. 106 sqq.
2. Laurent Cohen-Tanugi, "La démocratie majoritaire et l'État de droit," in *L'Interrogation démocratique*, Centre Georges-Pompidou, 1987, pp. 89 sqq.
3. I take as my basis John Taylor's article in "Don't Blame Me" in *New York* magazine, June 3, 1990, and Pascal Dupont's book, *La Bannière étiolée, op. cit.*, pp. 152 sqq.
4. Richard Morgan, *Disabling America, The Rights Industry in Our Times*, Basic Books, New York, 1984.
5. I refer, again, to the distinctions presented by Laurent Cohen-Tanugi in *Métamorphoses de la démocratie*, Odile Jacob, 1989, pp. 120 sqq.
6. Many authors have rightly said that insurance, by immunizing us against the effects of our own actions, encourages denial of responsibility. Among them are Alain Etchegoyen, *Le Temps des responsables*, Julliard, 1993, and Jean-Marie Domenach, *La Responsabilité*, Philosophie, Hatier, 1994, pp. 30-31.
7. In a fascinating study on new developments in civic responsibility, Ms. Laurence Engel, an auditor at the French budget agency, expresses her concern that the US model of rights and responsibilities is already taking hold in France, with all that that implies. Referring to consumer protection, she writes, "The ultimate criterion is no longer responsibility, strictly speaking, but the possibility of assuring the victim what has been judged to be just compensation: and so, the one who has the resources to pay, either directly or through insurance, will be designated the responsible party," (notes from the Saint-Simon Foundation, February 1993, p. 12.) As a direct consequence, the judges go through the entire chain of people who might be implicated until they find someone who can pay (this is called *deep-pocket liability*). Laurent Cohen-Tanugi and Maria Ruegg, in a rather harsh article, have contested Laurence Engel's representation of the judicial hell of America and its possible repercussions (*Le Débat*, no. 76, pp. 137 sqq.).
8. Odon Vallet, "Quand les moeurs changent le droit," *Le Monde*, January 20, 1994.
9. Jean-Marie Le Pen, during the May 1 parade in Dijon: "In our country, a virtual occupied zone is being formed in which the French citizens are deprived of some of their essential rights as regards their liberty and their security, and which is absolutely intolerable. The insecurity that prevails in our cities and housing projects and that provokes a veritable phenomenon of ethnic cleansing of the native French is only a conse-

quence, and not a cause."

10. *Le Monde*, January 20 1993. The National Front organized a colloquium in 1987, entitled: "One heart for France: an end to cultural genocide."

11. A National Front meeting at La Mutualité on October 26, 1994, with Bruno Gollnisch and Roger Holeindre. ·

12. According to a report by M. Maillard, prison chaplain at Looslès-Lille, there has been a change of attitude among prisoners in the past fifteen years: they no longer feel that they are locked up to pay a debt to society, but see themselves as being persecuted, wounded beings who are awaiting their liberation. "The entire prison regimen inclines the prisoner to deal with his grievance and never with his crime or his offence. The prisoners have a whole strategy and way of speaking to minimize their responsibility for their acts, to manage to make it look as though their role is minor. But this strategy always lays the blame on the other party and on society as a whole." The prisoners, concerned with getting the shortest possible sentences, don't talk much about the victims whom they injured but they do talk a lot about themselves in terms of being victims. (My thanks to Antoine Garapon for bringing this report to my attention.)

13. René Girard, *La Route antique des hommes pervers*, Grasset, 1985.

14. *Les Rêveries du promeneur solitaire*, op. cit., p. 83.

15. *Les Confessions, op. cit.*, Book II, p. 438.

16. *Idem*, p. 103.

17. On this subject I recommend André Glucksmann's very convincing book, *La Fêlure du monde*, Flammarion, 1994.

18. Must we be afraid of the power of the judges and fear that jurisprudential creation ill de-legitimate popular sovereignty? Philippe Raynaud warns against the figure of the judge as an "oracle of truth "and asks that we not yield to an angelic conception of the law that ignores the conflicts and the attributes of sovereignty. (*Le Débat*, no. 74, March-April 1993, pp. 144 sqq.).

19. Irène Théry has rightly observed that "Rights have destroyed the law, since they do not reinforce but dilute the law," (*Le Démariage, op. cit.*, p. 354).

20. Frank Nouchi gives an excellent synthesis in "Les balbutiements de la nouvelle responsabilité médicale,"[The Garbled sense of the new medical responsibility] *Le Monde*, April 6, 1994.

21. "The judges basically authorize Americans to bring charges even before any harm has been done, as soon as they have suffered any anguish. . . .

The fear of being harmed has itself become an immediate and tangible harm." (Laurence Engel, *Notes...*, *op. cit.*, p. 13.)

22. Luc Ferry demonstrated that this radical environmentalism is actually a form of anthropocentrism masquerading as something else, in *Le Nouvel Ordre écologique*, Grasset, 1992.

23. Laurence Engel, following François Ewald, suggests we de-couple the question of responsibility from that of indemnization, and to not lose sight of the needs and the well-being of the victims; in other words, to facilitate the reparation for damages while reinforcing the sanction and maintaining the notion of fault, a solution whose character she concedes is somewhat paradoxical (*Notes...*, *op. cit.*, pp. 31, 37, 38).

24. Pierre-Yves Pétillon, *Histoire de la littérature américaine*, Fayard, 1993, p. 244.

25. Knut Hamsun, *La Faim*, Cahiers Rouges, Grasset, p. 17.

26. In fragment 113 of *Aurora*, Nietzsche asserts that the ascetic's torment is "a secret will to control," a desire to distinguish himself in order to better subjugate his neighbor. Moreover, he distinguishes in the Christian taste for mortification, for pain, "a pleasure in power," "the vast array of psychic vices to which the desire for power was delivered" (*Aurore*, Pluriel, pp. 82-83).

27. Here, I am borrowing a distinction from J. R. Seeley, cited by Christopher Lasch, *Le Complexe de Narcisse*, Robert Laffont, 1980, p. 31.

28. In a study from Credoc, "La maladie grave fait de plus en plus peur," no. 51, August 31, 1990, R. Rochefort strongly emphasizes how medical progress has amplified our fear of grave illnesses that are seen more and more as forms of malediction.

CHAPTER 5

THE NEW WAR OF SECESSION

(BETWEEN MEN AND WOMEN)

"An erection is in itself already a phenomenon of aggression."
> Robert Merle, *Les hommes protégés.*

"The two sexes will die, each on its own side."
> Proust, *Sodom and Gomorra.*

You see them strolling together down the street, pushing children in strollers, laughing, eating and dancing in public, even embracing each other. But behind the smiles and the kisses, underneath the friendly, well-ordered appearance of daily life a devious, all-out, and merciless war is being waged. Between which camps? Men and women. On one side is a coalition of the conservatives, the media, men of the church, and the industries of movies and mass culture, all banding together against women to force them out of the work force and back to the home, to their roles as mothers and wives. On the other side is the divided ensemble of these same women, young and not so young, who are both victims of and accessory to their oppressors; they are punished ruthlessly for having dared to raise their heads and claim equal rights.

FROM HITLER TO *PLAYBOY*

This specific confrontation is only the latest episode in a war that has set one sex against the other since times immemorial. For the male, endowed with that mortal weapon that is called the penis, is basically aggressive. "Violence is the penis and the sperm that comes out of it. The penis has to do its job forcefully, for a man to be a man."[1] Equipped with that curse that hangs between his legs, man thus has only one obsession: to kill, to destroy. He brings barbarity as the cloud brings the storm. "Male sexuality, drunk on its intrinsic contempt for life, especially for the life of women, can become wild, springing in pursuit of its prey, using the night as cover, finding its consolation, its sanctuary, in darkness."[2] Making love, for a man, is almost always synonymous with brutality, with murder. "The American culture — movies, books, songs, television — teaches men how to be regarded as killers, to identify sex with the act of killing, with conquest and violence. That is why so many men find it difficult to distinguish between rape and making love."[3]

What is the common feature that connects the Third Reich to *Playboy*, and even more to *Penthouse*? It is pornography, which certain liberals insist on defending and which is worse than Hitler.[4] For the industry of the X-rated is nothing but "an instrument of genocide" or, to put it another way, "Dachau introduced into the bedroom and celebrated."[5] But take a look at Picasso, Balthus, Renoir, and Degas, too: these famous artists reek of hatred of women, whom they depict as lascivious little girls or as idiotically

ethereal dancers or whom they cut into pieces, whom they mutilate in order to mock them, to degrade them — as does most of
the abstract sculpture of the 20th century.[6] Rape thus summarizes
the general tone of relations between the sexes. "From prehistoric
times until today, I believe, rape has played a particular function:
it is nothing less than a process of intimidation by which all the
men keep all the women in a state of fear."[7] Yes, the immense majority of men, not to say all of them, mistreats women in one way
or another and it is recommended that women be particularly
wary of those whom they love: loving relations are nothing but
"rape embellished by suggestive glances,"[8] a disguised relation of
power,[9] and only by discouraging him can you acceptably live in
peace with the man in your life.[10]

Victim of a vast plot that unites television and institutions
against her[11] and that aims for nothing more or less than her destruction,[12] woman is thus the paradigm of the oppressed: the
slave of the slave, proletarian of the proletarian. She embodies the
most abyssal suffering and a woman to a man is like a Jew to an SS
officer. The phallic elite's hatred of her is so radical, its will for
extermination so powerful that "in most parts of the world,
women and children have become an endangered species"[13]!

FEMALE DICTATORSHIP

That's not true, the politicians, pastors, intellectuals, fathers
of family, and professors retort indignantly. The real martyr in a
couple is the man and not the woman. By destroying marriage,

the feminists only push men to despair, to alcohol, to suicide. "The celibate man is like a prisoner on a rock with the sea rising. He is a biologically shipwrecked man, with desperate dreams. . . In terms of criminality and mental illness, depression and mortality, the single man is the victim of the sexual revolution;"[14] the feminists, or "feminazis" as Rush Limbaugh's populist far right movement calls them,[15] form "a socialist, anti-family movement that encourages women to give up their husbands, to kill their children, to practice sorcery, to destroy capitalism and to become lesbians."[16]

Who is responsible for the disintegration of the family, the Social Security deficit, and the mass production of delinquents? Unwed mothers, American and British conservatives answer in chorus, "those girls who get pregnant only to jump the waiting list for subsidized housing."[17] Who is guilty of the genocide perpetrated on the persons of embryos and fetuses? The partisans of free abortion, of course. And Cardinal O'Connor proposed (in August 1992) to set up "a tomb of the unborn child," like the tomb of the Unknown Soldier, in every catholic diocese in America.[18] The feminists? They are the equivalent of the Khmer Rouges, said Professor Allan Bloom, who felt he was being harassed by them in his university like a Kampuchean refugee by his tortureres.[19]

So it's the men who are the real losers: as fathers, they are systematically deprived of their children by the legal machine that evinces "racism" and "tyranny" against them and even subjects them to "a silent and perfidious genocide" (Michel Thizon, founder of S.O.S Dad). Moreover, they are hounded day and night by narcissistic and avid creatures who lure them into the trap of marriage, bitterly claiming their right to happiness and the orgasm, and then leave them to seek consolation with any passing gigolo. And they can be certain, too, that in the event of litigation, justice will always side with the woman.[20]

For women are everywhere; they have toppled men's strongest bastions, and have transformed the family and the school into a vast gyneceum. Moreover, they are infantilizing and feminizing our children and even our precious cars are being subjected to this horrible female anatomy, since all the manufacturers have shifted to using rounder, softer forms (Yves Roucaute). A future devised by women? A gigantic political-social structure for mothering. "From the law against tobacco and alcohol advertising to the prohibitions on smoking, from seat belts to the obligatory helmet, citizens are being transformed into children who need to be protected from themselves; and I call the State that is being built, the 'preventive State.' Dare I say that this is *the most insidious form of totalitarianism that humanity has ever encountered?*"[21] (author's emphasis.) Not only have the women won, but they have the nerve to live longer than men and still they dare to complain.[22] Haven't they always been perfidious and dishonest? From gentle Frédégonde to the widow of Mao Tse-Tung, the history of women in power is only a succession of crimes, lubricity, and unequaled perfidy.[23] The truth that should be proclaimed is that "men suffer more than women," that they are crushed by the success of the ladies who, as frantic careerists, transform their male subordinates into slaves.[24] Lastly, it should be acknowledged that men are not men anymore:

softened, emasculated, gentler in their contacts with the second sex, they must find themselves again, retreat into the forests and isolated places to awaken their lost virility, to rediscover the "beast lurking within them,"[25] the great primitive creature that has been stifled by sisters and wives.

In short, both sides in America (and to a lesser degree in France) use such bellicose speech that, through its excesses, it adds up to only one thing: coexistence is no longer possible. It's either fight or stay apart. *What is left of male-female relations when each side claims to be the offended party? War or secession.* Indeed, it is a law of the victimist contagion that any group or class denounced as guilty declares itself in turn to be oppressed, in order to escape the charge. However, in this discourse of enmity, it is the very existence of the other that constitutes an affront. The rift between the sexes is thus transformed into a strict border that separates two species who are as foreign to each other as snakes and wolves. The male or female adversary has the right only of expiation, the right to apologize, to affirm publicly that s/he "refuses to be a man"[26] or a "liberated woman."

Let us clear up one misunderstanding right from the start: from this standpoint the gulf seems immense between America on one side, and France and southern Europe on the other. And this is for the simple reason that the laws in Europe are infinitely more favorable to women and children than on the other side of the Atlantic where, in addition, the conservatism of the Reagan-Bush years exacerbated the all-out attitude of the feminists. However, it still would be presumptuous to think that Europe will remain immune to the American contagion. Due to its magnetism, America has a knack for propagation and an ability to export its worst while reserving for itself its immense virtues. This chasm separating the two cultures, however, should be elevated to the rank of a theoretical difference: from this standpoint, the difference between the United States and France is not the difference between puritanism and libertinage, it is merely two ways of expressing the same democratic passion, the passion for equality.[27] In the name of the ideal of equivalence between man and woman, America preaches a kind of maniacal coding of their relations, tinged with hostility and mistrust; France, on the contrary, while not ignoring this concern, emphasizes the affinities rather than the divisions. In the name of emancipation, America breaks up; in the name of civility, France connects. Depending on which approach carries the day, the entire face of this fundamental alliance may be upset.

FREEDOM, EQUALITY, IRRESPONSIBILITY

Two things, said Montesquieu, kill a Republic: the lack of equality, and extreme equality. From this perspective, we still live in a world dominated by male values, in politics as well as in the workplace and the sharing of domestic tasks.[28] It is also true that a certain form of brutality toward women persists, ranging from forced incestuous relations to assault and battery.[29] The few women who attain positions of responsibility, especially in public office, must armor themselves to be accepted there, they must become, as the expression sums up so nicely, an Iron Lady. Ben Gurion said of Golda Meir, "She is the only man in the government." That says it all; and in many Western countries it is still valid. Without even getting to the inequality that goes with ageing, or the tyranny of beauty, a woman in government or in a company will always have to prove herself, that is, to do something extra to excuse herself for her success. It is as though it was assumed that imitation was the way to get from the state of subordinate to that of equal: to beat the men, you have to play on their turf and accept the validity of the procedures that they use. Because the masculine remains "the universal human,"[30] the standard of reference, many women executives, journalists, and professors have had to become dragons or viragos to be taken seriously (contrary to Mrs. Thatcher who, anxious to remind everyone that she was also a wife, had herself filmed while baking a pie for her husband).

Recognizing the persistence of male legitimacy makes it laughable to lament the decline, the universal debauchery, the destruction of the family, etc.. Thirty years after the feminist explosion, it is still easier socially to be a man and the principal levers of control remain in men's hands (even if on certain points, the right of custody of the children after divorce, for example, justice prefers women in an often abusive way — a trend that is, in any case, changing).[31] For sharing power does not mean abdicating, and making some concessions is not the same as making a revolution.[32]

That posited, it would be absurd to ignore the importance of

the changes that have occurred in recent years. We have indeed
seen, in the course of the century, the end of the automatic principle of authority being granted to men. Once they have admitted
the idea of equality, it is becoming more difficult for men to keep
their partners under supervision, to refuse them a privilege that
they grant themselves. The man, who used to see himself as the
quintessential human animal, the incarnation of Reason, relegat-
ing the woman to the side of nature and brutishness, now sees
himself constrained to moderate his supremacy. And what if
anatomy were destiny for him too, as Napoleon said?

What has changed in the last two decades is our partners'
tolerance for violence, suffering and trouble; gone are those long
retirements where our grandmothers frittered away their lives
because of morals or the respect due to their sex, gone is the stoi-
cal endurance of blows from choleric husbands; and gone is the
worship of unilateral fidelity that forced a girl to belong to one
man for her whole life; gone is the secular equivalence of women,
waiting, and resignation. The divorce rate is accelerating because
wives no longer hesitate to leave their husbands for the sake of
their individual success or a certain idea of happiness. And who
can blame them? Why should they be obliged to stay, kept from
remaking their lives? In the past fifty years, the greatest event in
this field is the visibility of women who have stepped away from
hearth and home and moved into the corporation as well as the
university, even into the highest positions. Conversely, what is so
shocking in certain traditionalist Moslem countries is the male
omnipresence, the absence or the discretion of the female element,

enclosed, contained, shielded, veiled, and kept to a subordinate role. What a sinister spectacle these women present, walled behind a piece of fabric if not an iron grill, and the cafés and streets teeming with young men whose faces reflect erotic misery and the certainty of an interminable life of frustration.

The achievements of the second sex diminish or weaken the picture of catastrophe that many feminists, especially American, present of their condition. Too often the enormity of the charges damages the credibility of the claim. Susan Faludi shows the extent to which antifeminist women in the United States act according to the same values that they challenge: independence of judgment and action, financial and professional autonomy, etc.. The neo-conservative is already a feminist in her rejection of feminism, and her lifestyle contradicts her call for women's return to the home. Marilyn French suggests that women do not enjoy any freedom, that an immense cobweb hinders their every gesture; how is it, then, that feminist protests meet with such an echo and such popularity? Isn't it a gross distortion to compare the anorexia from which certain girls suffer (victims of the dictatorship of fashion that constrains them to stay thin) with the Nazi death camps (Naomi Wolf)?[33] If the backlash against women in the United States, seeking to send them back to the household and maternity, is as relentless as Susan Faludi says it is, how can we explain that these same women continue to "enter the workforce in great numbers," to "postpone marriage," to "limit the size of their family and work while raising their children"? How can we take such a battle seriously when the author, after having stigmatized the string bikini and the miniskirt for imposing "a political vision of sexuality," writes triumphantly: "The designers have not succeeded in subjecting (women) to the most frivolous diktats; in spite of the plethora of garter belts and teddies displayed in the stores, they continue to buy cotton underwear." When was a significant war won by purchasing cotton panties and boycotting fine lingerie? Are we meant to associate this with the diatribes of the Church against female nudity, the bra and the corset?

> "What must one think of those women who use artificial means or corsets to accentuate the protuberances of their bodies, to increase them or simulate them somehow?" thundered one Reverend Father at the end of the 17th century. "Some confessors require that such blouses be covered with a kerchief, a scarf or a shawl. This remedy seems to us rather to encourage the evil than to destroy it . . . It would seem preferable to use these shawls and scarves, and to reject any artificial intermediaries as not being appropriate at all to Christian women. In this way what is missing will not be noticed, chastity will not be wounded and the salvation of souls will not be in any danger."[34]

We begin to suspect that certain feminists' rage comes not so much from a retreat as from progress — from the certainty that the attainments of the movement are quite irreversible. If the women have conquered "a new right, that of being unhappy,"[35] if they are torn between their loves, their careers and their children, it is because they have become, after the men, private people, forced just like them to struggle to invent themselves. However, this is a disappointing victory: not only has autonomy failed to remove the old burdens related to their condition, it has deprived them of the special regard that was their were due; but moreover it results in the distressing feeling of every man for himself. We have already seen that liberty disillusions and isolates whereas liberation unifies and exalts; one contrasts with the other like prose with poetry, like abiding by the law versus merrily over-throwing prohibitions. In other words, the feeling of futility and lassitude that many women (and men) feel comes not from an ob-struction but on the contrary from an achievement.

Still, the heinous philippics heard on both sides do not fore-bode anything good: as if relations between the sexes necessarily had to be poisoned as their conditions became more similar. It remains to us to prove that the liberation of morality does not lead automatically to war or recrimination. The patriarchal order and marriage used to be, above all, guarantors of peace between men and women. Feminism always had two components, a liberating anti-authoritative component and a cult component crystallized in resentment and uterine chauvinism. While it is possible to be-lieve in the first and to reject, with our partners, everything that smacks of discrimination, everything that prevents them from controlling their fertility and inhibits their free choice (what is feminism if not women's demand to attain the dignity of the sub-ject?), it is difficult to avoid seeing a certain inconsistency in the other position. While the women's movement is not supposed to fall under the rubric of revenge but rather that of rights, it is obvi-ous that certain militants are calling less for equality than for "preferential treatment,"[36] and act like a lobby anxious to use every possible means to increase its assets in the race for power.

Reading them, one understands that nothing will ever satisfy their aspirations, that the least setback immediately will be ascribed to the phallus-bearers — obvious scapegoats that are constantly sacrificed and resurrected in order to deflect attention from one's own role question. The Malicious One must be stigmatized, which makes it possible to forge tighter bonds within the group. The heterosexual white man is afflicted with three irremediable flaws: his sex, his skin color and his desperate normality that is, in fact, an appalling pathology (by contrast, the ideal, untouchable victim would be the black lesbian, thrice protected because she is a woman, homosexual and African-American). The monster, the white male, should be depicted as both formidable and ridiculous, brutal yet threatened by the least claim, a giant with clay feet whose weakness is as much to be feared as his strength.[37] It does not occur to our friends that they could treat their targets on a hierarchical basis, that the situation might call for a more nuanced understanding, and that in one's rage one should not confuse the Western countries (the only ones where women have rights) with traditional cultures, especially the Moslems', where the fate of their colleagues is often atrocious (to be born a woman in an Islamic land is to be born under a cloud of suspicion, and there is no greater ally than women in the fight against fundamentalism). But the underling is the narcissism of rhetorical effect, donning the garb of an insurgent without paying the price, describing independence under signs of absolute oppression to give oneself a factitious appearance of resistance. As though the obstacles, however severe, outweighed the attainments and as if one could equate an Algerian condemned to death by the fundamentalists for refusing to wear the veil and any Frenchwoman or American who runs into marital or professional problems. By doing so, we out off for as long as possible the entry into the age of responsibility, in order to enjoy the double position of the winner and the loser, and we continue to agitate mindlessly for equality, freedom and immaturity. Used carelessly, the rhetoric of the oppressed is like a person in good health who passes himself off as ill and hurts the true victims, those who need a suitable language and the right words to defend themselves.

MY ROOTS, MY GHEITO

Departing (often in spite of themselves) from the roles that used to be reserved for them, but without giving them up completely, men and women now find themselves in a state of uncertainty where they have to piece together new models from the old. This is a nerve-racking struggle. It explains some women's nostalgia for the traditional macho even as they revile it, leaving men astonished to find themselves with partners who are simultaneously so traditional and so liberated. (The Other is disturbing when he steps out of his role and doesn't play one part consistently.) Emancipation has made us into disconcerting beings, vagrants who fluctuate between several roles, several vocations. In this respect seeking "real men" or "real women" simply reveals one's own fantasies, searching for the security of a stereotype, trying to get a grip on the turmoil that engulfs us. Femininity is no longer defined as only the bluestocking, the whore, the Muse or the mother, any more than masculinity is seen as only the boss, the athlete, the owner, the paterfamilias. Feminism has mixed up our perception of women and men, a perception that was neither nor so modern nor so antiquated as we think. Which is why both sides are looking for more clarity: tell me who you are so I'll know who I am. What both sexes miss is not their former relationship, it is the simplicity that used to preside over their divisions: they'd like to end the torment of indecision, to assign the other to his place, to settle into one definition. A timeless order has been overthrown without a new one taking its place, and we suffer from living in an era of flux.

This leads to a twofold and symmetrical temptation: for each side to turn inward and focus on its own qualities, or to sweep them away with a swipe of the hand. The first position celebrates sexual difference as an irrefutable determinism that marks us for life. And while the little males, following the example of Robert Bly's fans, convene in the forests to pound their chests and sniff their armpits, the eco-feminists and other earth mothers sing the praises of the female body, the exquisite female secretions, and the female softness that they hold up in opposition to the brutality of the patriarchate based on "sacrifice, crime and war."[38] The fact of having been born by chance man or woman becomes a fate from which one cannot escape. Each person, depending on whichever category he landed in, has only to fulfill what Aristotle called his *telos*, his essence and his goal, as one point in a succession that preceded him and will carry on after him. At the same time both heir and transmitter, the individual is imprisoned for life in the restricted ghetto of his impregnable difference. He is nothing, his group is all and, as in reactionary romanticism, this membership determines who he is like an implacable command.

This tendency to see sexuation as destiny is often accompanied by a dream of purity that leads one to expel from oneself all that is hybrid, out of fear of being a mixed gender (like a half-caste). Some women like to imagine a world finally rid of men, who would be reduced to 10% of the world population after an energetic extermination,[39] having been rendered redundant by the development of unisexual reproduction through cloning. In this wonderful new world, the mother-daughter relationship represents the quintessence of human relations and an exclusively female language and civil code could be devised (Luce Irigaray), in which one would, for example, say "ovulars" instead of "seminars" and get away from the narrow "ego-testicular" mindset that corresponds to the male vision of existence. Certain radical lesbians take the rage for gender-cleansing so far as to describe the dildo in terms of floral or plant forms, in order to avoid recalling in any way the shameful phallus. In the other camp the males, haunted by fears of castration, are invited to separate from their mothers, sisters, and lovers, to remove themselves from the world of female attraction that softens them and perverts them. (Robert Bly's disciples exclude members of the female sex from their meetings.) Rejected as a friend, the woman is also rejected as a partner in pleasure. As the English poet Philip Larkin brutally expresses it:

"I have no desire to go out with a girl and spend 25 bucks when I can jerk off at home, for free, and spend the rest of the evening in peace."[40] A gloomy Utopia that makes mixed-gender activities inconceivable: sexual affiliation takes on the same status as race, barring any form of mingling. Each sex is a piece of humanity closed in on itself: men and women form two great tribes camped on opposite sides of a river, who can neither speak with each other nor be understood, much less try to come together.[41]

There is a contrary movement as well, that consists in denying any barrier between the masculine and the feminine, asserting that sexual identities do not exist, that they are artificial constructs, the fruit of historical domination. Let us forsake these divisions, forget the highly contingent fact that we have either a rod or a vulva at the base of the belly, and let us follow only one creed: that what a man can do, a woman can also do, and vice versa. Pushed to its extreme, such reasoning (which has often wrongly been ascribed to Sartre and Simone de Beauvoir) makes the distinction between genders as futile as "the color of the eyes or the length of the toes."[42] There are no more men or women, only unique beings, with no past, with no roots, indifferent to their biological constitution and capable of reinventing themselves every morning. Therefore, it is time to end the absurd segregation that has governed relations between the two sexes: from denying women access to all the trades that had been reserved to men (including the most brutal) to the expurgation of any trace of chauvinist supremacy in our vocabulary. In English, this means saying "chairperson" instead of "chairman," "police officers" instead of "policemen," and instead of "No man's land," "neutral territory"; in French it means feminizing all the professions and abjuring the grammatical law that prefers the masculine over the feminine when it comes to such designations. In other words, the iniquitous old division between male and female should be reabsorbed into the unisexual as quickly as possible. This is a blatant reductionism that addresses the tension between men and women mostly by declaring that there basically is none.

So in one case the genders are defined as separate nations, distinct from each other; in the other, the ancient demarcation of the sexes is erased and humanity is decreed accessible to all without regard for the ridiculous attributes that nature confers upon us at birth. For some, the sexual divergence is radical and implies irreconcilable lifestyles, for others it is an artificial border to be forgotten in our urgent campaign to achieve universal equality. It's a dead end either way, erecting insurmountable barriers or removing them with a stroke of a pen. The overthrow of the traditional separation leads one to believe that sexual identity is nothing but a smoke screen, the product of our faulty history. The partition survived intact the liberation of manners that has dissipated neither the mysteries nor the fears. The heady difference becomes all the more loaded since it presents all the features of false resemblance (including in those trades that are least gender-specific). We haven't changed; the closest are still the most remote. Today as yesterday, man-woman relations are still spun from clichés that are both contradicted and confirmed by experience, and that form the stock of their reciprocal animosity. Men continue to dump the most antiquated prejudices on their partners, viewing their sexuality with a mixture of fear and fascination, if not even repulsion; and the worrisome proximity of the second sex in our world sometimes pushes them to compete in boorishness, to adopt the solidarity of a clan in league against the intruder.

FORGETTING WHERE YOU COME FROM

Still, a return to the *status quo ante* is inconceivable. Post-feminism men, however macho they remain, have no more virile patriotism to defend anymore and no longer allow themselves to be reduced to a few stereotypes. On this level it seems clear that we have made progress vis-à-vis centuries past, and that the privileges foregone were also yokes that weighed down our elders. The terrible martinets that some of them were, maintaining iron discipline at home, terrorizing women, children and animals, were hardly attractive. Where was the joy in a life that oscillated between the brothel and the marital bed, finding only fakery here, feigned docility there? Men, too, have learned to be flexible, within certain limits. If we were to add up everything that they owe to women's emancipation, just in the intellectual, professional and cultural fields, we would discover indisputable contributions without which our era would have neither juice nor genius. All the jousting and the mistrust notwithstanding, these essential contributions weigh in favor of the current movement. Thanks to education and work, women have gained in intelligence, subtlety, profundity, and unconventional thought and behavior; they now display multiple facets in areas where convention, habit and religion used to confine them (especially if they belonged to the poorer classes) to the sole destiny of mother and housewife. Being able to interact with one's wife or one's lover, and with women friends, savoring the pleasures of the senses and of conversation, enjoying brains, charm and humor in one person, is an incalculable benefit of our era; and it was the brilliant 18th century — led by the libertines, all the high-ranking people and the courtiers — that paved the way. How vastly that outweighs having to relinquish the meager privileges of yesteryear, the sad happiness of growing old beside a porcelain vase or a doll who is angry at the whole world for having wasted her life and whom age has transformed into a shrew or a harpy! How could we side for even a moment with the sniveling prophets of maleness, with the resentment of the grumpy old boys? There is something grotesque and even repugnant in their search for a culprit on whom to blame their ill-ease, as they seek to transform their woes, their tribulations of the heart, into a case against women in general. The male order mutilated men themselves above all, and we must agree with Charles Fourier that "extending the privileges of women is a general principle of all social progress."

If relations between the two sides of humanity have not improved (liberation is hardly a synonym for serenity), they have become more and more complex; if they have not become easier, at least they are more interesting since they bring beings of (more or less) equal power face to face. Long before we are men or women, we are individuals subject to the same imperative: to construct our identities, to realize ourselves apart from any crutches of belief and custom. It is this need to invent ourselves as autonomous individuals, accountable for our actions and our failures, that bonds us with the others — with all that that implies in terms of anguish and loneliness. Being a woman is not a complete definition of a person: once the other's difference is recognized, we still must avoid reducing the other to that difference alone. Unless we descend into communitarianism, I can become a singular being only by forgetting my roots, by inaugurating a new history that belongs only to me. "A free spirit," said Nietzsche, "is what we call the one who thinks differently than we expect him to because of his origin, his milieu, his condition and his job, or because of the prevailing opinions of our day."[42]

In other words, being free means unshackling ourselves from the circumstances of our birth, while at the same time assuming them. We do not come from nowhere but we have the option of inventing our lives, of imprinting a course on them that is not an exact transfer of our heritage. Our acts are not simply the consequence of our affiliation, they add up to a definition of us because we are unlike anybody else. When Allan Bloom reproaches the feminist movements for "not being based on nature,"[43] he is perfectly right — but he forgets that all of humanity was built by emancipating ourselves from nature.

To be a man or a woman thus does not happen of its own accord anymore. The concepts of female and male persist without our knowing exactly what they mean. Generalizations about the one and the other may have had a certain relevance at one time;

now they are neither true nor false, merely unlikely. Since we cannot qualify either one without hesitation, we are constrained to suspend judgment. A certain number of virtues and flaws are divided equally between the sexes, as a common patrimony. The traditional models have not disappeared, they have been diluted among other options; they no longer dominate (thus the ironic return of the vamp and the macho, the sex bomb and the bodybuilder who parody their stereotypes by exaggerating their hallmark signs). In short, we are no longer following a trail that has already been blazed; that is what has changed, and its implications are enormous. Thus there is no need for women to give up their femininity since, on the contrary, they are free to invent new ways of being feminine (and if the occasion requires it, they can pick up their old roles). *As narrow as the margin of innovation may be, and as powerful as the inertial force of history may be, a range of destinies has become possible within the ancient polarity.* The new Eve will go on resembling the old one for a long time, but we would be blind not to see the things that, within this similarity, differentiate them already. Miniscule as it is, this revolution is decisive. Rather than trying to come up with a new identifying construct to mask this slight shift, why not celebrate it as a chance to explore roads that have never been traveled? Since nothing makes sense inherently — that is both what is great and what is excruciating about modernity — it is up to each one of us to create himself, in distress and enchantment, without using the manners of the past as anything more than starting points, supports, but neither shelter nor refuge.

WOMEN AS FLOWERS, AND THE PORNOCRATS

Everything is rape, and rape is everywhere: in the eye of the passers by, in their gait, their gestures and the air that one breathes, it hovers over every woman as an immense and constant threat. Such is the message that comes to Europe from the United States (relayed Europe by Germany and England), where the ultra-feminists' concern coincides with the neo-conservatives' desire to place sex under surveillance once again. Since rape, according to the new canons, can now take one of four forms (the legal one, between husband and wife; acquaintance rape, date rape and street rape), it increasingly is identified with any form of sexual activity. Whereas in France the legislators had the wisdom to limit the offence of sexual harassment to the professional context alone, in order to penalize abuse of power,[45] in the United States the same penalty extends to smaller everyday actions. A companion to the rape that it anticipates, harassment supposedly occurs in a "hostile environment," a gray zone thus named by the lawyer Catherine MacKinnon, who is a leader in the fight against pornography. In the vast catalogue of human attitudes, any ambiguous behavior, indelicate gesture, racy joke or persistent gaze is suspect. There can be no more admiring of callipygian Venuses, slender-waisted lasses or ladies with nicely-shaped lips — these are acts of odious racism,[46] a pathological attachment to appearances. Workmen must be prohibited from whistling when a pretty girl goes by. And let's not forget the small fry: teasing the girls, pinching them, pulling their hair becomes rape in play clothes, but rape nevertheless. The least electricity, the least gesture toward a person of the opposite sex is already pregnant with a malignant ulterior motive that must be sterilized at its source. Even certain works of art offend the eyes and constitute acts of aggression that should be hidden from sight. In short, the enemy in this case is desire, which is violent and bestial since it is male. Naturally, sexual harassment is unilateral, and to imagine that women could harass men can be only the work of a sick mind or, more precisely, that of a potential Nazi. Thus Jessica Manu, a journalist from the *Sunday Telegraph*, describing Michael Crichton's 1994 book *Disclosure* (about a company director's sexual harassment of one of her male employees), writes, "*Disclosure* is an evil book that plays on the antifeminist trend that is so much in vogue. Reading it, I felt like I was inside the skin of a Jew reading an anti-Semitic book under the Weimar Republic."

There's no point going into the possibilities of extortion and blackmail that this concept of harassment opens up. But the most sinister aspect of this all-out pursuit of rapists — practically all of the so-called stronger sex — is that it begins to exonerate authentic rapists. Criminalizing the least contact, the most modest advance, minimizes and even nullifies real rape, swamping it in an environment of indignation that is so generalized that one can no longer distinguish real rape when it happens. And our zealots don't care since, for them, what is essential is not to punish such and such an offence but to denounce a fundamental anthropological attitude: today's sexual relations. That is the monster to be eradicated, the abominable crime to be wiped from the surface of the earth forever. "Compare the remarks of a rape victim with those of a woman who has just made love. They are very similar," says Catherine MacKinnon. In light of this fact, the principal distinction between the normal sex act and abnormal rape is that the normal one takes place so often that you can't find anyone who finds it objectionable."[47] "Physically," Andrea Dworkin adds, "the woman in the sexual relation is an invaded space, literally an occupied territory, occupied even if there was no resistance, even if the occupied woman said, Yes, please, hurry up, yes again."[48] And what do you call a woman who allows such things? A collaborationist, of course, since she introduced the enemy into the territory! *Conclusion: heterosexuality is a bad habit, to be eradicated.* Thus one can maintain, without blushing, that most women are violated without realizing it and one may regard as a rapist any man who has made love with a woman "who did not really want it, even if she did not let her partner know."[49] Coupling is thus always rape, even when the woman consents: to lower oneself to participate in an act of such ignominy you would have to have been indoctrinated, brainwashed, and mentally raped, so to speak. Anyone who consents to a despot with balls is indeed a slave since the slave is incited by her master to enjoy her servitude.

Such a line of reflection leads to a suggestion that women suspend their heterosexual liaisons in the long term, that they put an end to a form of erotic relations that does not correspond to their profound sensibility, in short, to gradually evolve into total dissidence with men.[50] Women must be dis-intoxicated from male culture and its solidest base — that is, ordinary fornication — must be discredited, for it perpetuates allegiance under cover of giving pleasure. The normal must be labeled infamous, because it is already in itself a horrible perversion, "deviant behavior."[53] In their maniacal hunt to trap the most minor of libidinous inclinations, and by making women obsessed with a fear of rape, these feminists have stumbled onto the paradox of the ascetic that Hegel observed: seeking deliverance from his flesh and his diabolic temptations, the Christian ascetic focuses his attention on it, keeping an eye on it day and night, and while he thinks he has liberated himself from it in fact he falls into a mad fixation on his own body. In short, he triumphs only by succumbing, he remains hopelessly captive to that from which he would like to escape. In the same way, these militants make women terrified and distrustful, inviting them to reject the company of men, to suspect their tender words, their sweet compliments and their caressing looks as a sign of the will for aggression. As Katie Roiphe very precisely notes, sex is becoming again what it was in the Victorian age: a vice, a trauma, an abomination.[52] And it is a given, in this approach, that the only sexuality is male, the woman being satisfied to submit to the attacks of a bestial monster whom she can never desire in return, unless she has been subtly coerced into it. The consequence — the army of victims is growing exponentially, statistics on rape are sky-rocketing, and all of us are sexually harassed. (According to a study quoted in the *New York Times* on December 23, 1993, 75% of women doctors say they have been subjected to sexual harassment by their patients.)

But the paradox of this *lecherous prudishness* is that lunatic hunt for the equivocal, for ambiguity, has the reverse effect of sexualizing everything, giving everything a hint of perversity and indecency. Michel Foucault pointed out that puritanism is not so much the fear or the dislike of sex but a way of making it into an object of licit speech in society, the love of revealing all the embarrassing details and pornographic scenarios. If at least it were about decency! But no, they whip up a frenzy, they flush out the details, licking their chops over crude expressions and vulgarities, they rake up obscenities with a greediness worthy of the Inquisition, they exhibit panties and female nether regions in court, they wallow in smut the better to ban it. Thus Paula Jones, the woman who accused Bill Clinton of sexual aggression during the time when he was governor of Arkansas, claimed to be able to identify "distinctive marks in Clinton's genital area." And how were the Anita Hill scandal and Lorena Bobbit's trial used in America? As excuses to talk about sex, day and night, on all the media, in complete frankness.

EROS BOUND

Without immediately being able to impose a complete rupture between the sexes, the most extreme of the militants are trying in the immediate future to subject the relations to a contractual basis as much as possible. The first commandment: no coupling should take place without conforming beforehand to a definite code. Thus Antioch College in Ohio promulgated a charter

regulating the sex act that, from now on, must be regulated if possible by a written agreement. The warning to womanizers, phi-
landerers and other young Casanovas is clear: "You must obtain
consent at every step of the process. If you want to remove her
blouse, you must ask her; if you want to touch her breasts, you
must ask her."[53] That doesn't leave any room for improvisation,
for the free deployment of gestures and desires — everything must
be meticulously detailed. And when will loving embraces be codified in agreements sworn before a notary,[54] specifying which fantasies are authorized, how many orgasms are required (with a
penalty in the event of deficiency)? Why this state of "contractual
belligerence"[55] (François Furet) between the sexes, analogous to
that which governs the various social groups vis-à-vis the ruling
power? Because it is a weapon against oppression and must correct the perverse effects that weigh upon the minorities and particularly on women.

This is the dream of a society that has been entirely recreated
and refashioned by the law, right down to its smallest aspects,
and that bans habitual action — that is, our involuntary heritage — that rejects tradition and its relations of force sanctioned
by centuries of subjugation. This contractualism, a consequence of
the litigious nature of American society, may be perfectly legitimate within the context of marriage and tolerable within the
framework of the "prenuptial agreement" in vogue among American stars and certain others (in which a lawyer is hired to draw
up a contract guaranteeing that in the event of divorce, the richer
of the two will not be bled dry), the fixation on contractual agree-

ments becomes more problematic when it is used to govern the vague field of feelings and passions. Not only is there a danger of interjecting the law in cases where relations are harmonious, but a danger of casting a shadow between partners who are always prompt to brandish the law book at the least hitch. Private quarrels, domestic squabbles must, as far as possible, be resolved without any public authority intervening. The law is not competent nor welcome everywhere. But especially in the sphere of love, a mutual benevolence is required that allows for total abandonment, play, discovery, and the invention of an understanding specific to the lovers.

It is true that in the act of love the woman is the one who brings slowness and refinement; she resists haste and simplicity. She teaches the man the value of time, the linkage between patience and sensuality; she teaches to him to defer his pleasure, to go beyond the simple, too simple mechanics of the penis. Deliberation and leisureliness accompany the unfurling of a pleasure that needs time and attention to blossom and unfold. The young male learns at puberty to restrain himself, i.e. to oppose nature. Female eroticism, a factor of civility and complexity, holds off the crudeness of the brute and the precipitation of the adolescent. When a woman decides not to give in immediately, to make her suitor wait, and when a couple places various obstacles between desire and fulfillment (not to kill the pleasure but to increase it), they are absolutely within their rights. Since when has anyone considered it necessary to make a general law to govern this? In this field, the individual's whim is supreme, and nothing, nothing should obstruct it when the arrangement is between consenting adults. Lovers are free to abandon themselves entirely within the scope of certain rules, staging their own scenarios; any agreements that link, for example, sadists, wife-swappers or the heroes of Sacher-Masoch remain purely private arrangements, concluded according to micro-strategies of pleasure. Until proven otherwise, one does not present himself before a lawyer to deliver himself as a slave to his mistress, or organize a pleasure party or taste joys of a ménage à trois. In the same way, governing any bedroom behavior by written regulations (as required by the code of conduct at certain American universities), negotiating the least territorial concession step by step, means placing the sexual union under the eye of an all-powerful authority that has of absolute control over the emotions of its administrates. At least it could address the subtleties of eroticism, playing with the interdict as was the case in earlier times with the rule book administered by the confessor: they allowed the woman certain carnal concessions that were rigorously circumscribed. These permitted impudicities reduced the force of the taboo in a context of overall condemnation of the flesh that has been maintained by the Church up until our day.

But the pointillistic "sexually correct" approach in America confines love within the alternatives of yes or no and cheapens hesitation and procrastination. It ignores the importance of "maybe" (Georg Simmel), that hangs between agreement and refusal, it overlooks the fact that desire proceeds by various ways and responds well to ambiguity and uncertainty, and that one is not always sure of his desire beforehand. To require coeds to plan in advance everything that they will do, to invite them to "think about what they say and say what they think," is to believe naively that one can plainly spell out his desire and program it like a computer. The rule is there only to tell us what we should do and to reduce the burden of a freedom that terrorizes us. (In the same way the erotic codes may betray the inability of American men and women to communicate otherwise than through coercive regulations.) No doubt our love does obey tacit laws; but sensual happiness is also the ability to forget these laws, to transcend them, to play with them all the better to subvert them. Eros must remain a child of the imagination or it will fade away.

In no case can we allow with the public administration to regulate our turpitude, to lie in bed with lovers and spy on their frolicking. If we have gained anything in the last century, it is that society overall has ceased interfering in our love lives; and to reintroduce it by means of the judges would be a terrible step backward, authorizing everyone to interfere with everyone, ringing in the reign of mutual surveillance. The charm of our era is that it permits every approach to love, including the most enigmatic of all: abstinence. We should not be agitating for such and such form of eroticism, neither libertinage nor conjugality, but for a world where every inclination can be satisfied, a world that delights tender hearts as well as perverts. (The decision to remain chaste and pure is perfectly right if it is made with complete freedom, as an individual choice and not a collective constraint.) Pleasure must remain the sole arbiter of its excesses and its limits — or else we will find that we have wrenched Eros from the influence of the priests and doctors only to subject it all the more thoroughly to the control of lawyers, opening up a new field of legal expertise.

That the embrace of love allows one to delight in degrading oneself, that the lowest and the highest may come together, that is what repels the bigmouthed hypocrites, the sanctimonious cold fishes and the new den mothers of the feminist movement. It is normal to want to reinforce legislation against rape and to punish it for what it is, in other words, a crime. But it is with the aim of preventing lubricity and licentiousness that the new prudes and the old churchgoers are mounting a guard at the bedroom door and launching their crusade between the sheets. Both groups, in spite of their differences, have as their only goal to keep women in a state of inferiority, even if it means picking up again the most well-worn arguments of sexism.[56] As though a woman, victim of her own weakness, her charm, and the perfidious seducers that surround her, cannot survive without a guardian. Both groups utter the same paternalistic statements, declaring women to be passive, impressionable, and unable to govern themselves, foolish geese who are the target of coarse fornicators, brainless little beings who need to be warned (against drinking too much at a party, for example) to compensate for their fragility, their lack of maturity. This type of advice is summarized in one assumption: we know what is good for you, better than you will ever know. What is intolerable in a certain form of feminism (like the male chauvinism of which it is often just the mirror image) is that it dictates how a woman should be and labels this dictation an emancipation, defining for her a revealed truth that is as coercive in liberation as it used to be in oppression. Who then should receive prize as the best censor? All the prigs who want to rein in the fair sex, or her alleged liberators who cherish woman only as a miserable, crushed being, the better to control her? There is something intensely dubious in their solicitude that mostly consists in terrorizing their protégés and keeping them in a state of infantile fear, forbidding to them to pull themselves out of their condition. And one senses these muses' terrible impatience to stand as candidates, after the fathers, the masters and the priests, for the position of supremacy over the fair sex. This "sexual correctness," can be reproached not only for heaping stupidity on top of stupidity, but most of all for harming the cause that it claims to support, for being nothing but an aggressive form of resignation supporting the notion that it is still a woman's lot to submit, to suffer. And finally for wavering in regard to carnal pleasure between the most ridiculous prudery and the most contemptible vulgarity, making stunningly base remarks on the subject, and being unable, for want of culture, to grasp the symbolic and poetic dimension of eroticism. Learning about love is mostly a matter of learning how to talk about love, and one never learns that as well as from poets, novelists and philosophers.

CURING THE HEART OF ITSELF

In the great game of passion, men and women both claim, in turn, that they bear all the burden of sadness and declare the other sex unworthy of their devotion. Each one claims to suffer from a particular torment, declares himself or herself the big loser and accuses the other side of not understanding anything about the misery of loving. This type of argument, which can be levied in either direction, argues in favor of abstention or a redefinition of love since it has been so badly damaged by centuries of injustice. "Women who love too much" (as they are called in the eponymous best-seller by Robin Norwood) are wrong, according to Susan Faludi, to blame their vexations on personal reasons.[57] For sentimental disappointments have a social and political origin, and those who ignore this fundamental law are condemned to become "relationship addicts" or to remain alone, brooding and harping on their misfortunes.[58] Behind this warning lies a recurrent idea found with all the reformers of passion since Charles Fourier: that there is a political or legal solution to unhappy love affairs, that instead of each one crying in his (or her) own corner over these disgraces everyone should band together, overthrow the system, and give birth to a new idyllic world. It is the same therapeutic obsession that led the prophets of the sexual revolution in the Sixties to ridicule love, to reduce it to an old fable that would be tossed into the shadows of the past by a new free play of the senses and a flourishing of the flesh. It is still this same fear of dependence in love that encourages certain feminists to denounce sentimental ties — how can we preach equality when everyone persists in misleading each other, in humiliating each other, instead of engaging in collective combat? Those women who admit to sometimes giving in to rage or jealousy are looked upon with condescension and pity, they are made to feel guilty for wallowing in their misfortunes, they are urged to join their sisters and friends in the fight.

However, whatever the state of equality in a given nation and whatever the justice of its laws, putting happiness to death is not the way to do away with the pain. In the first place, love adds to the pleasure of life the privilege of winning an election without meriting it. That some being likes me, and that I cherish him/her in return, has nothing to do with the virtues of either party. No particular quality or nobility of heart enters into the choice in love; it can be fixed just as passionately on a villain, a coward or a hero. By the same token, the most democratic of societies cannot correct the fundamental iniquity in passion that consists in being preferred over every other — and for purely arbitrary reasons. Love is an obvious denial to all the Utopias of justice. It can reach the heights of splendor or the abyss of infamy, and it does not respond in the least to the concept of progress or merit. I never deserve to be loved, the affection that is given to me is something extra and unearned, like an ineffable grace. Seeking to cure the feeling of itself, of its shadowy face, sterilizes it. The heart, in its capacity to transform any being into a "being of escape" (Proust), the heart confers upon the loved one, however humble, a plenitude, a majesty that sets him above the common run of people. The cherished being, by the ardor that we dedicate to him, becomes a free and frightening force that we vainly try to domesticate. The more attached I am, the more he eludes me, the more obscure and distant he seems, until he takes on a fantastic dimension.

Loving means granting to another, of our free will, power over us, it means making ourselves dependent on his or her whims, putting ourselves under the control of a despot who can be as peculiar as s/he is charming. With one word, a simple about-face, the beloved can elevate me to the zenith or toss me into the dust. Tying ourselves to a man or woman whom we no longer know because we adore him or her means making ourselves vulnerable, and discovering that we are naked, captive, defenseless. Loved ones not only transform themselves into strangers as our relations gain in intimacy; they represent an equal possibility of ecstasy and disaster. Listening to them, venerating them, waiting for them is tantamount to yielding to an absolute verdict: I am accepted or rejected. Thus we can fear the most from the people who are most dear to us — their loss or their leaving would mean a mutilation of an essential part of oneself. Love redeems us for the sin of living; when it fails, it shocks us with the gratuitousness of this life. The atrocious thing about suffering in love is being punished for having wanted to do everything possible for the others' good because we loved them; it is a punishment not for a fault but for a rejected offering. And the "No" that rejected lovers hear cannot be appealed; they cannot blame it on anyone else, they are left to their own solitude.

Of course there is happiness to be found in love, the happiness of having someone always at your side, a feeling of complicity, shared trials, and the happiness of being able to lower one's guard and to surrender oneself in all confidence to the other — but it is a happiness that bears within itself the germs of its own destruction, if it degenerates into a predictable calm. Certainly it is always possible to dislodge the other from his/her position of eminence and in the course of a shared life to make him predictable, as familiar as a piece of furniture, or a plant. But that is a sad progression and we waver in our liaisons between the fear of not understanding our partners and the despair of knowing them too well. The first wound that our beloveds inflict upon us comes when they seem so rich with intense, attractive energy, and we exhaust ourselves in following or trying to anticipate them. The second wound comes from the excessive transparency of others who become too human, too easily anticipated, and who by losing their superb aura, their unexpectedness, also lose all interest. In this arena, victory is no different from a rout and we vacillate constantly between the violence of the unknown and the dullness of the too familiar. In one case the other eludes me and I hopelessly strive to catch up with him; in the other I elude him, in that, to the extent that he made himself available he became a part of the normal course of my existence. I had been blown away, off-balance; here I find myself again, I recover my equilibrium. But in exchanging failure for security, I also lose a necessary tumult. For the worst horror is to survive as a couple in quiet automatism. Once the maddening enigma that the other represents has been resolved, he becomes banal. I have tamed him so well that I suffer from his excessive distance no more than I suffer from now from his annoying proximity. Just yesterday, I couldn't grasp him even inside of the closest carnal conjunction and I lived in terror of being left; now he is predictable, reduced to a mechanical "darling" who has lost any capacity to surprise me.

Certainly, not all our loves are unhappy, but they are all haunted by the specter of their extinction. Thus there is no solution to suffering in love: like insomniacs, we are satisfied to shift from one side to another, to swing between the distress of breaking up and the distress of monotony, between happiness as a tension and happiness as tedium. There is no wave of passion that is not enhanced by a fillip of worry and love is nothing but a state of euphoric pain, intolerable as it is divine. Such is the paradox: it is an anguish that generates pleasure, a marvelous serfdom, a delightful evil whose disappearance upsets us.[59] If you don't risk suffering, you will never know love. And wasn't a man, Marcel Proust, the finest dissector of the catastrophes of love and the failure of love? Neither gender has a monopoly on this exaltation or this despair; sharply training our sensitivity onto one person brings doubts as much as delights. To love is to experience the insoluble alliance of terror and miracle.

It will be said that it is better to forget passion and its false magic spells and antiquated pathologies rather than to prolong a state of subordination that locks women in desolation and distracts them from the real fight for emancipation. The more so as love is the quintessential opportunity for treason, betrayal, and inconstancy and that, as an Italian proverb says, "below the belt, there is no religion and no law." However, the ambition to abolish all ambiguity and all risk of loss may be a more monstrous Utopia than that melancholy and depression into which lovers sometimes fall. Even though it generates affliction, this state of constraint is often preferable to the calm heart and we find many people who, as soon as they get out of one painful relationship, dive into a new torment and pursue it with great gusto. Their insane attachment resists the most persuasive argument. We may disparage love, and curse it, but the fact remains that love and only love gives us the feeling of living at high altitude and condenses into urgent, heady moments the most precious stages of a life. A demanding freedom is not a freedom that protects but one that exposes us to the fire. Passion may be dedicated to misfortune; but it is a greater misfortune still never to feel passion. "Humanity, after the season of love, only vegetates, becoming numb to the wishes of the heart; women with too little to do bitterly feel this truth and in their declining age they seek in religious devotion some support from that God who seems to gone away and taken their cherished passion with him. Men manage to forget love but they cannot re-place it. The fumes of ambition, the tenderness of paternity are no equivalent to the truly divine illusions that love provides in our best years. Any sexagenarian exalts and regrets the pleasures that he tasted in his youth and no young person would exchange his loves for the amusements of an old man"[60] (Charles Fourier).

BEING SEDUCTIVE, OR BEING FRANK

If Europe has placed any bet that sets it apart from the United States, it is in seeking to reconcile modernity with the most flexible fidelity to tradition. It is in declaring that habit is not uniformly oppressive, and innovation is not uniformly liberating. Certain customs that evolved over the centuries deserve to be preserved, for they constitute a civilizing process, the genius and the memory of many generations. The extraordinary diversity of the arts of living, in Europe, probably comes from the fact that an intelligent conservatism is practiced there, and that the present egalitarianism is combined with some of yesterday's ways. The past, in France, was in many regards emancipating and there remains even today the condition of change: courtly love, the poetic tradition of heraldic blazons, Louise Labé's work that is special in every sense, the Précieuses, the salons, and libertinage were periods of freedom for women that laid out the parameters for what is occurring today. Sovereigns, at least in the field of passion, they have anticipated their emancipation as people. To preach a *tabula rasa* would in many regards make the current situation incomprehensible.

While in the United States the coexistence of the sexes always seems to be on the verge of explosion, Europe appears better protected from this hostility by a genuine culture of seduction. Heiress, perhaps, to the "erotic of the troubadours" (René Nelli) that wove a whole ritual of allegiance and subservience between a knight and his lady, seduction is not only propedeutic with courtesy, it civilizes the desires by forcing them to advance under cover. It is the basis for the two sexes' common taste for conversation, for exchange, the lively spirit that gives their interactions all the depth and lightness of banter. It is also the pleasure of pleasing, of playing with the other, of allowing ourselves to be played with by him, of misleading him with our assent or being led, ourselves, by the nose. This stands in contrast to the puritanical and often Protestant will for frankness, where transparency of the mind should be accompanied by simplicity in manners. (The sensual and emotional element of Roman Catholicism, together with its secular compromise with human weaknesses, may explain why the Latin countries have accommodated better than some others the shocks of modernity to their culture.) However, the attempt to tell everything about oneself at the first meeting, to be open with the other so that she or he will reveal him/herself to you is naive and disappointing. It supposes (supreme illusion!) that we know ourselves, that we are only one-dimensional, and that our contact with the other will not change us, that it will confirm us in our being. To present oneself that way (here I am, and this is how I will be for all eternity) is not to reveal ourselves, it is in fact to conceal ourselves, to solidify one image; by a strange misinterpretation, extreme sincerity then becomes the height of the lie; we end up lying to the other because we change, in spite of ourselves, or we lie to ourselves by refusing to acknowledge the change. When the art of courtship is reduced to a reciprocal declaration of love, it falls into platitudes and destroys the magical capacity of our meeting to awaken a world that slowly opens to us and the perception of which overwhelms us.

While it is salutary in politics, the duty of clarification is fatal in love. Love requires indistinction, subtlety, and surreptitiousness that make it possible to distill the revelations and to better discern the stunning novelty of the other. There is splendor in the secret that the other appears to enclose within himself, and landscapes that he suggests that should not be exposed to strong light under penalty of profaning the sentiment before it can come to life. Love wants to be born covertly, masked by a coat of light as much as of night; chiaroscuro is its preferred tonality, hiding as much as it reveals, proceeding by allusion. It needs obstacles, even fictitious ones, to grow in strength; it needs to have the outcome delayed, the too ready clarity of hearts and bodies postponed. Tricks and schemes serve the cause of feelings much better than sad sincerity. The hunt, the capture, danger and chance, downfall and transfiguration will always be part of the panoply of passion. Frivolity and pretence can be profound, the shimmer of appearances can be far more moving than the baring of intimacy.

We in Europe also live in an urban civilization and the art of the city is above all theater, the art of putting ourselves on display and appreciating the spectacle offered by others. Watching each other, sizing each other up, admiring each other (especially in the Mediterranean countries) is an important aspect of public life. Observing the young women who stroll in front of the café terraces is a delicious pastime, while being stared at, looked at, and wordlessly lusted after is a pleasure for these same young women who in their turn measure up and eye their observers. All of that creates an atmosphere of complicity between the female and male parties, made up of winks, smiles, and allusions, a kind of superficial eroticization but without erotic goals, and it instills in even the most neutral relations a kind of disconcerting intimacy. That also explains the extreme coquetry of certain European women, the art of making something special out of nothing, the talent for making oneself look good, all compatible with total freedom; this love of artifice and make-up is diametrically opposed to the ideology of naturalness and it transforms our big cities into a fascinating spectacle. The multitude of faces that pass by are like so many access roads to beauty: not all are ravishing but all are enchanting in some detail, an instance of allure that ends up creating a true visual fairyland.

In other words, the will to seduce prefers linkage versus separation, passionate attraction versus mute hostility, oblique speech versus simplicity; it supposes, finally, that the misfortune of being treated as a sex object is nothing compared to the misfortune of not being desired at all. It is the wisdom woven of indulgence and irony, that does not try to remove the thorns from love but strives to use its defects in the service of its development, to civilize it using its impurities as a base.

COMPLICITY OR DEAFNESS

We are not through yet with the women's movement, especially in a time when the temptation is great in Europe to send them back to the home and get them out of the labor market. The old battle for equality will go on, and there is no reason to slow it down or censure it. We should retain feminism's function as a criticism of the prejudices and imbalances existing within our societies. Again, there are two competing logics: an American type that is suspicious and litigious, and a French logic of complicity, of intelligence that emphasizes common values more than divisions. (These are broad generalizations; the two trends run through each country to differing degrees.) It is characteristic of North American civilization that it remains handicapped by the spirit of segregation, even among the keenest adversaries of the Establishment. Women's Studies for the women, African-American for the Blacks, Judaïca for the Jews, Men's for the men, each is invited to stay home and shelter himself within his birth group. It's like a form of house arrest that hints at the rule of apartheid. The minorities are so full of themselves that they can no longer converse with each other. However useful these "ethnic" or gender alliances may be for their members, in Europe it is not forbidden for a Jew to take an interest in African cultures, for a man to be interested in female studies, or a heterosexual in homosexuality; in short, to see these particularisms as so many paths toward the universal. For these "identity politics," as Edmund White calls them, under the guise of restoring dignity to the outcast groups, quickly degenerates into micro-nationalisms, a proliferation of heteroclite congregations looking for special treatment.

How many feminists are trying to impose in literature and cinema a positive image of woman? (Representing a female as a member of the malicious or perfidious gender is compared to racism.) In this respect it should be mentioned that violence and cruelty are by no means purely male prerogatives. Women have partly escaped until now because of their social relegation; but what was taken for virtue turns out to have been a provisional prevention from doing evil. And it is not clear what angel would keep women forever secure from committing foolish or malicious acts, as if being born female removed them from the errors and pettiness of the human condition.[61]

And finally, what about those who don't feel any affinity for his/her "kind," who do not want to ally themselves with their brothers or sisters? What happens to the millions of men and women who value above all their similarities, and whose fidelities are not chauvinist or feminist but related to the marital, the family, to love? On what basis should we maintain the "old edifice of iniquity" (Hegel), the outdated relation between the sexes? Solely on the basis of the happiness of being together, because the enemy we are fighting is also that which we want, and separating men and women would mean amputating from each one an essential piece of itself.

Even with concessions and dialogue, it is not true that the two aspects of the human species will be able to be reconciled and live in harmony around republican principles. The division of tasks, and anatomical destiny — the potentialities allowed at the ones and denied to the others (for example the faculty of child-bearing, and the difference of the pleasures) — are permanent obstacles to perfect communication or an idyllic state of agreement. Each gender remains undecipherable to its opposite, neither so different nor so near as he believes. But this proposal should be reversed at once — with respect to other half of humanity, the source of the fear and the source of wonder are one and the same. The door that separates is also the bridge that connects, the essential point being that the rapprochement does not obliterate the distance nor does the distance prevent each side from fellow feelings. Every relationship begins in ambiguity, in the vague combination of attraction and fear. Equality is an insatiable monster that is always likely to drag all and sundry into a relentless spiral of desire and competition. Therefore it is necessary to moderate the demand for parity by the desire to cohabitate, and the wish for equality by that of shared pleasures. Asking for a common world means acknowledging that what binds us together is stronger than what divides us. We will not see the end of discord between the sexes but it is up to us to avoid fanaticism on both sides, the readiness to raise the standard of the martyr, to avoid the outbursts of hatred and vileness that regularly overtake the public scene in America. It is up to us to generate new relations, to maintain ourselves in a state of passionate tension.

Let's not underestimate the sufferings and the failures that have caused the slow disintegration of the patriarchal system over the past half-century, the crisis of masculinity that followed, and the painful lessons that their so recent and fragile freedom has brought to women. Still, it is wonderful to be living through this period of change in sexual identities. It is easy to imagine that some are distressed by the traitorous and perfidious scum, cursing their disloyal sisters, and that others dream of an apocalyptic revenge on the so-called stronger sex. One group's cowardice is as laughable as the others' rancor. In spite of the deafness and inevitable disappointments on both sides, we must preserve at all costs this atmosphere of erotic and loving friendship that makes today's Europe not the continent of debauchery but a place of high civili-

zation. In this domain, the Old World may be the future of the
New.

CENSURE OR RECIPROCITY?

There are two strategies for correcting the most glaring disparities
between the sexes: prohibition or reversibility. Take beauty: it hangs
over women like a *diktat* and for them physical disgrace is too often a
metaphysical disgrace. How can we thwart this aesthetic blackmail, "the
new theology of weight control" (Naomi Wolf)? Some think that we
should encourage women to ignore the injunctions of fashion, lingerie
and lace, to disobey the culture of the eye that imposes canons that are as
arbitrary as they are exclusive; others (in a tradition closer to Latin
Europe) think it is enough to ask men to share with the fair sex the same
preoccupation with their body image. In earlier times, the man alone was
judge and the woman was what was judged; why not turn them both into
watcher and watched at the same time? Why shouldn't the male participate in his turn in the extenuating asceticism of the spectacle, discovering the pleasure and the anguish of dressing, perfuming, and contemplat-
ing himself? This shared narcissism would make everyone equally vigi-
lant, and the care taken to maintain oneself would have less to do with
being in love with one's own body and more to do with being concerned
about one's image. Like the wealthy, they have a treasure to lose, they
must maintain their capital in a constant battle against age and time.
But, however imperfect this approach may be, is there any other way to
attenuate the dictatorship of appearance but to extend it to men? It
would be a lesser evil in any case; it would be preferable to the cult of
naturalness, the carelessness that flourishes in democratic countries and
invites everyone to display and to expose himself shamelessly. Isn't it
healthy, on the contrary, not to be resigned to one's deformities or little
imperfections but to try by all kinds of artifice to correct them, to mitigate them? At least the requirement of minimal elegance has the merit of
fostering emulation between people who compete in grace and inventive-
ness.

And still: man, from time immemorial, has regarded woman as his
prey. But to be hunted in his turn, evaluated, measured up and even
transformed into a *Go-Go boy* in a nightclub for the pleasure of women

spectators (consider the success of Chippendale's); to be displayed naked in magazine spreads, a beautiful beast captured and thrown on the stage as a vulgar object of pleasure... Shall we have brothels for women, paid gigolos, red light districts where males will solicit passing women for paid erotic interludes? Shall we extend prostitution for both the sexes? Won't that entail boorishness, indelicacy? Of course; but women's accession to equality is also the right to coarseness and brutishness like the men's; don't worry, women will get there as well as us. Conversely: shall women make a wholesale entry into the market of seduction, taking the initiative, approaching men they like? They expose themselves to the risk of rebuff. Everything that had been the prerogative of one sex becomes the privilege and the curse of both. Admittedly, by doing this we settle for extending the dominant tendency, not canceling it; but this strategy of reciprocity is better than the utopian will to repair love, to correct immorality, to sweep away the flirt, to prosecute the coquette. These subtle shifts do not herald any enchanting future; they may be more decisive than the absolutism of virtue envisioned by so many reformers who are ready to censure and punish, to make mankind happy in spite of himself.

Footnotes

1. Andrea Dworkin, *Pornography, Men Possessing Women*, E. P. Dutton, 1989, cited by Pascal Dupont, *La Bannière étiolée, op. cit.*, p. 281.
2. Andrea Dworkin, *Letters from a War Zone* (Secket and Waeburg, London, 1988, p. 14), cited by Katie Roiphe, *The Morning After*, Little Brown, New York, p. 179.
3. Marilyn French, *The War Against Women*, Hamish Hamilton, London, 1992, p. 179.
4. Catherine McKinnon, cited by Katie Roiphe, *The Morning After*, *op. cit.*, p. 141: "Even Hitler couldn't make sex into a murder weapon the way the pornography industry has done."
5. Andrea Dworkin, 1981, cited by Lynn Segal in *Dirty Looks, Women, Pornography, Power*, B.F.I. Publishing, London, 1993, p. 12.
6. Marilyn French, *The War Against Women, op. cit.*, pp. 165-166.
7. Susan Brownmiller, *Against Our Will: Men, Women and Rape*, Bentham, New York, 1975, p. 5, cited in Katie Roiphe, *The Morning After, op. cit.*, pp. 35-56.
8. Andrea Dworkin, cited by Charles Krauthammer, "Defining Deviancy up", *The New Republic*, November 22, 1993, p. 24.
9. Marilyn French, *The War...*, *op. cit.*, p. 184 and 189.
10. Susan Faludi, *Backlash, The Cold War Against Women*, Editions des Femmes, 1993, p. 88.
11. *Idem*, p. 106.
12. Marilyn French, *The War...*, *op. cit.*, p. 184.
13. *Idem*, p. 10.
14. George Glider, cited by Susan Faludi, *Backlash, op. cit.*, p. 317.
15. *Times Literary Supplement*, June 1993, p. 14.
16. Pat Robertson, cited by Robert Hughes, *Culture of Complaint*, Oxford University Press, New York, 1993, p. 31
17. Peter Lilley, then Minister of Social Security in England, cited by *Courrier International*, no. 161, December 1993.
18. Cited by Robert Hughes, *Culture of Complaint, op. cit.*; trad. *La Culture gnangnan*, Arléa-Courrier International, 1994, pp. 52-53.
19. Cited by Susan Faludi in an interview with Allan Bloom, *Backlash, op. cit.*, p. 323.
20. Yves Roucaute, *Discours sur les femmes qui en font un peu trop*, Plon, 1993.
21. *Idem*, p. 13.
22. *Idem*, pp. 141 sqq.

23. *Idem*, pp. 270-308.

24. Warren Farrel, *Why Men Are The Way They Are*, cited in Susan Faludi, *Backlash, op. cit.*, pp. 329 et 332.

25. Robert Bly, *L'homme sauvage et l'enfant*, Seuil, 1992.

26. John Stoltenberg, *Refusing to Be a Man*, Meridian Books, New York, 1992.

27. While it is an extremely prudish country, the U.S. is also home to a highly developed pornography industry and features a morality that is so liberated, in some locations, as to be unequaled. Éric Fassin shows that in comparing France and America, if we wish to avoid falling into trite stereotypes on both sides, we must remain critical, as each of the cultures inclines toward adopting an external point of view on the other: "Le féminisme au miroir transatlantique," *Esprit*, November 1993.

28. The wage gap between men and women was 33% in 1981 and 30% in 1993 for workers with equal qualifications. According to *L'Express* (August 5, 1993), men who worked one hour longer than women every day performed two hours less domestic work. And, while in France 60% of the judges are women, women constitute only 5.7% of the National Assembly; in Denmark they constitute 33%.

29. Georg Simmel, *Philosophie de la modernité*, Payot, 1923; republished in 1989, Book 1, P. 70.

30. According to a report by A. Spira and N. Bajos (*Rapports sur les comportements sexuels des Français*, La Documentation française, 1990, pp. 217-218), almost one woman in twenty claims to have been a victim of forced sexual relations, the most dangerous period being from the age of 13 to 15 years. Similarly, according to Antoinette Fouque (who opened *l'Observatoire de la misogynie* in France in 1987) two million women were beaten in 1991, one woman or young girl was murdered every day, and 5,000 rapes were reported in France in 1992, up from 2,200 in 1982.

31. Over the last twenty years, the natural family in France has been becoming a matriarchal family from which the father is excluded. According to S.O.S Papa and the New Movement for the Paternal Condition, 1.7 million children live without their father and 600,000 never see him any more. In 85% to 90% of the cases (in France), the child is systematically entrusted to the mother following separation. We are very slowly re-thinking this pattern of granting preference to the woman, and the magistrates tend more and more to balance the responsibility between the father and the mother in order not to penalize the child. (On this subject, see Irene Théry's very moderate analysis, *Le Démariage, op. cit.*, pp. 226 sqq.)

32. The masculine, as François de Singly has observed, can take the appearance of the neuter insofar as it is disguised as the general interest. The defeat of ostentatious machismo is just the abandonment of a superficial prerogative for better resisting the women's offensive, *Esprit*, November 1993, pp. 59-60.

33. Naomi Wolf, *The Beauty Myth*, Vintage, London, 1990, p. 208. Naomi Wolf courageously abandons the victimist rhetoric of her last work, *Fire with Fire*, Random House, New York, 1993, to plead in favor of a positive feminism that would focus on power more than on recriminations.

34. Cited by Guy Bechtel, *La Chair, le Diable et le Confesseur*, Plon, 1994, p. 184.

35. *Newsweek*, March 7, 1960.

36. Lawyer Owen Fiss explains that the war against discrimination is a rhetorical formula, a strategy for gaining an advantage in the workplace: *What is feminism?*, November 14, 1992, p. 7.

37. "Masculinity seems to be a very delicate flower, an orchid that needs to be constantly nourished and tended, . . . apparently, nothing wilts the petals of masculinity so much as a sprinkling of feminism, which is immediately perceived as a deluge." (Susan Faludi, Backlash, *op. cit.*, p. 91.)

38. Luce Irigaray, *Le Temps de la différence*, Livre de Poche, 1989, cited by Elisabeth Badinter, XY, Odile Jacob, 1992, p. 45.

39. Sally Miller Gerhart, cited by Naomi Wolf, *Fire with Fire*, *op. cit.*, p. 151. Since then, Sally Miller Gerhart has tempered her exterminator's fervor and envisions more peaceful solutions to limit male power.

40. *Times Literary Supplement*, June 25, 1993.

41. The French pioneer of feminism, Simone de Beauvoir, always rejected with disgust the notion of absolute differentialiation: "I completely reject the idea of locking women into a female ghetto. Women need not to affirm themselves as women but to become whole human beings." (*Tout compte fait*, Gallimard, 1972, pp. 507-508.)

42. Susan Okin, *Justice, Gender and the Family*, Basic Books, New York, 1992. Okin rejects using gender differences as a pretext for injustice and the establishment of hierarchies. On this subject, see Martha Nussbaum's objections, *Esprit*, May 1993, pp. 64-65.

43. *Humain, trop humain*, Folio, Gallimard, p. 207.

44. Interview with Susan Faludi, *Backlash*, *op. cit.*, p. 323.

45. On this subject see Alain Ehrenberg's article in *Esprit*, November 1993, pp. 73 sqq. France introduced the concept of marital rape in 1990, addressing vaginal penetration but also fellatio and sodomy.

46. See the special issue of *Partisan Review*, "The Politics of Political Correct-

ness," 1993, no. 4.

47. *Towards a Feminist Theory of the State*, Harvard University Press, 1989, p. 146, cited by Katie Roiphe, *The Morning After, op. cit.*, p. 81.
48. Quoted by Robert Hughes, *Culture of complaint, op. cit.*, p. 10.
49. Quoted by Pascal Dupont, *La Bannière étiolée, op. cit.*, p. 213.
50. The sexual separatism preached by certain feminists runs into considerable opposition within the women's movement. Many are repelled by the prudishness of the extremists and their highly suspect alliance with the religious bigots of the moral majority in their common fight against pornography. American feminism does not have any monolithic ideology. See on this subject Michel Feher, "Eroticism and feminism in the United States: exercises of freedom," *Esprit*, November 1993.
51. Charles Krauthammer, article cit., *The New Republic*, trans. into French in *Le Débat*, 1994, no. 81, p. 168: "In the vast field of moral leveling, it is not enough that deviance becomes standard; the normal must be regarded as deviant."
52. Katie Roiphe ironically details the fantastic and even insane forms that the fear of rape has taken on college campuses. No professor, for fear of being accused, dares to close his office door when a coed is talking with him; in certain establishments lists of rapists or supposed rapists are displayed on "walls of shame" without the defendants having any opportunity to defend themselves (*The Morning After, op. cit.*, p. 19). Many charges of rape are imaginary but they are encouraged for the good of the cause and any man is regarded as suspect *a priori* (*idem*, p. 41), a practice that recalls in a way the collective humiliation meetings inflicted during the Chinese Cultural Revolution (*idem*, p. 41).
53. *Sunday Times*, October 31, 1993 quoted in *Le Canard enchaîné*. NOW (The National Organization of Women), the principal American feminist organization, wanted to make the Antioch code the standard for sexual intercourse throughout the country. The immense majority of Americans reacted negatively to this code.
54. François Furet mentions this possibility in a very critical analysis of "political correctness," *Le Débat*, March-April 1992, No. 69, p. 83.
55. François Furet, *La République du Centre* (cowritten with Pierre Rosanvallon and Jacques Julliard), Calmann-Lévy, 1988, p. 21, in connection with the Communists and the Gaullists.
56. According to Katie Roiphe (*The Morning After, op. cit.*, p. 66, 149 and 151), feminist diatribes against rape are like the manual of good conduct of the Victorian era, describing girls as passive beings deprived of any sexuality

and whose virtue must be preserved by all means.

57. Susan Faludi, *Backlash*, *op. cit.*, p. 381.

58. *Idem*, pp. 376, 383.

59. Nicolas Grimaldi has analyzed the process of beneficial anguish in Proust, *La jalousie*, Actes Sud, 1993, pp. 34 sqq.

60. Charles Fourier, *Le Nouveau monde amoureux* (1808-1814), Slatkine, Geneva, 1986, p. 14.

61. According to the *Washington Post*, quoted by *Le Monde* (January 14, 1994), victims of marital violence in the United States between 1975 and 1985 were mostly men. Prisoners of their phallocentric prejudices, husbands and lovers seldom win sympathy, and refuse to admit that they have been beaten by their wives.

PART THREE

Victimist Competition

CHAPTER 6

THE INNOCENCE OF THE TORTURER*
(THE VICTIM, IN SERB PROPAGANDA)

> "The day when crime clothes itself in innocence, by a curious inversion that is specific to our time, it is the innocence that is called to justify itself."
>
> Albert Camus, *L'Homme révolté.*

> "Not being able to make powerful those who are just, we have managed to make just those who are powerful."
>
> Pascal, *Pensées.*

"We are the new Jews of the world, here at the end of the century. Our cherished Jerusalem is threatened by infidels. The whole world hates us; a protean enemy, a hundred-headed hydra has sworn to destroy us. All our children already wear an invisible yellow star sewn on their clothes. For we have suffered a genocide worse than that which the Nazis perpetrated against the Jews and the Gypsies, and like the Hebrews we must start our wandering in the desert, even if it goes on for 5,000 years." Who says such things? Some exalted Messianic leader, the head of some fundamentalist Protestant cult competing with Judaism in fidelity to the Bible? Not at all! These remarks have been made on a regular basis, in one form or another, for many years by partisans of the Milosevic regime in Belgrade. The novelist Dobrica Cosic,

* A longer version of this chapter appeared in the magazine *Esprit*, August-September 1994.)

the chief inspiration of Serb nationalism and president of the new Yugoslavia (Serbia and Montenegro) until June 1993, wrote that the Serb "is the new Jew, at the end of the 20th century — victim of the same injustices, if not same persecutions: the new martyr people."[1] But the Serbs are more Jewish than the Jews, to tell the truth, since they have been "victims of a genocide that exceeded the Nazi genocides in method and bestiality," as Cosic wrote in connection with the policy of extermination carried out by Croatian Ustashis against his compatriots between 1941 and 1944.[2]

A FUNDAMENTAL ERROR

For the war that has been devastating the territory of ex-Yugoslavia since 1991 and that was premeditated by Belgrade was based on a fantastic misinterpretation: the torturer displayed himself as the martyr and Europe, in agreement with him, rendered those under attack (Croatians, Bosnians, Kosovar Albanians) responsible for the tragedies that befell them. If they had a problem, they had brought it upon themselves — it was they who were guilty! Why this appalling error, why for nearly a year did so many Western intellectuals, politicians, and journalists get sucked in by the Serb propaganda, how could so well-informed a person as François Mitterrand still say on November 29, 1991 (at the very time when the town of Vukovar had just been razed and a quarter of the Croatian territory had fallen under the control of the ex-federal army), "Croatia, not Serbia, belonged to the Nazi bloc" (in an interview in *Frankfurter Allgemeine Zeitung*)? Because Milosevic and his people had the wits to capture public opinion and to justify in advance the war that they were going to launch, by endlessly propagating stories about the misfortunes suffered by the Serbian people throughout history. By constantly showing photographs and videos of women, children, and old men who had been massacred, trampled, and tortured, by endlessly reciting the list of those who died in Jasenovac during debates and at meetings (one of the most dreadful death camps of the Croatian regime under the pro-Nazi Ante Pavelic, where Jews, Gypsies Serbs and Croatian partisans perished by the thousand), this propaganda secured the moral high ground, and from the start it intimidated any possible contradictors: look upon my suffering and dare to show me its equal! This is a case study that obscured our comprehension of the conflict and was the spring from which later misjudgments flowed: indifference, hesitation, and the wait-and-see policy of Europe and America.

Thus the Serb rulers, before launching their offensive in Croatia and Bosnia, had already won the battle of the minds, had already been granted a certain benevolence by the international community. That explains why Belgrade, like few invaders in recent history, were allowed to proceed; why Belgrade was favored by having its theses discussed, commented upon, listened to, and assessed with so much attention; why it enjoyed such indulgence. Since 1991 countless documentaries, articles and reports have appeared, detailing the crimes committed during the Second World War by the Croats, the Bosnians, and the Albanians who joined the Nazi regime — as though a proper recollection of these horrors would somehow compensate for those made at the same time by the Belgrade militia. Admittedly, this exclusive preference for the Serbs was abandoned after about a year; but in order to avoid back-pedaling too abruptly, the foreign ministries invented this

other fable: that all the camps were equally horrible. Thus the
principle of equidistance triumphed: things were not put into
their proper perspectives, but all parties were smothered in the
same vague tribal brutality. And in May 1993, in connection with
the events in Bosnia, Warren Christopher made these confusing
remarks before Congress: "It would be easy to compare all of that
with the Holocaust, but I've never heard anything about a genocide carried out by the Jews against the German people."[3] Many
today still continue to find extenuating circumstances for Serb
nationalism and cannot approach the subject without immediately dumping mud on the Croats, Bosnians, Slovenes, Albanians
and Macedonians.

For the imposture worked. The Serb hypnotist, seeking final
acquittal for his heinous crimes, had only to disguise himself as a
victim to be forgiven. What have we started up with the Yugoslav
crisis? The same, eternal error that we already made with Communism and with our support for the Third World: *we allow ourselves to be blackmailed by the rhetoric of the victim*. The terrible lesson
of the century is this reversal that transforms the oppressed, once
they have arrived in power, into dictators, that transforms the
proletarians into tyrants, the colonized into new Masters. Those
who were persecuted have lost their innocence, and those from
whom we anticipated a new justice and redemption have instead
founded other despotisms, all the more frightening since they are
built under the auspices of freedom and justice. It is this potential
reversibility that we are unable to grasp — as if having been a victim once in history made you forever a victim, safeguarding you
from ever slipping into violence and totalitarianism. That was the
strength of Milosevic's propaganda (besides — or because of —

its fantastical aspect, which has been ascribed to a tradition of Slavic folklore. He invokes all the woes suffered by his people, especially between 1941 and 1945, and demands perpetual immunity, placing themselves above the law. Nothing was more discouraging than seeing this trickery accepted and swallowed by the public (and very often in the name of strict democratic vigilance). Very few, at least in the beginning, understood that these same people who were presented as resisters to fascism (the Serbs) had already borrowed fascism's methods, that the wolf had disguised himself as a lamb; very few remembered that victimist ideology had been part of fascism, which is a doctrine not only of a higher race but of a humiliated higher race.[4] With impeccable skill, the Serb extremists thus succeeded in masking their appetite for conquest as a concern for protecting their minorities, their bellicose will as a love of peace, their ethnic cleansing as a burning desire to preserve the Yugoslav federation. In short, as the proverb says: "The Devil, too, likes to quote the Scriptures."

THE EXALTATION OF DEFEAT

What is the victimist identity, for the Serbs? It is a tradition that is nurtured by literature and the Orthodox Church and that has taken root in a long tormented history, that of Turkish colonization and Habsburg suzerainty, which generated an exaggerated patriotism that spawns dramatic acts of heroism.[5] It is a feeling of permanent insecurity created by the constant migrations and borders changes, the anguished uprooting and exile of nationals who are driven through hostile territories. And finally, it is a hereditary feature that has endured since the defeat of Prince Lazar on

June 15, 1389, before the Ottomans at the battle of Kosovo Polje ("Field of Blackbirds"), a historic event whose legacy is remembered from century to century. The Serbs were worthy of a great destiny — they should have been the builders of a new Byzantine kingdom; but it slipped through their hands. Today, bruised heirs to an empire that never was, they remain inconsolable for this loss. There is pride and even beauty in this way of celebrating their defeats as though God had chosen this people precisely to bring it misfortune and to make it the instrument of his intentions, as if the terrestrial debacle were transformed instantaneously into celestial victory over the forces of evil. The Serbs appear to be intoxicated with the wrongs that have been inflicted on them and they cultivate, especially in their epic poetry, the exaltation of the trials endured, the rock-hard belief in their martyrdom. A whole people is immersed in the certainty that they are bound to suffer and they derive from this a sort of aristocratic dignity: to be so disparaged, mistreated since the dawn of time, can only be the work of God!

Since he came to power, Milosevic has been adept at reviving his compatriots' fear, at awakening this ancestral background to use it for a political and military plan for a Greater Serbia. (Greater Serbia, let us recall, doesn't mean simply bringing together all the Serbs into one State, it also and most importantly means expelling all non-Serbs from that State.) This obsession with mourning, death, and disappearance, perfectly honorable in itself, becomes highly suspect when it is used by the leader of a State and transformed into an ideological weapon to legitimate war. Thus Milosevic's Serbia, by the late 1980's, felt that it was hurt not so much by the injustice of the economic situation stemming from the misadventures of the Second World War and the dislocation of Yugoslavia but from an essential, metaphysical injustice that finds its roots in a 1000-year history. In this respect Serb national-communism is an interesting hybrid: from extreme nationalism it borrows the obsession over mixed blood (a recurrent theme in Dobrica Cosic's novels), the phobia over impurity, and the urgent need to separate, to know who is who. "Our heart and our identity," declared Karadjic, leader of the Bosnian Serbs, "can survive only through separation. You cannot mix water and oil. The Balkans are not like Switzerland or the USA. The melting-pot never caught on, in spite of a succession of foreign occupiers."[6] From Communism it borrows its style, its culture of lying and its claim to be fighting in the name of justice, a claim that is grafted onto an old cultural legacy, as we have seen. This bizarre mixture blurred the vision of our most astute antifascists: this is not nazism — Milosevic is not Hitler and ethnic cleansing is not the final solution — nor strict Stalinism, but the denatured product of their late marriage combined with a pluralist façade and a mafia-like economy. That is why the Serbian cocktail can be used as a precedent for the peoples lately emancipated from communism; its seductive power derives from the combination of two movements (that used to compete with each other) in a fight against their permanent enemy: liberal democracy. It pairs Stalinist methods with an insane celebration of the identity, magnified and exalted in its purity,[7] against contamination and interbreeding. And most of all, it gives a politics of resentment to countries that do not feel that they are their own masters and for which independence is mostly a sense of shattered foundations. It shows them how, in the name of yesterday's misfortunes, to fabricate a badge that makes them untouchable, that exempts them from paying their debts, and moreover that grants them permission to hate and to punish as they see fit.

However, standing behind smaller Serbia is the immense shadow of Russia, which is linked to Serbia by ethnic, emotional, and religious bonds — the shadow of a new pan-Slavic, Orthodox arc. To all those in Moscow and elsewhere in the debris of the Soviet empire who dream of taking revenge on the West and who feel humiliated, Milosevic's Serbia offers a successful model for exiting communism. That is where the true risk of contagion resides. The Belgrade regime's fault lies not so much in having expressed what may be legitimate objections — all the former Yugoslav republics were dissatisfied with their fate — but in having chosen to rectify them through ethnic violence and purification, thus making a mockery of the oath on which contemporary Europe built itself: the banning of war. *Never again* to invasions, to mass destruction, to exterminations on our continent — such is the pact that since 1945 has bound the nations of western Europe and that has governed the Franco-German reconciliation. Henceforth our disagreements must be settled by dialogue and arbitration, not by weapons. The "Yugoslav laboratory" (Roland Dumas) has re-opened a Pandora's box: the prospect of modifying borders by force. Believing it can buy peace by cutting up Bosnia, Europe only encourages war as a means of solving problems. (Moscow's brutal intervention in Chechnya would not have been possible without Vukovar and Sarajevo.) Finally, it again authorizes crimes against humanity as instruments of conquest in one's own land.

GENOCIDE AS A RHETORICAL DEVICE

This is not intended to play down the enormity of the massacres perpetrated by the Ustashis from 1941 to 1945 (which were appalling, but were conducted with the approval of only a minority of the Croatian population) and the terror that it planted in the hearts of the Serb people. Croatia under Pavelic remains, after Nazi Germany, "the bloodiest regime of all of Hitlerian Europe. Neither fascist Italy nor Vichy France nor Slovakia, Hungary, or Romania knew anything like it."[8] In this sense, one of President Tudjman's mistakes, at Croatia's moment of independence, would be that he did not offer a solemn apology to the Serbs for the Pavelic regime, that he did not go (as Willy Brandt, for example, went to the Warsaw ghetto), to kneel at Jasenovac, to assure them that the new Croatia would not produce any more such abominations. Such a gesture would not have disarmed Belgrade's aggressiveness at all, but it would have had an immense symbolic impact — it would have proven that the young republic, anxious to join Europe, was taking the position of reconciliation and justice. (Franjo Tudjman waited until on January 15, 1992 to condemn the Ustashis' mass assassinations of Jews — in a letter to Edgar Bronfman, president of the World Jewish Congress. Author of a book that is at the very least ambiguous about the genocide, Tudjman in addition repeated on several occasions during his electoral campaigns: "Fortunately, my wife is neither Serbian nor Jewish." He excused himself for his "negationist" book in a letter sent in February 1994 to the president of the American B'nai Brith. As is often the case with him, the good impulse comes along, but too late to erase the blunders that annul it.)

For the memory of the genocide always invoked by the Serbian extremists is an endless source of hatred, revenge, and rage. Infatuated with a misfortune that makes them special, these extremists have big eyes indeed: they claim not just one but three genocides in the 20th century alone. Thus a certain Petar Milatovic Ostroski, a Serbian writer defending his country against the "international plot," believes that "in the 20th century the Serbian people have been victim to three waves of genocide by the Croatians. The first took place from 1914 to 1918, the second during the independent State of Croatia, and the third since the inauguration (sic) of Franjo Tudjman, Tito's General and Pavelic's historian. To the greatest shame of the Serb, this genocide is still going on."[9] But Petar Milatovic Ostroski, in his great distraction, forgot another genocide: that to which the Serbs subjected the Kosovar Albanians. "The physical, political, and cultural genocide of the Serbian population of Kosovo and Metohija is the most serious defeat that Serbia has suffered in its struggle for liberation, from the battle of Orasac in 1804 to the insurrection of 1941;" so says the Memorandum of the Academy of Science dated 1986, a background document that is heavily laden with the ideas of Dobrica Cosic and that is said to have inspired Milosevic's "Cultural Revolution."[10] From a real genocide, by the Croat Ustashis, the wooden official language extends this term upstream and downstream to cover any type of remonstrance and challenge to Serbian policies. In January 1994, one Daniel Schiffer, a "philosopher" and propagandist residing in Western Europe and representing the Belgrade regime, accused certain French intellectuals of a new betrayal in their attitude with respect to Serbia. "The great majority of French intellectuals have thrown themselves into a moral geno-

cide of Serbia, practically a pure and simple cultural (if not spiritual) lynching, as if every Serbian were in fact or in potential a
nazi!"[11] For anti-Serbism can only be the contemporary avatar of
anti-Semitism, as Daniel Schiffer suggests again, apostrophizing
his interlocutors: "With the often virulent way in which you kept
accusing only the Serbs, thinking you were standing up against
crime, you only invented in the eyes of international public opinion a new type of racism: an anti-Serbism like the anti-Semitism
that existed in the 1940's, in our fathers' time." Already in 1991 the
writer Milorad Pavic was writing, "In this moment the Serbs in
Yugoslavia are once more on the lists for genocide the way the
Serbs and the Jews were during the Second World War. But this
is the first time that Serbo-phobia, in Europe and even in the
whole world, is more vehement than anti-Semitism."[12]

What is not genocide to the Serbs, I ask you? The least criticism, the smallest reservation takes on the dimension of total
crime: a fantastic exaggeration that destroys the impact of the
word by infinitely diluting it. If criticizing Milosevic makes one
guilty of "genocide," then this weighty word that should be used
with the greatest parsimony loses all meaning. The Serb ruler is
obviously not responsible on his own for devaluating the term;
this abuse of language is common among all parties in the Balkans,
where it tends to be used to describe the international tensions,
but even here in the West, as we have seen, it is wrongly used and
overused.[13] Let us simply note that, for followers of Milosevic,
whoever is opposed to them is a "nazi" and any kind of nuisance
that they encounter can be described as a "genocide." Addressing
the representatives of the EEC in Geneva and protesting the sanc-
tions against the new Yugoslavia, on December 9, 1993, Milosevic

declared: "When the day comes that your children learn the truth, I do not know how you will explain to them why you killed our children, why you waged a war against three million of our children and by what right you made twelve million inhabitants of Europe the basis for the last, I hope, genocide in this century." Thus the principal anathema, by a process of tragic distortion, becomes a rhetorical cliché in propaganda, a formula that has the simple function of disarming any possible objectors and suggesting that: *You owe us everything because of all the trouble we have endured; you cannot refuse us!* The idea that the whole world is in debt to such and such a group or country and must permit their every whim is also popular with the Russian extremist Zhirinovsky.

> "In the past, Russia saved the world from the Ottoman Empire by sending its armies south. Perhaps if there had been no Russia, all of Europe would have been Turkified, the Turks would have captured Budapest, would have besieged Vienna and it would have been a short road from there to Berlin, Paris and the English Channel. Seven centuries ago we stopped the Mongols.
>
> We could have let them pass or we could have submitted to their domination. What then would have remained of Europe? We have saved it many times: in the south, in the east and in the north when the fascistic plague was triumphing in Germany, Italy, Portugal, Spain, Greece. Thanks to the Russians, Europe was freed from fascism. . . . The other peoples must be grateful to the Russians for this."[14] And the late Greek Minister for Culture Melina Mercouri, anxious to defend the cogency of Athens' opposition to the recognition of Macedonia, also affirmed on January 6, 1993 that Europe "must discharge its debt towards Greece," "the Europeans are obliged to us," as it is Greece who gave them "the very idea of democracy and the roots of the development of [their] civilization."[15]

In short, every time a nation or a people wants to place itself above the law, in all good conscience, it invokes its high deeds and its past sufferings to affirm quietly that it deserves this small exception to the international standards!

A FALSE ASSIMILATION

Collecting genocides the way other people collect diplomas obviously makes it possible to draw a comparison between the Serbs and the Jews, a comparison based on the fate they both suffered in the Ustashi concentration camps. However, a bit of historical research would suffice to show the flaws in such an analogy. We must recall, for example, that in occupied Yugoslavia of 1941 there was a Serb government in collaboration with the German occupiers (led by Milan Nedic, the "Serb Pétain"), and that starting on October 5, 1940 — that is to say, well before the arrival of Wehrmacht — a law imposed a *numerus clausus* on the Jews for college and university admission and forbade to them to work in certain trades, in short, already restricting their rights; that before the war there was the fascistic party of Ljotic that later organized the Corps of Serb volunteers whose task was to round up Jews, Gypsies and partisans for execution; that on October 22, 1941 in Belgrade (under the nazi yoke) the Great Anti-Masonic exhibition opened, denouncing the Judeo-Masonic and communist plot to dominate the world — an exhibition that was a considerable success; that during the occupation, Orthodox dignitaries (in contrast to the Catholic clergy of Croatia) ordered the forced baptism of Catholics and Moslems but prevented Jews

from converting, thereby handing them over to the German extermination machine; that the Final Solution (and the first gassing of
Jewish women and children) were inaugurated and concluded in
Serbia thanks to the active cooperation of the local authorities,
the clergy, the National Guard and the Serbian police force that
led to the total liquidation of the Jewish community of Serbia; and
finally, that in August 1942, Doctor Harald Turner, director of the
nazi civil administration of Serbia, declared that this country was
the only one where "the Jewish question and the Gypsy question"
had been resolved.[16]

That doesn't take anything away from the fact that the Serbs
were the very first to resist, with Tito, as he himself publicly recognized; that doesn't erase or attenuate in any way the abominations of the Ustashi State at the same time; but it does render dubious, if not suspect, the automatic identification with the Jews
that the Belgrade nationalists are quick to claim. In Serbia like
everywhere else in Europe there was a strong anti-Semitic tradition that still persists to our day, at least latently among the orthodox clergy,[17] even though many Serbs shared the fate of the
Jews vis-à-vis the nazis during the war, even though the meager
Jewish community remaining in Belgrade is under absolutely no
threat (any more than that of Zagreb), both parties having enough
scapegoats never to fall short in that category.

THE JEW AS BOTH COMPETITOR AND ROLE MODEL

Just as anti-Semitism has outlived its object in a pinch by
Judaïzing the "goys" in places where all traces of the Jewish presence have disappeared or has been reduced to a handful of peo-

ple — as has happened to many peoples and groups — the desire to be Jewish in place of the Jews becomes acutely competitive as people struggle to attain the prestige of being the elect. Generally, two major types of anti-Semitism can be distinguished: the religious, of Christian inspiration, accusing the Mosaic people of having killed Christ and persisting in the error of their ways after the evangelical revelation; and the nationalist, denouncing stateless minorities as a source of impurity that is prejudicial to the health of the nation. A third, more surprising trend has been added to these two traditional objections in the last half-century: envy of the Jew as a victim, the paragon of misfortune. In this way he becomes the model and the obstacle, he usurps a position that should by all rights redound to the Blacks, the Palestinians, the Serbs, the Russians, the Poles, those of French extraction, etc.. Traditionally pan-Slavism and pan-Germanism (which have been imitated in this respect by many peripheral nationalisms) attribute to themselves a divine origin, a special alliance with Providence sealed by their trials and tribulations; this is usually designed as a way of setting themselves apart from the Jews. Calling itself the chosen people enables an unstable or dispossessed group to transform banishment into a basis for grandeur, for believing itself invested of a Messianic vocation. Thus Dostoyevsky, in his militant Slavophilia, made Holy Russia the Christ of nations, temporarily so that it could re-emerge all the better tomorrow in its full glory;[19] and thus Radovan Karadjic exclaims today: "Serbia is a creation of God. Its grandeur is measured by the hatred of its enemies" (March 1994).

It does not matter that this tribal mystique is founded on an error since in the Bible election is the burden that God transmits to Moses and his people — to institute humanity, since Judaism has "a moral sovereignty," "a responsibility that a nation must not shirk;"[20] whereas in these ideologies it becomes a new variant of racist thinking, a means of affirming one ethnic group's superiority over another. "The Serbs," says Radovan Karadjic, "are the superior people in the Balkans."[21] If people believe themselves to be marked and noticed by God, it is natural to consider themselves the best race and to see their neighbors as inferiors since, being something other than they, they must be lower. But in their metaphysical exaltation these nationalist movements invariably "run into the secular claim of the Jews in their path"[22] (Hannah Arendt). On the one hand their claim of divine election has "the Jews as the only serious rival," their "more fortunate, luckier competitors, because from their perspective the Jews had found the means of constituting a society of a new type, a society which by the very fact that it had neither visible representation nor a normal political application could become a substitute for the nation." In addition, this claim was reinforced by "a superstitious apprehension, a fear that after all, perhaps it was the Jews and not themselves whom God had chosen, to whom success was guaranteed by divine Providence. There was an element of absurd resentment against a people who, it was feared, had received the rationally incomprehensible guarantee that it would appear one day, against all appearances, as the final winner in the history of the world."[23] And nothing illustrates this form of envious hatred better than Hitler's famous statement to Hermann Rauschning: "There cannot be two chosen people. We are the people of God. That's all there is to it."[24]

But since the Second World War, there is another major reason for nations or minorities in difficulty to want to take the Jews' place: the Jews' suffering has become the standard of reference and the Shoah has become the benchmark event by which we judge and condemn crimes against humanity. "The victims of Auschwitz," Paul Ricoeur said, "are the quintessential representatives in our memory of all the victims of history." But through a fundamental misinterpretation, those who want to be the new bearers of the yellow star see the Genocide not as the height of cruelty, "darkening the sun" (Claude Lanzmann), but the occasion of being singled out by misfortune, a distinction, the potential for winning an inalienable immunity or irresponsibility. And that is why the term 'holocaust' has been so strikingly and shockingly misused since 1945: being able to say you are the object of a new holocaust mostly means shining the brightest floodlights on your own case; it also means purloining the maximum misfortune and declaring yourself its only legitimate owner, expelling all others.[25]

Instead of being a catastrophe and a warning for all of humanity, the Genocide then becomes, through a process of confiscation, a source of unlimited moral and political advantages, a magic key that gives you permission for all forms of abuse and that pardons the worst mistakes. To Judaïze yourself the way the Serbian extremists do (if necessary by declaring yourself more Jewish than the Jews, who are now unworthy of the role), secures you an inexpugnable situation, a kind of perpetual line of credit for immorality. This leads to the ambiguity of the ethnic theology that is based on identification, the Judeophile passion that, by incorporating the Jew in oneself, can reverse itself like a glove into its opposite.

EVERYONE IS AGAINST THE SERBS

The Serbs often complain that they are demonized, drummed out of the family of nations; and they see this universal execration as an *a posteriori* justification of their struggle. They are right, because they are alone against the world. But let's not forget that since 1986 Belgrade's propaganda was dedicated to systematically sullying the peoples they were out to beat: first of all the Albanians of Kosovo, "disguised fascists" according to the terms of the Memorandum and rapists of Serb women, "bestial terrorists."

> Talking about the war waged by the Kosovar Albanians against the Serbs since 1981, the authors of the Memorandum specify: "The insurrection in Kosovo and in Metohija right before the end of the war, organized with the cooperation of the Nazi units in 1944-1945, was crushed militarily but it turns out that it was not overcome politically. Under its current aspect, disguised under new contents, it develops with great success and is close to victory. We have definitively not settled our accounts with the fascistic aggression, the measures taken until now have removed only the external signs of this aggression whereas in fact its explicit goals, inspired by racism, have been reinforced" (quoted in *Dialogues*.) And V. K. Stojanovic, president of the Association of University Professors and Scientists of Serbia, wrote in an open letter in the daily *Politika* of February 8, 1990: "Today the bestial Albanian terrorists are erupting in Kosovo and in Metohija by attacking and destroying all that is Serb, burning Serb houses and terrorizing the few people who have stayed there," (quoted in Mirko Grmeck, Marc Djidara, Neven Simac, *Le nettoyage ethnique*, Fayard, 1993, p. 286.)

As for the Croats, they have been a genocidal people for four centuries, according to the Serb historian Vasilje Krestic,[26] a "rotten" people, according to the ultra-nationalist leader Sesjel who recommended on Serb television to cut their throats "not with a knife but with a rusty spoon," a suggestion that was applied to the letter by his militia, as much in Bosnia as in Croatia. Finally, the Moslems of Bosnia and Sandjak are "victims of rectal frustrations that encourage them to pile up riches and to take refuge in fanatical attitudes," according to the strong words of the psychiatric doctor Jovan Raskovic, another theorist of Serb nationalism.[27] Besides, Islam is nothing more than "sexual terror" founded on rape and "inherently genocidal" according to Bijana Plavcic, muse of the Serb regime of Bosnia.

> "Rape, alas, is a war strategy of the Moslems and certain Croats against the Serbs. Islam considers it normal since this religion tolerates polygamy. Historically speaking, during the 500 years of the Turkish occupation, it was completely normal for high-ranking Moslems to exercise a right of cuissage on Christian women. It should be stressed that the Islamic religion considers that the national identity of the child is determined by the father. . . . This sexual terror is also exerted on the men and takes on a genocidal character." (*Borba*, September 8, 1993.) It is rather remarkable that this leading Serb accuses the Moslems with exactly the same maltreatment that the Serbs apply on a broad scale to Bosnians and Croatians, specifically mass rape as a means of racial purification!

Just as there is hereditary transmission of the quality of victim, the torturers reproduce from father to son: fascism is a contagious disease, its gene passes from one generation to the next. It is an immutable property attached to a people and history cannot modify it no matter what happens. This propaganda has a farcical, pathological aspect that would be a good topic for psychoanalysis if the joke did not directly generate terrorism. Because it oscillates between puerile arrogance and moral delusion, Serb rhetoric has not always been taken seriously; and that is a pity, for she has always said what she was going to do and she always does what she says. The more insane it seemed to our Western ears, the more it should have been heeded. For these words were used as doctrines of State. They not only cast the seeds of fury into people's minds, they lit the bonfire. These words were weapons, these words killed.

So it wasn't that the world demonized the Serbs, it is the Serbs who began by demonizing all their neighbors and gradually the whole world (except for some friendly countries, Greece, Russia, Romania) by inventing a plot against themselves, a complex plot that includes (sorry the list is so short) Islam, the Vatican, the Comintern, Germany's "4th Reich," the freemasons and several Western secret services. And what is the constant of paranoid delusions? They go hand in hand with megalomania, making it possible to inflate its small country to a planetary scale. For the Serbs want to be a "cosmic people" that can start world wars and they are convinced that they are the object of a planetary aversion that constantly impels all men to harm them. "The whole world has been involved in demonizing the Serb people, an unprecedented phenomenon in the history of civilizations."[28] The plot against the Serbs is above all a plot against the truth; . . . the conscience of humanity. . . . as well as the destiny of the world are tied to the Serb problem.[29] Touched by delusions of grandeur, these nationalists (who include eminent and well-read men, professors and scientists) entertain a constant thought of the conspiracy that enables them to think they are important. "If the whole world is at war with Serbia, then a world cataclysm, a flood will drown this world in its entirety, except for little Greater Serbia."[30] This fantasy of being surrounded by a "Hitlerian-Vatican-Islamist conspiracy," this self-persuasion of "an infernal hatred against the Serbs. . . . that makes us, the Serbs of the diaspora, the real damned," these "monstrous anti-Serb rituals" that are part of "an incredible symphony of evil" (Komnen Becirovic) thus feed a radical Manicheism. Serbia finds itself alone, against the whole universe!

Derogating the ethnic groups upon which one intends to declare war, dedramatizing their exile or their death, is a way of casting their disappearance as an insignificant lapse of history. This kind of contempt needs to be ensured of the total abjection of the other in order to exalt itself and to elevate itself at the expense of the other. The more monstrous the crime one plans, the more the future victim must be made to appear monstrous: the crimes of which one suspects him are actually forecasts, they announce the crimes that one will perpetrate on him. And just as the far right always ascribed a superhuman power to the Jewish International — an aspiration to rule the world — the Serb extremists ascribe to their adversaries the blackest intentions and a fantasy of absolute power that makes their immediate elimination urgent (whereas, on the ground, the relation of forces has always played in favor of the Serbs, who are masters of artillery and fire power). The charge levied against the other is the vehicle of the assault that one contemplates unleashing. Suspecting him of ethnic cleansing simply means acknowledging and anticipating that you plan to do it to him. Thus all one has to do is to hit the future victim with accusations of the fault of which one is about to become guilty in his regard. (It was almost more painful still to hear the tune of calumny picked up unmodulated in the Western European media, for example the equations 'Croatian = Ustashi,' 'Bosnian = fundamentalis;' to see this propaganda blossoming under the pens of so many supposedly well-informed writers.

Consequently, aggression can dress itself in the uniform of candor: as a nation of archangels absolved until the end of time by their past torments, the Serbs never attack, they only defend themselves. They are just, even when they kill; they are protected by a glaze of absolute, impenetrable innocence, higher than any wicked deeds they might commit. If they remain impervious to repentance and remorse, it is because it was not they who massacred, they merely crushed some harmful insects, lice that are human in appearance alone. And a veteran of the Second World War, come to welcome Zhirinovsky to Bjelina (Bosnia) in February 1994, could exclaim in all innocence to an American journalist: "The Albanians, the Croats, the Moslems, and everybody like them do not deserve to live."[31] "This tragic sincerity of the killer" (Gaston Bouthoul) impels him to dehumanize his adversary so he can eliminate him in all good conscience and escape culpability (with the notable exception of the democratic Serb opposition that publicly apologized for the destruction of Vukovar, Sarajevo and Dubrovnik and for the siege of the Bosnian enclaves).[32]

THE RIGHT TO REVENGE

For the pack of assassins derives its certainty that it is acting within its rights by repeatedly invoking the past. Thus in the late 1980's, the Orthodox clergy and the public powers beat their war drums and went as far as unearthing the corpses from the Second World War in order to stimulate a desire for revenge.

> "We will unearth the bones of our martyrs and will give them a worthy site. The bones must rest closer to heaven since the Serb people have always been the people of heaven and the people of death," Doctor Raskovic wrote at the end of the 1980's.[33]

And this immense army of the dead was launched into an attack against the living in order to bathe in blood all the affronts that had been suffered. This is funereal propaganda, a worship of mass graves and skeletons, a scarcely veiled necrophilia that gives a new meaning to the well-known slogan: "Where a Serb has died, there lies Serbia."

In his very ambiguous paschal message in March 1991, intended "to revivify the spiritual communion and the communion of prayer with our sacred innocent dead victims. . . . from the past fifty years," Patriarch Paul of Belgrade quoted "Grand Archbishop Nikolaj of happy memory," saying, "If the Serbs were to avenge themselves in proportion to all the crimes that have been inflicted on them during this century, what would they have to do? They would have to bury men alive, roast the living on an open fire, skin them alive, cut the children into pieces under the eyes of their parents. The Serbs have never done this, not even to wild beasts much less to humans."[34] Now, what is amazing in this text is that it exactly describes the atrocities that the Serb troops would perpetrate from June 1991 onward, as soon as the war began. If tragedy, as Claudel says, is "a long wail in front of a tomb that is not well sealed," then all the Serb territory, irrigated by the sacrifice of martyrs, howls for revenge.[35] The roots of this tribal nationalism have bathed, so to speak, in the blood of the innocent who died for the fatherland over seven centuries. And this ground is holy "because it is a vast cemetery filled with those who died without gravesites."[36] That is why the Serb soldiers have headed to the front since June 1991, flanked so to speak with those who died in 1914-1918 and 1941-1945, themselves escorted by all the deceased from the previous centuries, in order to complete the unfinished business and to drown a millennium of insults in an orgy of redemptive murder. This immense lugubrious procession was accompanied by the prayers of the archbishops and the songs of the balladeers. For these killers are also poets, Karadjic himself teases the Muse in his idle hours; and in this conflict crime arrives on the wings of epic poetry and the worst of the raptors is able, between two slaughters, to sketch a modest quatrain full of darkness and fury. Milan Kundera identified a beautiful example of this alliance of lyricism and atrocity under Stalinism, "this war was fomented, prepared and conducted by writers and was carried out by the hand of the writers" (Marko Vesovic). This vindicatory rage explains, finally, the appalling nature of this conflict in which, at least in the beginning, an army of professionals confronted unarmed civilians, with campaigns of throat-slashing, torture, mutilation and the assassination of prisoners and innumerable acts of sadism lengthily detailed in UN reports, this will to annihilate the other, to wipe from the surface of the earth even the memory of his existence.[37] For the record, it should be known that the leader of the Bosnian Serbs, Radovan Karadjic, a former psychiatrist, was working before the war with his patients in Sarajevo on the fantasy of the body cut into two pieces — which he believes is present in all men.[38]

In its benign version, victimization is a paradoxical form of snobbery. In its insane version, it is the active negation of the concept of humanity, the open call to murder.

WHOLESALE PLOTS

Defending the 1993 law that obliges Greek citizens to mention their religion on their identity cards, the spokesman for the Holy Synod accuses "the American Jewish lobby" of seeking to destroy Hellenic national unity by disputing this law (which was highly desirable for the Orthodox Church) [April 9, 1993].

When his film *Do the Right Thing* narrowly missed winning the Golden Palm in Cannes in 1990, black American director Spike Lee immediately blames his failure on white racism.

The leader of the political and legal commission of the GIA (Armed Islamic Group), one of the principal terrorist movements in Algeria, Saif Allah Jaafar explains: "We attack the Jews, the Christians, the apostates because they are the henchmen of a profane colonialist plot. They are the living symbols of the occupation in Algeria as well as in other Islamic countries; in the land of Islam, these foreigners are only non-believer spies."

Zviad Gamsakhurdia, the late president of Georgia, blamed his ousting from power on a transnational plot that was remote-controlled from Washington, which was seeking to establish its reign over the whole world: "The scenario of the permanent coup d'etat in Georgia had already been tried out more than once in other parts of the world. . . . This all happened to us because we did not want to be subject to the *diktat* of the Western countries. . . and become a colony. Only a servile power is convenient for the West. That is one of the reasons for the military coup d'etat that brought to power the figure of Shevardnadze, who is an agent of the CIA, a direct agent of Euro-American imperialism."[40]

Leonard Jeffries, director of the department of Black Studies at City College of the State University of New York, explains the slavery from which his people suffer in these terms, in May 1991: "The Jews are the principal leaders of the slave trade, and they were its financiers. They are the leaders of a conspiracy planned and organized from Hollywood in order to bring about the destruction of the Blacks."

On August 12, 1994, while the Italian lira is plummeting, Minister for Labor Clemente Mastella, a member of the National Alliance (far right), blames the "international Jewish lobby," which he suspects of hardly loving the Italian neofascists.

Again, during the summer of 1994, the bi-weekly Egyptian Islamist *El Chaab* denounces at the UN Conference on Development and Population which is to entertain in September the American and European attempts to impose "libertinage and abortion" and "to exterminate the oppressed peoples, including Moslems, but without spilling blood."

Ivan Czurka, leader of the Hungarian populist right and a nationalist, emphasizes the existence of a cosmopolitan world plot "against the Hungarian economy" as the reason why international backers continue to grant appropriations to the former communists who still control some of the State apparatus. He is mad at the Jews for having filled some of the important positions in the old Nomenklatura.[41]

For Alexander Zinoviev, a former dissident who favors the restoration of communism in Russia, the West was out to cause the downfall of his country by paying Yeltsin and Gorbachev to dismantle Sovietism and to crush Holy Russia in one fell swoop. "They represent the fifth column of the West, which ideologically bought them to finish of them once and for all with Russia."[42]

The theme of the plot is reassuring in that it explains all the events as being the action of occult forces. But designating the Great Satan can work two ways: either it is a form of giving up (what good is it to fight when a higher intelligence is directing infernal intentions against us?), or it identifies a scapegoat, an enemy who should be destroyed in order to restore the lost harmony (as in Serbia or Algeria today). The notion of a conspiracy is irrefutable since any argument against it can be used as proof of the pervasive powers of the conspirators. (As the paranoiac says, "Is it my fault that I am always right?") The idea of the conspiracy inoculates those who think they are its target against the pain of criticism, of questioning. And then, it offers them a supreme consolation: it allows them to feel that they are important enough for someone, somewhere on earth, to try to destroy them. Ultimately, the worst conspiracy is that of indifference: how many of us would survive the idea that we do not engender enough love or enough hatred to justify the least ill will from someone else?

THIEVES OF DISTRESS

With the rhetoric of Greater Serbia, one must always look at things in reverse, interpreting every sentence in the opposite of its manifest sense; one must get used to the idea that violence speaks the language of peace, and fanaticism that of reason; one must get used to seeing the repudiation of genocide being used as the vehicle of a new crime against humanity. Nothing summarizes Greater Serb behavior better that the sentence that George Steiner ascribed to Hitler in one of his books: "You will adopt my methods while disavowing me."[43]

Thus, through a huge swindle, those who should be seated on the defendant's bench are found seated with the prosecutors; thus Serb nationalism, which excels in disguising its horrors under the noble cloak of the fight against fascism, culminates in the most contemptible revisionism. In Belgrade the war in Bosnia was called "an anti-genocide liberation movement," and in the Serbian detention (and extermination) camps, the Bosnian and Croatian prisoners were tried for "crimes of genocide against the Serb people" when their only crime was to have been born Croatian or Bosnian; in Belgrade during 1992 a book was published entitled *Sarajevo, Concentration Camp for Serbs*. By mid-August 1993, when Sarajevo had been surrounded for more than a year and 70% of the territory of Bosnia was under Serb control, the federal republic of Yugoslavia (Serbia and Montenegro) asked the Court of the Hague to demand that the official government of Sarajevo put an end "to the acts of genocide against the Serb ethnic group." Serb tour operators organized trips to Vukovar to verify the "on the spot" the genocide perpetrated by the "Ustashi" forces. Lastly, the height of wretchedness, in January 1992 at the Yugoslavian Cultural Center in Paris (and simultaneously in Belgrade) an exposition was scheduled that was entitled: "Vukovar 1991, Genocide of the Serb Cultural Heritage." (The exhibition caused a unanimous outpouring of indignation, and never opened its doors in France.) Whereas the splendid Austro-Hungarian city of Vukovar was entirely razed by the Serb army in 1991, and its population liquidated or driven out, the aggressors shamelessly maintained that they were its defenders and that its inhabitants had destroyed it piece by piece!

We know how much this propaganda has distorted the meaning of the word "genocide." However, it has also enriched it by giving it a new meaning: from now on any people that has massacred or destroyed another can pride itself on having suffered from genocide. Most of the outrageous crimes committed by the Serb troops have been blamed on their victims: there is something Christ-like in this racket for souls, in this diversion of martyrs — but it is an obscene Christ, an Antichrist, in fact — who assassinates and then wants everyone to feel sorry for him. This is a supreme refinement of the Evil One: blaming one's victim for evil that one has inflicted upon him. From that viewpoint, the Germans would be justified in claiming to have been the target of a genocide at Auschwitz on behalf of the Jews and Gypsies, the Turks could accuse the Armenians of massacring them in 1915, the Hutu extremists could accuse the Tutsis, etc.. This is a shocking inversion of the truth: the murderer is his victim's victim, and if I kill you it is your fault — it is actually you who kill me. (Another alternative of this attitude: castigating the malicious victims who oblige you to make them martyrs.) It's a double blow: one takes on the drama of the oppressed and at the same time erases all traces of one's crime. Thus you can enjoy the solicitude that surrounds the loser while enjoying all the benefits of being the winner. (In certain cases, the vampirism is complete. According to the Association of Threatened Peoples, many Serb war criminals hid abroad after taking on the identity of those whom they had liquidated.) An archangel covered in blood, the torturer can then cry over himself in all good conscience, even in the midst of a heap of corpses!

ANGELIC KILLERS

Of course the conflict in ex-Yugoslavia is not only between the Belgrade regime and its neighbors; it pits a pluralist, liberal, open Serbia against another Serbia, mostly rural, which is backward and very proud of its barbarian primitivism which vomits at the ethnic mixing, the impurity in Belgrade and more generally in all the cities, "those pigsties where bastards are born from interethnic marriages" according to one Serb extremist.[44] (This exactly parallels the way in which the Croatian nationalists of Herzegovina baited themselves against Mostar, symbol of Turco-Slavic syncretism, where they completed the destruction after the Serb bombardments.) And the "friends" of Serbia, in France, would have been well-inspired to support the most enlightened faction of the Serb people, the ones who aspire to peace and a unified Europe, instead of supporting a sinister dictatorship that brought the country to shame, hysteria and a military adventure that likely to engulf the entire region in flames.[45]

Finally, the drama of former-Yugoslavia is that, with Europe unable to impose the law, the law of the killers became the law of all the ethnic factions, and purification became the common denominator between the three camps. What is obscene about war is the inevitable complicity that it ends up weaving between enemies who think they have nothing in common but who end up resembling each other more and more. Without a democratic tradition, without a leader who could compete with the diabolic intelligence of Milosevic, poorly armed and driven mad by the exactions made on their close relations and the total indulgence that the aggressor enjoyed, and especially abandoned by the people whom they begged for assistance (the Europeans and the Americans), the Croats and Bosnians, each to a differing degree (and without ever reaching in scale and scope the level of bestiality of the troops from Pale and Belgrade), turned on the Serbs first, and later on each other (during the war that went on until February 1994) the savagery that they had endured from their common aggressor. Milosevic's perverse genius is that he was able to divide his adversaries, to inject them with the poison of ethnic hatred, and to have them find that as a kind of *a posteriori* justification: "See how despicable (or fanatical) they are? How right we were to separate from them." A stunning imitation of the victim's role: the model of the conqueror has (partly) contaminated that of the vanquished and the general confrontation justifies that for which the war was supposedly waged — the idea that it was impossible for the two communities to live together. And it is just miraculous that in Sarajevo and other enclaves of Bosnia (and in Croatia, where hundreds of thousands of Bosnian refugees live), the Serbs, Croats, and Moslems succeeded in coexisting for so long, succeeded to maintain their dignity and tolerance in spite of the bombs, the shortages and the hunger. In this matter, despite the insanity that seems to have been propagated by all sides, the culpability of the Milosevic regime is beyond doubt (even though the regime now, through political opportunism, preaches as an apostle peace, an Al Capone disguised as Mahatma Gandhi). However it fared in war or diplomacy, the Serbs have definitively lost the halo of martyrdom that their past history had earned them. As the Serb opposition leader Vuk Drakovic observed, "In this atrocious war that is still going on and whose end is difficult to foresee, the great, the divine boundary that separated us from our tormentors, that made the difference between the book of shame and the book of the lamb, has been erased at every point. And that is the greatest Serb defeat, the only real defeat of our people in the history of their existence."[46] And Milosevic's Serbia carried out "Hitler's posthumous victory," as Marek Edelman phrased it so well!

Throughout this conflict, in every case, nothing was done (by the international community) for those under attack, whose least legal infractions were maniacally analyzed while their attackers enjoyed a free hand from the start. The Bosnians' only crime (and the Croats', before them) in the eyes of the Western governments was to have resisted instead of allowing themselves to be led to the slaughterhouse, wrecking the calculations of the large capitals that had counted on a quick victory by Serbia, the only power that could maintain order in the Balkans after the disintegration of Yugoslavia. To punish those who were attacked (who were also separatists), we used and abused that fatal sophism that suggests that any victim is a potential future miscreant, and refused to help them because of the malicious people that they might become. What could be a worse perversion of justice!

Is a child drowning under your very eyes? Let him go; or he'll surely turn into a monster later on. Why should the victims be without blemish and beyond reproach? Have we forgotten that the French resistance and the Allies committed sometimes terrible crimes? Neither the Croats nor the Bosnians acted like angels; but no one would ever help anybody if we insisted that the damaged party should be white as a lamb. We don't condition our assistance to people in danger on whether they "deserve" it!

Thus a pattern of conflagrations has developed wherein we avoid becoming engaged, at least when our interests are not directly concerned. Just recently, the least scowl from Saddam Hussein would set in motion a fantastic military armada, without anyone worrying overmuch about the democratic nature of Kuwait; similarly, the Serb atrocities and the genocide of Tutsis in Rwanda were met with nothing but prudent half-measures. In this great night of indetermination where all the combatants are gray, we avoid understanding so that we can avoid having to engage. This triumph of the principle of equivalence — they are all barbarians — is nothing but plain negationism. Just imagine if we should reinterpret the Second World War according to the same principles: in that case, it would no longer be possible to distinguish the good from the evil, and the Shoah would be just the counterpart to the Soviet threat (as in the thesis preferred by the German revisionist school). The "rejection of Manicheism" on which some people pride themselves as if it were an intellectual exploit, the refusal to get in the middle, scarcely dissimulates an active sympathy for the aggressor. Not taking sides in a confrontation between the strong and the weak is equivalent to siding with the stronger party and encouraging it in its enterprises. That neutrality is another name for complicity. And too bad for the victims, who are robbed even of respect for their suffering — by confusing them with their tormentors; and too bad for the victims of Prijedor, Omarska, Sarajevo, Vukovar, and Gorazde, killed and mutilated a second time by our incomprehension. Not satisfied with having abandoned them, we expropriate their affliction, we deprive them of the right to remain in the memory of the living!

PERVERSIONS OF MEMORY

Princess Bibesco was in the habit of saying, "The fall of Constantinople is a misfortune that happened to me last week," and she cultivated "the faculty of coming and going, of inverting the hourglass, of moving back the hands of time, of living in other bodies. . ." There are indeed certain people and certain beings who maintain a carnal intimacy with their past that remains eternally present; beings and people who express an unforgotten aptitude to be contemporary with the past centuries, the adventures of which they tirelessly revive like so many episodes of their day-to-day life. And it is no passéism or nostalgia when the nations of Central and Eastern Europe look to re-appropriate their history, to rejoin the sons of the relation broken by decades of communist propaganda and lies. Recovering one's memory is the first stage of freedom: emancipation is first of all the acceptance of one's traditions, even if it is only in order to be able to detach oneself from them or to set them in a new context.

Memory can also be used to promote not reunion but traumatism, to commemorate catastrophes that have befallen a people and for which they cannot mourn since they literally do not go away, they do not line up nicely in the warehouse of history; they continue to hurt many years after their occurrence. Then memory becomes a warning, the auxiliary of vigilance. "Remember," say the great museums of genocide (Yad Vashem in Jerusalem, Tuol Slang in Phnom Penh). Never forget what was done in the name of race or revolution by the Nazi regime, the Pol Pot dictatorship. These millions of men, women and children who were killed to expiate the sole crime of having been born must remind us that a terror took place to which no one can be indifferent. That is why the Holocaust, by its unique nature, became the genocide of reference, the absolute crime compared to which we judge similar crimes. Not the cruelty reserved for one specific people but pure evil which bears many faces and which scorns all of humanity, using the person of the Jew or the Gypsy as an example. A crime against "the hominidity of man in general" (V. Jankélévitch); a crime against the fact that men exist.

But memory in its turn can be perverted in two ways: by resentment and by intransigence. When, far from being the resurrection of martyrdom, it subjects itself to the *diktats* of an aggressive nationalism and becomes a catalogue of events to be avenged, when it restricts itself obsessively to a revival of sufferings, to reopening the wounds in order to lend more legitimacy to a will for punishment. Then it becomes the handservant of anger, of resentment: it becomes insane, it reconstructs the past the way one reconstructs a face, it degenerates into myth, into fable, a mercenary memory that is less concerned with remembering the dead than with launching reprisals against the living. It will dig up obscure conflicts that go back to the dawn of time, it will re-ignite the tensions and exacerbate the animosity as if all of history were only a slow fuse that is destined to explode today.

This is why there is something of very profound in Érnest Renan's expression: "Anyone who wants to make history must forget history." If all the people who have been harmed would keep on re-visiting their respective complaints, there would be neither peace nor harmony on the earth. Every nation, region, even village could cite some damage that has occurred within the past 500 or 1000 years, and for every hatchet that has been buried, every family would be torn apart for the same reasons, by being unable to overcome mutual disagreements. Once the culprits have been judged and punished, and reparations obtained, if necessary, and forgiveness accorded by the victims if they judge it necessary, there comes a moment when, time having done its work, we must draw a line, leave the dead to mourn the dead, and to leave their hatred and quarrels buried with them. If we wish to live in peace with our contemporaries, we cannot dig up all our historic sore points. Forgetting is one of the things that makes room for the living, for the new arrivals who do not wish to carry on their shoulders the weight of ancient resentments. As Hannah Arendt says, it gives the arriving generations the ability to begin again.

There is another form of defiant memory that paradoxically celebrates a new harshness. In our day, indeed, repeated commemorations of yesterday's massacres are interspersed with confusion and nonchalance over today's massacres. The more we make a big deal over the torture victims of the past, the less we care about those of today. There is a way of "sanctifying the Holocaust" (Arno J. Mayer), of making it into an event that is so closed on itself that we have not the least consideration for victims of other misfortunes. We seal up the dead of Auschwitz with their dreadful secrets and we push away everyone else. Guardians of the unbearable, nothing in today's events satisfies us, nothing measures up to the enormity of the beautiful hell that we cultivate: today's wars, contemporary slaughters, we brush them aside with the back of our hand. Trifles, frivolities compared to the all-out drama of which we are the agents.

Such an attitude, instead of increasing our aversion to injustice, closes us to compassion: what should be the vector of clarity becomes that of detachment. The danger thus exists that the exclusive commemoration of Auschwitz would imply an indecent indifference to the calamities of the present. What good are our anti-totalitarian incantations, as if we were trying to remove Hitler or Stalin retrospectively, instead of facing today's despots and bloody charlatans who create appalling devastations at their own levels? Should we wait until a hecatomb reaches the dimension of the Shoah before we react? Real courage does not mean being a hero after the fact and decrying nazism in 1995, but fighting the ignominy specific to our time. It is, rather, a question of opening the commemoration of Auschwitz to all who have been massacred and tortured, with the proviso that we not amalgamate one crime with another, but recognize that diverse manifestations of genocide exist, that they are all equally wretched but that they do not challenge the singular character of the Shoah, "that monstrous masterpiece of hatred" (Vladimir Jankélévitch).

In other words, two mistakes must be avoided: 1) the idea that everything is equal, the tendency to elevate the smallest crime to the height of a wholesale extermination, without understanding that there are degrees in infamy, that not all murders are the same; and 2) discrediting any other atrocity for the reason that it is not the Holocaust and doesn't stand up to comparison with the Gold Standard of terror. It's not a choice between memory, which keeps alive secular antagonisms, and lapse of memory, which erases tragedies and pardons the torturers. *The only indispensable memory is that which keeps alive the origin of the law:* it is a pedagogy of democracy, an intelligence of indignation. The injunction that is made to those who were born after the Shoah and the Gulag is not so much to stoop under the weight of an appalling memory as to do everything in one's power to make sure that these horrors, even in some attenuated form, are never repeated. That is our fundamental debt to the martyrs of the century: to prevent the repetition of the abomination, whatever dimension, form or face it may take.

But to achieve that, memory is not enough; memory is not certain. For men at a given moment in their history to resist cruelty, some imponderable element is needed, a breakthrough, a miracle that would save them from dishonor and push them to say "No," to stand up to the insupportable. It is this breakthrough, this decision which absolutely inaugurates freedom, on which a generation will be judged.

Three capital crimes have taken place since 1941 in the mental space of the Southern Slavs: that of the Ustashis — the worst of all, until proven otherwise; that of the Tchetniks — about which too little is known; and finally that of Tito and the communists — from the Liberation until the death of the red dictator. None of these three crimes, because of the official truth imposed by Bolshevism, was tried or expiated, nor correctly analyzed and explained (apart from the propaganda accounts) right up until the outbreak of war in June 1991. The accumulation of these three painful events explains the fierce rancor in the Balkans and the fact that every community wavered between amnesia and the will for revenge. Hatred and rage have flared up again over the maddening odor of mass graves, and the friendship between the peoples has not withstood the floods of blood that date back through time. That is why it is imperative to punish the fourth crime, that of Milosevic — to judge the assassins from every party; this is an unavoidable condition of any reconciliation between the peoples and a suspension of the vengeful rhetoric that collectively accuses everyone since it is so difficult to identify those who are truly responsible. May the Yugoslav example at least make it plain to us: as soon as a people aspires to saintliness because of its sufferings, as soon as it starts displaying its wounds and counting its dead, watch out. It is planning a foul deed and memory, instead of preventing a return to mass murder, is invoked only to perpetrate it once again. By draping themselves thus in the mantle of saintliness, the killers, before sharpening their knives, are asking the civilized world's permission — while waiting, perhaps, to turn on them, too, some day.

Footnotes

1. Dobrica Cosic, *Le Temps du réveil* [*Time to Wake Up*], interview with Daniel Schiffer, L'Âge d'homme, 1992, p. 30.
2. Dobrica Cosic, in a brochure distributed by the Information Ministry, Belgrade, 1992, p. 5.
3. Quoted by Roy Gutman, *Bosnia: Testimony of a Genocide*, Desclée de Brouwer, 1994, p. 64.
4. In an unpublished interview with J.-C. Guillebaud, René Girard emphasizes the naivety of Nazism, which terrified everyone by talking like an executioner, like a rough blond thug, whereas Communism dissimulated its expansionist penchants under the defense of the disinherited. This is a brilliant distinction which, however, encounters two objections: until the end, the Nazi regime spoke with two mouths, that of a Germany humiliated by the Treaty of Versailles and the Judeo-Masonic conspiracy and that of triumphant Aryanism. And it was Hitler's genius, and his vulgarity that were his best passports to power. Nobody took him seriously, nobody believed that, "starting from so modest and so contemptible beginnings" (Hermann Rauschning) this low-level political agitator would become Chancellor and actually apply the program outlined in *Mein Kampf*. Hitler did not hide his intentions and it was his coarse frankness that served him best as a screen.
5. Orthodoxy itself, says François Thual (*Géopolitique de l'orthodoxie*, Dunot, 1994), always regarded itself as persecuted by Rome, by the Turks, by Communism. Believing itself the object of an Islamo-Vaticanesque plot and seeing itself as the only authentic agent of Christianity, it developed a dolorist undercurrent that the author calls "the complex of the suffering Servant."
6. Interview with Robert L. Kroon, *International Herald Tribune*, October 19, 1992.
7. Cf. B.-H. Lévy, *La Pureté dangereuse*, Grasset, 1994.
8. Paul Garde, *Vie et morte de la Yougoslavie*, Fayard, 1992, p. 79. Garde points out the principle that governed the Ustashis' principle vis-à-vis the Orthodox Serbs: "A third of them must leave, a third convert to Catholicism and a third die"(p. 75).
9. P.M. Ostroski, "Nouvelle valse sur le Danube noir," *Serbie - Nouvelles, commentaires, documents, faits, analyses*, January 1992, p. 21.
10. Memorandum published in the review *Dialogues*, September 1992, p. 20. Let us recall that the Albanian majority in this part of Kosovo were de-

prived of their rights and of their status of autonomy by Belgrade in 1989 and since then have been subjected to a regime of apartheid.

11. Daniel Schiffer, "An Open Letter to Pascal Bruckner, Alain Finkielkraut, André Glucksmann and Bernard-Henri Lévy," *Le Quotidien de Paris*, January 14, 1994.

12. Milorad Pavic, *Discours de Padoue, l'Europe et la Serbie*, Belgrade, 1991, p. 4.

13. At the Golden Globe ceremony in Los Angeles in 1994, Tom Hanks (who received a price for Jonathan Deme's film, *Philadelphia*, in which he played the role of a lawyer infected with AIDS and whose firm fires him), thanked the jury in these terms: "I am proud to receive this price since this film talks about a genocide that is going on today." Until proven otherwise, a virus, however fatal it may be, has nothing to do with the deliberate will of one group to eliminate another. That is about as absurd as saying that AIDS is God's punishment for our sins. Michel Roux notes that in the Balkans the word genocide is used extensively: "Any population expelled from an area says it is a victim of genocide, even when there has been no extermination caused by the ruin of its culture and its places of sacred memory." ("La question serbe," *Hérodote*, p. 54, 1992.)

14. Vladimir Zhirinovsky, *Un bond final vers le Sud*, p. 123, translated by the Commission des Affaires étrangères de l'Assemblée nationale.

15. *Le Monde*, January 6, 1993. By the way, if Europe and modern Greece are in debt, they both are, with respect to ancient Greece.

16. This information is taken from an article by Philippe J. Cohen, a doctor in Bethesda, Maryland: "Anti-Semitism in Serbia and the exploitation of genocide as a means of propaganda," the European Messenger, 1992, No. 6. Cohen points out that the Jews, who enjoyed considerable tolerance in the Ottoman Empire, were persecuted as soon as the Serb State emerged and all throughout the 19th and 20th centuries. He also explains that the Tchetniks, the Serb monarchist guerillas, not only collaborated with the Italians and the Germans but directed most of their efforts to massacring Moslems in Bosnia and in Sandjak. On the final solution in Serbia, also see Raul Hilberg, *La Destruction des juifs d'Europe*, Idées, Gallimard, volume II, pp. 589 sqq.

17. In addition to rehabilitating major figures from the collaboration — Nédic, Ljotic and especially Mihailovic, a more ambiguous personality (leader of the monarchical resistance, shot in 1946 by Tito for providing intelligence to the enemy) — the current regime in Belgrade maintains close relations with pro-Slav, anti-Semitic and anti-liberal Russian nationalist and ex-Communist circles. And following the publication in

Serbia of *the Protocols of the Elders of Zion* in 1991, a notorious anti-Semitic forgery that was concocted in tsarist Russia, and the emotion stirred up within the Jewish community by this work, the Ministry on Religions published an official statement. After having recalled that the Jews in Serbia had always been honest citizens and that the two peoples were linked by historical bonds through their common tragic destiny during the Second World War, it specifies: "In France and in other Western countries today, certain intellectuals and philosophers of Jewish origin are taking part in anti-Serb campaigns ignited at the very moment when the Serbians are fighting for their elementary rights in their secular homes against the same people who formerly were the authors of the genocide against Serbs and the Jews. But that is not a reason to develop an anti-Semitic sentiment and national and religious intolerance"(April 1994). The ambiguity of the last sentence will be appreciated!

19. On this Slavophile theology, see especially the last part of *The Idiot* and the excellent foreword by Alain Besancon on Dostoyevsky's anti-Westernism (*The Idiot*, Folio, Gallimard, 1972).

20. Emmanuel Levinas, *Difficile Liberté*, Livre de Poche, p. 313.

21. Quoted by Florence Hartmann, *Le Monde*, February 25, 1994.

22. Hannah Arendt, *l'Impérialisme*, Fayard, 1982, pp. 198-199.

23. *Idem*, p. 202.

24. Quoted by François Bédarida, "La mémoire contre l'histoire," *Esprit*, July 1993, p. 9. In his January 30, 1945 speech, Hitler would say, "All-mighty God created our nation. We even defend His work by defending its existence" (article in the *New York Times*, reproduced by H. Arendt, *L'Impérialisme, op. cit.*, p. 187).

25. Even in the very heart of Judaism (and Christianity), various interpretations of the Holocaust tend to see it as a divine message addressed to all the children of Israel so that they would return to the promised land. In a wonderful article, Jean Daniel clarified "this mystique of privileged persecution" which sees the Israeli miracle as the meaning of the Nazi curse and pretends to reserve to Jews alone the memory of the Genocide by refusing other people the right to commemorate it as a drama belonging to all of humanity (*Le Nouvel Observateur*, July 8, 1993).

26. Quoted by Ivo Banac in *Vukovar, Sarajevo*, Editions Esprit, 1993, pp. 169-170. Vasilje Krestic's assertion led to a polemic with Slavko Goldstein in the Croatian newspaper *Danas*.

27. In his book *Pays fou*, published in 1990, Raskovic exalts ethnic purification and the use of force to free Krajina from the Croatian yoke.

28. Pavle Ivic, *De l'imprécision à la falsification, Réponse à Paul Garde*, L'Age d'Homme, 1993, p. 15.

29. Komnen Becirovic, in *Vercenje Novosti*, September 9, 1993.

30. Mavce, a naïve painter and a member of the Assembly of Serbs of Bosnia, quoted by Veronique Nahoum-Bunch, in "Poétique et politique, le nationalisme extreme comme systeme d'images," *Tumultes*, 1994.

31. John Pomfret, in *International Herald Tribune*, February 7, 1994.

32. Via personalities such as Bogdan Bogdanovic, Ivan Djuric, Vesna Pesic, Ivan Vesselinov, Vuk Draskovic and more generally the intellectuals of the Club of Belgrade and the Centre Anti-Guerre. That earned them a charge of treason from the ultra-nationalists, and some had to go into exile.

33. Raskovic, *Le Nettoyage ethnique [Ethnic Cleansing]*, p. 310.

34. Even if Patriarch Paul did not explicitly call for revenge but for 'remembrance,' it is shocking way to see this quote from Archbishop Nikolaj, dating from 1958, on behalf of a Christian whose religion teaches forgiveness and love of one's neighbor — especially in the explosive context of the spring of 1991, a few months before the outbreak of hostilities (in Raskovic, *Le Nettoyage ethnique, op. cit.*, p. 277).

35. Nella Arambasin correctly analyzed this right to revenge as seen among the Serbs, in *Esprit*, July 1993, pp. 156 sqq.

36. Veronique Nahoum-Grappe makes an excellent study of this patriotism based on man's kinship with the nourishing earth, and the son's with the father, with the obsession for substances that convey the identity: blood, sperm, and sap, which should not be spoiled or contaminated. Thus the mass rapes to create little Serbs in the bellies of Bosnian and Croatian women. (In Ivo Banac, *Vukovar, Sarajevo, op. cit.*, pp. 73 and 75.)

37. The Serb opposition writer Vidosav Stevanovic depicted this horror in his novels *La Neige et les Chiens*, and *Christos et les Chiens*, Belfond, 1993.

38. I owe this information to Patricia Forestier, a member of the Citizens Commission for Human Rights in France and who received it herself from Narcisa Kamberovic, a psychiatrist and former colleague of Karadjic at the University of Sarajevo.

39. Interview with *Al-Wassar*, Lebanon, quoted in *Libération*, February 3, 1994.

40. Interview in *Narodnaya Pravda*, the nationalist newspaper of Saint-Petersburg, October 1992, quoted by *Le Monde*, October 30, 1993.

41. *Politique internationale*, 1993, p. 147.

42. *Le Point*, May 27, 1993

43. George Steiner, *Le Transport d'A.H.*, Biblio, Livres de poche, 1981.

44. Quoted by Ivan Colovic, intellectual and Serb opponent in ICE, Ex-Yugoslavia, Conference 1992, p. 11, November 1993, Advanced Teacher Training School.

45. See on this subject the excellent issue of *Temps Modernes* on the Serb opposition, "Un Autre Serbie" , February-March 1994.

46. Second Congress of Serb Intellectuals, April 23-24, 1994, quoeted in *Liberation,* May 25, 1994.

Chapter 7

THE ARBITRARY REIGN OF THE HEART

(The Misadventures of Pity)*

> "I love humanity, but to my great surprise, the more I love humanity in general, the less I love people as particular individuals."
>
> Dostoyevsky, *The Brothers Karamazov.*

A vital document compromising a high-ranking person has gone missing in the royal apartments. We know who took it; it was one of the ministers. He was seen taking the letter; and we know that he still has it in his possession. The Paris police prefect is in charge of the investigation. He has the thief's apartment searched from top to bottom, in vain; he has the minister assaulted by thugs who strip him from head to foot. The letter cannot be found. Only a private detective, alerted by the prefect, unravels the enigma: to be so sophisticated, the hiding place can only be one of total simplicity. The letter has eluded the police sleuthhounds because it was too obvious: "To hide the letter, the minister used the cleverest expedient in the world, which means, basically, he did not try to hide it." In a word, the thief had left the document on a table, under the nose of the whole world, so that no one would notice it.

---

* A shorter version of this chapter appeared in the magazine *Esprit*, December 1993.

We could almost transpose the plot of this tale by Edgar Poe (*The Purloined Letter*), word for word onto our apprehension of suffering: in the democratic countries where the freedom of information reigns, other people's misfortunes little by little become invisible to us, because they are exposed and broadcast so incessantly on the screens and newspapers of the world.

1. THE LAW OF FLEXIBLE FRATERNITY

Routine of Insults

Once upon a time, the truth would burst out like a revelation: Albert Londres detailing to the French the reality of the Cayenne prisons, André Gide denouncing the mining companies' misdeeds in the Congo, the Allies discovering the death camps in 1945, Solzhenitsyn confirming the existence of the Gulag in the Soviet Union, the Vietnamese broadcasting the Khmer Rouge's atrocities: all these facts leaped from the shadows into broad daylight almost instantaneously. The shock came from the sudden revelation of such immense ignominies: how could we have lived without knowing this? We will never leave this era completely: most tyrannies continue to spin systematic lies and misinformation and in the presence of a journalist or cameraman express a great reluctance to torture, beat or kill. For a long time yet, great crimes will need to be kept secret in order to eliminate not only the people or the peoples who are deemed undesirable but even the evidence of their disappearance. However, another trend has taken shape in our day: the reign of over-exposure, which leads to equating one event with another, and to our getting used to them.

Tragic events have a radiant state when they burst freshly onto the screen, overwhelming us. The rush of adrenalin makes us giddy and stuns our minds. Such intense horror (murder, carnage, assassination) hauls us out of our torpor, wounds us like a profound personal offense. But other scenes cause the preceding ones to fade: the skeletons in Somalia, the common graves in Rwanda are dissipated in a flood of news juxtaposing the Council of Ministers, a new car model, a fashion show. We have hardly given our passing attention to the disappearances in Chile and the battered children of Brazil when other incidents claim our attention. Because they come one after another, current events compete with each other, and little by little the abomination that had upset us so much degrades into anecdote. The principle of rotation has done its job and the quick procession of the planetary dramas means we can only give short shrift to each one. Information being constrained by the double requirement of renewal and originality, one spectacle drives out the other, the next one takes the place of the first. Delivered in gusts, unrelated, barbarous acts and futile enterprises appear in a baroque sequence of frames that nullify and cancel out each other. Every evening a new episode, a new crusade soon relegates yesterday's to a lapse of memory; and the media have the unique ability to create, as much as to use, the event.

The news catalogue format also tends to render the representation of terror banal. Twenty years ago a televised spot was enough to catch our attention, but now the flood of shocking scenes has raised our threshold — no abject scene can survive or withstand repetition. The exhibition of frightful images, far from moving us further, especially encourages one specific impulse: voyeurism. The continuous chain of images to which we are treated on a daily basis, and which display other people's distress, is basically pornographic. It gives all of us the right to see everything; nothing can escape the indiscretion of the lens. (And the right of optical interference, free access for cameras at any scene of carnage, is a prelude to the right of interference plain and simple.) But there's no use in showing more and more scenes of mutilation, death, and disease, in seeking the limits of the unbearable, in striving to accentuate the effects and to inventory with maniacal attention every form of atrocity; at the end of all the gore, apathy reappears. Excess reaches a saturation point; even hell becomes monotonous. And then the media give us home delivery of wholesale packages of bad news. All these starving people, these plague victims that appear before us (usually while we are having dinner) swamp us in their sheer volume and diversity. The unemployed, telling their tales of woe, Blacks from the "townships" of South Africa, oppressed Kurds, child prostitutes combine voices to form an improbable chorus. How can we ponder all these unrelated tragedies together?

These victims all seem to address us in one language, that of the conscience, and they command us to worry about them! But the main effect of this hodge-podge is to crush the TV viewer under the size of the task. Beyond shame and a slight nausea, he doesn't know what to make of all these dramas about which he knows very little and which come in such great numbers as to escape our capacity to grasp them. Our immediate co-presence at every misfortune of humanity leads straight to inertia: in a universe where every group of people seems to be in the grip of a fatal madness, competing in fratricidal hatred, our sensitivity follows a parabola going from terror to nonchalance. The media achieve the miracle of making us tired of phenomena over which we have no power (although we occasionally try to do something with our feeble checkbooks). Far from mobilizing us, they mire us in an environment of permanent catastrophe. The anguish that this generates is gentle in two senses: both superficial and, in the end, pleasant. The most appalling plagues, far from upsetting us, only make us prize our good fortune and our peace of mind.

Pain: Upping the Ante

In the past hundred years the two world wars, the Shoah, the Gulag, the Kampuchean genocide have given us a terrible barometer by which to measure atrocities. The enormity of these slaughters has driven up the volume of spilled blood to a level that is not easily grasped, in line with a typically modern perversion — the love of big numbers. Since there are now billions of humans groping around on this earth, the coefficient of injustices has been multiplied to a fantastic degree. We now measure the figure of deaths on a scale inflated with several zeros: to get a reaction from us, at least a few hundred thousand would have to be killed. At best, we change channels. Thus our ambivalence vis-à-vis massacres: by a spontaneous calculation, we compare the total number of victims to that of the preceding calamities, we ponder, with a skeptical pout, whether they really deserve our attention. Macabre math? Certainly. But every day we absorb via the media the idea that mankind is quantifiable, that he is a commodity that is available in such great supply that it can be wasted without any harm. On the one hand, in Europe and America we emphasize the individual life to the extreme, on the other hand we perceive the globe as an over-populated space where man proliferates like a vermin. Our ideal of the eminent dignity of each person is in conflict with the influence and the terror of errant multiplication. Where numbers triumph, morals capitulate!

And since 1945, "genocide" has been the unit of measure when it comes to mass homicide. Instead of thinking that a crime is odious long before it reaches the stage of extermination, we even discount it if it doesn't count as genocide! And we set the bar so high, we are so famished for large-scale destruction that mere monstrosities can leave us cold. Thus during the war in former Yugoslavia, we looked askance at the Bosnian and Croatian prisoners in the Serb camps: they were not emaciated enough, there was still too much fat on their bones, they hadn't been sufficiently maltreated. In the court of universal suffering, the Bosnians were dismissed. You've got to do better than that. Under the pretext that the Serb camps were not Treblinka, we decided that they were nothing, we ignored them. If, when we say "never again!," we mean the Shoah in the exact forms that it took between 1942 and 1945, "it" probably never will return and we will be able to sleep in peace, diluting the terror of current misfortunes in the knowledge of previous misfortunes that make them pale in comparison. What ought to horrify us leaves us unmoved, but this is a terrible impassivity, for it pretends to be profoundly human and masquerades as lucidity. It is our perspicacity that renders us blind, our mistrust that is wary of everything but itself and that is armored with an excess of suspicion. Truly a strange perversion: the memory of evil, instead of sensitizing us to injustice, reinforces our indifference to it!

The Impotent Image

So it is no longer true that an image can launch an army, rock a dictatorship, or overthrow a totalitarian regime; and there is no point in calling for more photographs and more footage, because their overabundance only reinforces our tolerance for the intolerable.[1] We ingest such a high volume of daily dramas that we lose any sense of revolt or discernment. The convenient myth that suggests that only what we see on film really matters — the rest just vegetates in a state of "cathodic death" — ignores the fact that the lens transforms the object into fiction. Since Timisoara and the Gulf War, photography has entered the era of suspicion: airbrushing, computerized imagery and montages can fake the most moving cliché and the day is gone when there was "a moral message on every reel" (Jean-Luc Godard). The means of mass diffusion of information has shaken the categories of truth and forgery. The truth gives way to credibility and even live broadcasts, instantaneous uploads, can be manipulated. It is naive to think that what we see is reliable and can be the basis of knowledge: this idea, inheriting the pedagogical optimism of the 19th century, blames all the evils of society on ignorance alone. A veil darkens the mind: let it be raised and all prejudices will fall away, men will mobilize instantaneously in each other's behalf. If the workers, as Rosa Luxemburg said, really understood their condition, they would commit mass suicide or would revolt without delay. All the effort of the revolutionaries thus consisted in tear-ing away the shadows of ideology to hasten their awakening.

But seeing has long since ceased to oblige us in any way, especially the inattentive way we watch things on television. The eye has no particular power of penetration and while we may have lost the ignorance that was our fathers' alibi, we have acquired another that is more frightening still: that of "useless knowledge" (Jean-François Revel), of futile information. A people ceases to be innocent as soon as it is enlightened; such is the democratic creed. But what we know about (usually dimly and confusedly) seldom becomes anything that we can do something about. The image neither lies nor tells the truth, it unravels: it holds us at arm's length, the TV screen becomes a visual screen and the universe can penetrate our life without influencing it. It is perhaps time to admit that the media (and especially television) have a limited power; their influence on events is small. Contrary to their narcissistic view, they can neither resolve the great questions nor set off massive mobilizations. Rather, they always leave us well-informed yet impotent.

When is an image effective? When it crystallizes a vague feeling in public opinion, when it confirms our choosing sides: during the Vietnam War, just one photograph (that of a completely naked little Vietnamese girl running down the road, out of her mind with terror, as the bombs were falling (Huyng Cong Ut, 1972), did more damage than all the earlier reporting and it corroborated the Americans' unwillingness to continue pursuing the conflict. An image works when it anticipates and justifies a political decision or accompanies a precise action, when it is reduced to a means (although it can be falsified to serve the ends of propaganda). Otherwise, it has no value of indoctrination and its role is one of pure contemplation. We should limit the "CNN effect" to its proper proportions: it's not these unbearable glimpses that cause historical decisions; in fact it is political decisions that lend a historical character to certain stereotypes. The bombing of the marketplace in Sarajevo in February 1994 did not cause the Western response, it reinforced the determination (especially in France) to put an end (temporarily) to the most trying conditions of the siege. In short, television is the best antidote to the ability of its own images to mobilize public opinion; and the most apocalyptic messages, if they are delivered just as they are, without prolongation in reality, become perfectly digestible and compatible with the life of a normal man.

"What was unique between 1940 and 1945," said Emmanuel Levinas, "was the resignation." What today's martyred people are suffering, all over the planet, heralds another disaster: now, knowing that a crime against humanity is going on under our very eyes leaves us in doubt. The fantastic progress that has been made in broadcasting news, and all the testimony of the international humanitarian organizations, floods us with data that paralyze our comprehension and, alarmingly, raise the threshold of what is tolerable.

This ability to live with horror began with the war in Lebanon; it was prolonged with Sarajevo, whose daily bombardment was quickly integrated into the droning murmur of daily events; and it reached its apotheosis in Rwanda. A genocide took place under the gaze of the whole world without sparking anything but a kind of sad stupor (at least for the first two months, enough time for the assassins to complete their work). *We abandoned them in broad light of day* and it was only because it was so very overt that this barbarity finally was ended. Such is the corruption specific to the overwhelmed viewer: the more often indignation is aroused, the weaker his response; the worst becomes normal; and indifference is never based on lack of information (which defuses events even as it reveals them to us). And it is a media cliché to denounce our lack of memory of the dramas that are covered in the daily chattering. But that admonishment is itself part of the lapse of memory; it consecrates it.

So there is no need to turn our backs, to close the newspaper, to shut off the TV: we hold our horror the way other people hold their liquor. The world that stood by dumbly while Jews and Gypsies were being exterminated now protests eloquently when it comes to other peoples. In an extreme case, a dictatorship that was well-acquainted with our mindset could conduct liquidation campaigns in all impudence, could broadcast its crimes loudly and clearly. The complete frankness would be a better cover than lying. Perhaps fifty years after Auschwitz we have entered the era of banal genocide (provided, obviously, that it affects only the peoples who are "marginal" in the great sweep of history, and provided that it is done quickly, in a few months). And this is even worse, for these "final solutions," however primitive they may be, perpetrated with machetes or sticks, will be carried out in broad daylight and with our tacit assent (especially if, as in Rwanda, the killers are our allies). Everything in the open, everything broadcast, everything exposed: that is the best means of immunizing us against the calamities the media report to us.

Intermittencies of the Heart

And so it is with our recurring fatigue with the catastrophes that envelope the planet. It is not the fatigue of a rescuer who has been exhausted by the vastness of his efforts, but that of the witness wearied by the same and sempiternal scenes. How can we feel accountable for dramas that take place thousands of miles away and that are connected to us only by an infinitely thin causal sequence? It's not that nothing touches our hearts; *everything* touches our hearts, moving us one way and another: a slaughter in Burundi, a famine in Ethiopia, dogs dissected in a laboratory and the birth of quintuplets in a private clinic. Our concern for the downtrodden, worldwide, is as powerful as it is instantaneous: one beautiful sob immediately driven out by another. These volatile demands do not produce any specific effect, just a skin-deep sentimentality that can be set of by all sorts of different causes. There is something inhuman in the swirl of disasters that crashes down on us: it does not leave anything stable in its wake and governs only short nervous jolts. Compassion, that eminently modern faculty to suffer along with the needy, is now subject to a law that is even more changeable: that of caprice.[2] We become so close to all the world's tragedies that we lack the distance to see them; we are so close to the other that we no longer have real neighbors. And we commune with reflections that slide by in front of us. That is why our concern for the other is so fickle.

Why do we latch onto one cause, and shun another? It's a mystery! The criteria of attachment and antipathy are innumerable and follow only one rule: that of the intermittencies of the heart connected to the galloping rhythm of the news. Suffering isn't enough to satisfy us; we want that *je ne sais quoi* that moves our heart. We only respond by infatuations, about-faces. Europe cried more in August 1993 for Irma, a little girl from Sarajevo who was wounded by an exploding shell, than for all the earlier victims of the war together. But we forgot the cause as quickly as we took it up. Images do affect public opinion, but ten times in a row, and the same people who called for immediate intervention in Somalia (1993) upon seeing the shriveled bodies of children were soon after calling for the repatriation of the American troops the moment the first soldiers were killed. As Mandeville said, "Sometimes trifles horrify us, and sometimes atrocities leave us indifferent."[3] Compassion degrades into a vague pity for all the unfortunates lumped together. Television eliminates geographical isolation but distances us emotionally by drowning all the victims in the same sea of information. In the realm of information, we have gone from a logic of restriction (and even of censure) to a logic of saturation. It is because they are too familiar, too predictable, in a way, that the distresses of the other have become banal. They have ceased being poignant since they are no longer overlooked; we are choking under a plethora of investigations, statistics, cries of alarm. And the pathetic calls to wake up produce a kind of exaggerated, insulated insensitivity that is born of excess and not of lack, or rather an ecliptic sensitivity that half-opens sometimes under the gusts of a transitory emotion only to close up all the better afterwards.

FOR EVERYBODY, OR JUST FOR "FRIENDS"?

The will to be responsible always runs aground in one of two ways: satiety and bulimia. It is true that we are principally accountable for anything that depends on us, that the responsibility for a drama lies with those who could have prevented it — a responsibility that is circumscribed but that is total within these bounds. Duty lies with those who are closest, before extending to those who are farther removed, and we cannot be blamed for every misfortune on earth. But responsibility is not satisfied with this containment: it also implies an obligation of each man towards all, a feeling of co-membership in the same species. Thus appears an absolute requirement: however ignorant I am as to the dramas of the world, I am concerned with the injustices perpetrated on other humans. I cannot say I am indifferent to their fate; their wounds affect me as if they were my own wounds.

Universal solidarity is, however, threatened in its turn by Irenism and disincarnation. It exists as a vague concept, without contents, boundaries or limits, like a perfect love that floats in the sky. But we cannot espouse every cause and meet every drama with the same level of emotion. To those who abjure us, when we are concerned with Bosnia, Rwanda or Armenia, not to forget Afghanistan, Angola or Abkhazia, we must answer that these thousand sources of indignation become a thousand reasons to withdraw; that by telling us not to prefer one cause over another, you incite us to a global engagement that is the height of disengagement. A solidarity that is solidarized in general supports dissimilar causes with the same enthusiasm. This is a routinized fidelity to outside figures: Albanians, Tibetans, Kurds parade in turn through the plaintiff's stand, in a rite that is pre-scripted for various observers. And the same ones who supported the Bosnians in December support the Tutsis in July, as they will defend the Algerian democrats six months later. Our attention to the world is patterned on the vibrating rhythm of the news, it gives a once-over to all the hot spots in the world. We are already pulling back the hand we reached out, and our Pavlovian offers of assistance are soon withdrawn and fade away due to our inability to make choices.

It is when we are everybody's brother that men become so cold. We cannot do everything; we have to share the work; and that means that we can only fulfill this ideal through friendship, and give up the idea of helping and being helped by everyone. I can only be men's friend if I establish closer relations with some, to the detriment of others; that which prevents me from loving them all equally is also that which enables me to help some of them. Partiality contradicts altruism, which, however, presupposes it — since it is a contradictorily essential condition of it. It's as though, to be effective, responsibility had to choose a limited field of fraternity and a geography of its own (not based on physical distance), or else it will remain undefined, that is, blind. This segmentation not only establishes boundaries, it gives us an entry point into the world, serving as both a barrier and an instrument. Other men certainly call for our assistance; but as limited beings, we cannot give ourselves to everyone, we have to give preference to permanence and fidelity.

Universalism, however, injects a stream of remorse into this partial philanthropy. Worldwide engagement can only be superficial, yet exclusive commitment to one issue alone seems narrow-minded. Required to pay attention simultaneously to certain people in particular and to humanity in general, action cannot live up to all expectations, cannot end all suffering and dry all tears. And so responsibility becomes hateful and tragic: its mission is endless; no matter what we do, we are never free of other people's misfortune. And we continue to swing like a pendulum between universal sympathy and the limits of incarnate beings.

A Big Spoon

But it would be wrong to blame this hard-heartedness on some kind of abuse by the supposedly biased media, on illusory spectacles, misleading reporting, and over-emphasis on the entertainment value of the news. The evil is more profound than that, and is part of the democratic hubris: it is the desire to be informed on every issue that is insane. Information requires each one of us to experience all the current events as dramas that affect us personally. However, you cannot feed John Q. Public all the world's news by big spoonfuls every day without causing a salutary reaction of rejection, you cannot ask him to bear the weight of all of humanity's troubles on his shoulders. That is the terribly monotonous absurdity of the media: by constantly submerging us under still more facts, at all hours, in continuous floods, they exceed our capacity of absorption. Our attention cannot keep pace: it goes along as far as it can, then disengages for reasons of intellectual health. Withdrawing, retiring, is a way of maintaining our senses in the face of an information monster that has neither a head nor tail. Here we are, thanks to the communication technology, overwhelmed by a duty that is boundless and that can only be met with a boundless resignation.

By inviting us to consider the Earth as one village, where

every inhabitant would be as familiar to us as our next-door neighbors, the media impose on us a kind of unreasonable every-day concern for the world. This outrageous expansion of the conscience is basically a hemorrhage: trying to stay abreast of world events, to be an informed citizen who can emit a judgment on the affairs of our day, is a full-time job. It takes a lot of work to read one or more newspaper every day, not to mention listening carefully to several radio and TV news programs! True, the written press requires effort and patience to read, which slows down the stupefying effect produced by TV. However, even the best newspaper, far from being a morning prayer (as Hegel thought), is like a fan that disperses the wisps of our ideas and forces us to ingurgitate a myriad of topics that are diametrically opposite to our concerns: we succumb under the weight of a monstrous encyclopedia of the moment that is inflated and at the same time inadequate.[4] (The more so as the press too can drown the reader in piles of paper and endless stories and journalistic investigations that verge on graphomania.)

Skimming or Selecting

Of course it would be impossible, unthinkable to do without the media, which has become the air that *homo democraticus* breathes. The news they report is essential to our understanding of the present. But to take in today's news, we first have to forget yesterday's. And however enthusiastically we go through a weekly magazine or a daily newspaper, we feel embarrassed, too, because the task is endless and it is hard to keep up with the flow of facts, to keep one's head above water. Unlike a book, a finite, limited object, a mechanism that resists time and which, by its concision, reveals essential truths to us, any newspaper no matter how talented its writers is out of date as soon as it is printed. Journalists sacrifice themselves every day to a goddess, an intransigent fantasy: topicality. It badgers them, forcing them to rush, to try to catch up. (It is interesting in this respect to look at the news from a more literary standpoint: international reports, regular columns, background articles, leads and editorials all start from a different inspiration but their sometimes exceptional quality slows down this feeling of wear and tear. For the newspaper, too, wants to endure, even if at the end of 24 hours it is only an illegible scrawl.) Scintillating with thousands of names, statistics and incidents that are arbitrary and ever changing, "current events" has turned into a bottomless pit, an unfathomable well. This gigantic mass (that has already been filtered down through the editing process) crumbles even as it accumulates. The small size of the book seems like a guarantee of enrichment; the openness of the newspaper leaves the impression of disjointedness and vacuity. We are unable to reconcile the need to make reality intelligible with respect for its complexity; we are *not so much ill-informed as disoriented.* We are running after a world that is in a state of perpetual transformation (especially since the fall of communism).[5] Thirty minutes, an hour or two for the whole planet, it is both too much and too little. These daily digests offer us syntheses that are both final and futile. Where the experts themselves acknowledge their embarrassment and are often mistaken, how can we ask the average to individual to make informed choices and have an informed say in politics? Even the model citizen, with plenty of leisure, examining the press with the meticulous care of an entomologist, could have only a very small idea of the convulsions that rock his era; even the most objective, the most pedagogical newspaper would still oblige us to filter the news, "to shop around" in the immense labyrinth of events. The scope of the information that gets away from us keeps on growing even as we learn, and we come out of this effort struck by our terribly erudite ignorance.

Why should we bother to be informed about the state of the world? Out of elementary courtesy towards others, since courtesy is already a "political policy in microcosm" (to paraphrase Leo Strauss), because as cohabitants in the City, I have a duty to my contemporaries. Through information, all of humanity (as a collective person) is put in possession of its ugliness. The media are thus the transmitters of a heroic morality and they lay upon us a crushing, if abstract, burden of guilt. Since every day we witness live broadcasts of all the baseness of the world, no matter what we do, we can never do enough; we will always fall short of the essential solidarity that should link us to our neighbor. How can we be our brother's keeper when we belong to such an extended and turbulent family? Quite simply by channel surfing. Every day we drink the wine of fraternity via the television screen or the tabloid but it is a superficial intoxication that ends up in a fantastic hangover. This burgeoning solidarity chokes on an overload of sufferings: and it is a crisis of aerophagia, for we are never in contact with flesh and blood beings. Everything can reach us but nothing touches us. If the fact of living in a universe that is "more present to itself in all its parts than it ever was before" (Maurice Merleau-Ponty) prevents our being totally unconcerned, we discharge our burden by reducing it to a spectacle. We bleed, but as in the fables, the wounds close again instantaneously! Once again this shell is essential: the media technique and its universal "visibility" neutralize the idea of responsibility by dilating it to planetary dimensions.

Consequently we waver between two dead ends: either we follow the electronic frenzy and its daily shows, getting drunk on an inflation of miseries, in real time, in a strange carnival of compassion and detachment; or we concentrate on a few burning issues of the day, at the risk of arbitrarily overlooking certain others; we lock ourselves into a two-sided process of deceleration and rarefaction. It's a terrible dilemma: a love that embraces all but holds nothing, or incarnation that restricts itself to one or two fields and doesn't want to know anything about the rest. Being human, today, means having to choose between two kinds of inhumanity: by skimming the surface or by zeroing in. For engaging always means excluding, practicing a shocking lapse of memory about other causes that we deliberately ignore. And what is true for the individual is true for the UN as well, deluged as it is under innumerable missions since the end of the Cold War and constrained to treat its interventions on a hierarchical basis too, and prudently to leave aside certain zones or populations that are under threat — despite its officially universalist rhetoric.

2. LOVING INDIGENCE

The Transcendence of the Victim

We like to think we are nice to the needy; we keep putting them on pedestals, we keep reminding everyone of the scandal of their distress, exalting the heroes of the sacrifice. To the point that we no longer have public opinion but public emotion, as if our fellow-citizens were only a troop of Good Samaritans with hearts overflowing with love for their wounded brethren. On the ruins of great political plans a charitable discourse is flourishing that bathes everything in a kind of irrepressible kindness. What princess, actress, super-model doesn't have her cherished Indians, Kurds, homeless, pandas or whales, as if each one had reached into the immense well of misfortune to choose a totem? Leagues, foundations, organizations stumble over themselves — anything related to suffering has its own committee. Even the magazines are rife with benevolence contests, where the readers are invited to elect and reward the most generous men and women. There is no major entrepreneur, singer or actor who do not sponsor the fight against cancer, AIDS, or myopathy, or does not lend his name to fundraising appeals in the name of Ethiopia or Bangladesh. What is a star, today? A Mother Teresa who makes movies, who sings a little.[6] All these sublime creatures dream of only one thing: becoming saints! This emphasis on the heart seems to be an essential asset in every artistic career. You have to show that you "have heart," and when making your rounds of the official receptions, make sure to surround yourself with handicapped or starving people who make you look good by contrast. It is a kind of reverse ostentation where the obsession with appearances is maintained *mezza voce*: the nobility of a cause must reflect onto anyone who promotes it. In the 1950's, it was the great "heroes of over-consumption" (Jean Baudrillard) who triumphed — highly skilled spendthrifts leading excessive lives dominated by expense, luxury and disproportion. Nowadays it is the heroes of compassion who get top billing and inspire ardent sympathies by their commitment to the disinherited.

However, let's not be in a hurry to laugh at these machinations or to see them as simple publicity stunts. We should congratulate ourselves, on the contrary, that in some recess of his psyche contemporary man can still build a small altar to benevolence; we should rejoice that there exists, even in a wan, caricatural form, a bond with the disenfranchised. Society would be intolerable without this multitude of small gestures of mutual aid and friendship that impel people to support those less fortunate. It is the positive side of the crisis that more and more citizens come to the aid of their compatriots in need without waiting for government subsidies.[7] There is nothing shocking in the idea that famous or wealthy people might devote some of their time to the poor, as a way of thanking Providence for the benefits with which it has blessed them: voluntary aid inspired by vanity is better than no voluntary aid at all. This appetite for misfortune is more than snobbery or a marketing strategy. Nowadays the damned are no longer the bearers of a Messianic plan that would aim at reconciling humanity with itself; but our age, wild and frivolous as it is, continues in its noisy way to celebrate the transcendence of the victim, to salute in his adversity the face of a scandal and a mystery. We no longer consider misery and disease to be destiny or a just punishment, we no longer believe in the constructive value of pain but see it as a plague to be destroyed or attenuated, we no longer think (as Bernanos did) that "the poor will save the world . . . without wanting to, . . . in spite of themselves."[8] For the degradation of a human being obliges me, in every sense of the term. His destitution becomes my law, as soon as I take note of it; it engages my responsibility. His torment is a summons, and evading it would be shameful. Offences made to others are a blow to my own humanity. Better yet: if humanitarian aid is progress, compared to charity, it is because, far from extending our solicitude only to those who are near, it expresses a potential concern for mankind in its entirety and proclaims that other people, everywhere, are my neighbors, even when they are far away. However problematic it may be, this is a significant change.

The quasi-divinity of the weak that persists in our day, the obscure glory born from insult, prohibits us from rebuilding, word by word, our century on the previous one, the Victorian Era that was so hard on the needy. Nietzsche saw this concern for the destitute as the worst heritage of the slave morality (i.e. Christianity), which he felt was guilty of having made the victim a god; on the contrary we know that it constitutes the prerogative and the pride of civilization.[9] (And the horror of certain passages in Nietzsche, where he decries the ill and the impoverished, when he exclaims in *The Antichrist* "May the weaklings and the losers perish," where he preaches the worship of the superior man, the selection of the strong and the elimination of the rest, weakens his otherwise luminous criticism of certain excesses of pity, a critique already suggested by Rousseau.)

TELETHON MADNESS

A telethon is hysterical generosity as a theatrical production. While the beneficiaries may be children with genetic diseases (or AIDS victims), the heroes are the donors themselves, and the whole society applauds itself for its generosity. The spectacle conforms to the principle of exaggeration and celerity: of course the event is full of smiles and good humor, an astonishing joviality, for time is precious. This Yom Kippur of the finer feelings has to make up, in two days, for a year of egoism; it's a kind of blend of the marathon and the village fair. Here kindness must be announced, proclaimed, acclaimed; gone is the antiquated concept of quiet and discreet charity. You have to scream, to be full of noisy enthusiasm, in a tournament where cities, towns, colleges, communities, and hospitals line up to offer the biggest check. The real pleasure is in contributing together, in publicizing the smallest gesture. It's all a matter of pacing, and emulation: everything has to be played out in such a way that there is no down-time; the pressure has to be constant (especially since, someday, any one of us might find ourselves the beneficiary of the medical research). The goal is to collect more than in any of the previous years, which explains the suspense and frenzy. The day's tally is constantly displayed and the number to beat is always on the screen. But signing checks and collecting money is not enough. Charity has to be defined by a superhuman effort. By contrast with the handicapped, heroes of fundraising set out in an outrageous hyperbole of useless exploits: thirty hours of intense tennis or basketball, rock'n'roll marathons, scaling the Eiffel Tower (solo), an elite team of federal troops rappelling down the Radio Tower (upside down); the firemen of Marseilles simulating a daring rescue from the top of a bell-tower. In 1993, a group of lawyers in Lille organized the longest pleading in legal annals (24 hours); in Soissons, a cyclist beat the world record for exercise bikes by covering 800 kilometers in less than 20 hours; a butcher in Arles made the world's largest sausage, 150 lbs., etc.. You think you are with the Evangelists, and you find yourself in the Guinness Book of World Records. What is the relationship between all this prowess and breast cancer? None. What counts is to make a lot of noise about it and call attention to it. On stage, even the presenters seem afflicted with a palsy: they bounce up and down while announcing the results, they stamp their feet, howling and laughing with mouths wide open, and point the cameras at the few kids lined up in wheelchairs to witness the euphoria.

In fact this itching mobility is a kind of test by absurdity: the more inert the patients are, the more the benefactors gambol about, running, climbing, pedaling as if that would ensure the continuation of their perfect health. How can you not like these sweet little disabled people? They infuse the nation with ingenuity, they are the expiatory victims on which the harmony of the community is restored. If there were no genetic diseases, they would have to be invented so that we would have occasion to mount these telethons and enjoy two days of collective élan. For it works — and the effect of such drives is that in 48 hours a whole country gives itself the means of making scientific progress on one specific topic. A combination of obscenity and effectiveness, jokes and faith, the telethon summarizes all our ambivalence towards the victims. We are sincerely sorry for them but we need them to love us and redeem us through their trials. Finally, in contrast to the old and unpleasant form of philanthropy, it inaugurates a new form of entertaining charity that combines games, performances and competition. A blend of two moralities: the utilitarian and the ludic. Being good becomes both advantageous and amusing!

The Actor's Pain

What characterizes the disinherited in our societies? The fact that we do not see them, or rather, that we see their failure too well to look at their faces. The poor must add the disgrace of exclusion to their material poverty; they are literally transparent, they walk in broad daylight as if it were night. They have all the traits of an individual in negative: not a property owner, not a citizen, not married; they have fallen out of the community of men. This phenomenon only becomes all the clearer as poverty starts to become more visible in the big cities again, as it spreads like a hideous sore. In the poor, we only perceive the indigence, not the man. Consequently the charity volunteer always starts by giving the miserable an identity and a human face, by selecting a few representative samples from the crowd of losers. The star (or the benefactor) lends his name to those who have none, forcing people to look at them. This approach can be shocking, but misery always needs some theater if it is to arouse pity.

In the Middle Ages, begging was an industry based on the manufacture (or the imitation) of sores and ulcers; that persists nowadays in many poor countries (for example, the family may mutilate the weakest child so that he can make himself useful by begging). Exhibiting their tortured bodies is the last, the atrocious recourse of those who must be further harmed if they are to survive. On a less dramatic level, the same scheme holds true, for example, for panhandlers in the subway, who plow through each car asking for coins, striking the imagination of the passengers with a brief and percussive account of their tale of woe. To avoid annoying passengers who have already been bombarded by a thousand similar stories, one has to present himself with eloquence, look contrite, demonstrate talent, and slip if necessary into melodramatics. And the same theory impels crushed people and minorities to play up their distress and in general to add some luster to their own sad stories. They have to become more or less the actor impersonating their own sorrows, to embody their tribulations in the eyes of others. A good pauper shouldn't suffer too much, for that would be distasteful; but he has to suffer enough to spark our interest! He has no chance if his misery is not obvious and disappoints our intention to do good. Prove to me your despair! Not only does the oppressed have little chance to reach us, but he runs into competition from the other oppressed people who also wish to be heard. In the waiting room of the world's conscience, millions of afflicted people trample and jostle each other in the hope of being heard and helped. And this, too, adds to the terrifying prestige enjoyed by the word "genocide" and its ability to capture our attention, at the risk of weakening its own impact through over use and inappropriate use.

In the same way the great media charity shows serve to extract the handicapped from the night of anonymity and to put on display models of courage, good citizenship, and kindness that are in theory accessible to everyone. To be seen and heard, to incite compassion (which is always addressed to a single being[10]) the needy must be extracted from the mass, must be individualized and sponsored (by a TV channel, a brand, a famous figure, a newspaper). This leads to what I will call the cosmetic makeover of the victim who is prepared and refined for presentation. He is refashioned, worked over again and again so that he will be heard and seen better than the beggar on the street corner. The same principle works for humanitarian organizations that use mass mailings to fabricate the biographies of abandoned little boys or girls who address donors directly to request their assistance. The disinherited must always be a precise person with an identifiable face and whose destiny one follows; for example, a poster from the AICF in 1994 that showed two photographs side by side: that of an absolutely skeletal girl and then a plump and smiling picture with the caption, "Leila, $50 later." Even the skinny ones must be dragged out of the sea of famine, and used as specimens; even skeletons must be made photogenic, selected and sorted according to a rigorous casting call for horror.[11] However, this reconstruction, this framing is principally the consequence of a responsibility that must retain its human dimension to be effective. No one cries over statistics and the overall facts of poverty are less touching than the sight of a man or a woman broken by hardship and disease. To become effective, charity requires tasks that are on its own scale, it has to remain a face-to-face altruism, we have to meet the recipient. People exist for us only if there are occasions for us to encounter them. Certain people expect immediate help from us because they are close to us, and these expectations define privileged lines of action.

It is not surprising that the greatest gestures of generosity coincide with natural catastrophes (cyclones, storms, floods) that hurt specific communities: our sense of fraternity is triggered most of all by the sharing of a disaster that constrains us to provide mutual aid and support.

A Narcissistic Commotion

Still, it is hard to really espouse the poetic and sympathetic rhetoric that our era uses in regard to itself. For the charitable person, according to an ancient perversion denounced as long ago as the Gospels, always tends to confuse the end with the means. The abolition of suffering is first used to promote the benefactors, who shine the spotlight on themselves, ahead of the people who are to be helped. When charity bands together with publicity, it betrays its first commandment: tact and secrecy. "Do not practice virtue ostentatiously, to be seen by other men," says the New Testament. However, according to its partisans, the law of decibels is justified by a concern for effectiveness. Getting media coverage facilitates the "insurrections of kindness" as Abbot Pierre called them*; it instantaneously mobilizes a crowd. The argument is unassailable. But there is a strong temptation, for some people, to confuse the commotion that must be made around the victims with a delicious hubbub of attention to their own person. There are two types of benefactor: the good one who, through his actions, sets an example and acquaints us with the needy, and the bad one who is there to show off and who stands between the poor wretches and the public. The benefactor should be as transparent as crystal. The thickness of his ego blocks our view; it is he in particular who cares about the image and he will only make a sacrifice if it leaves a trail on film. His golden rule is self-exhibition: comforting the downtrodden, hugging a baby, carrying a sack of grain, giving an injection. Knowing how to handle the public, and a talent for make-believe, win out over real commitment that is ungrateful, complex, and not very spectacular. Photographs, however, give the rescuer a flattering aureole. There is, as they say, an immediate symbolic return in terms of recognition.

Narcissism, a venial sin, you may say, is the one thing in this world that is most widely shared — only actions count, not intentions and not the inevitably impure repercussions. True! However, we run the risk of seeking out the poor not to help them but to elevate ourselves by stepping on them, to polish our images, to enjoy the delights of public benevolence. I am good and I want you to know it. It's no longer the needy who look for a helping hand, it is the impatient benefactor who drops everything to go looking for a victim to help. This type of kindness smacks of cannibalism, hungry for outcasts to feed its image of generosity. How many charitable organizations are fighting over the wounded and the desperate like market shares, nest eggs that bring them revenue? The homeless are at best only a foil; they enhance, by contrast, the heroes who comfort them, nourish them, soothe them. They serve to elevate a few individuals above the crowd, who stand out and shine against a backdrop of misery, madness and distress. Thus in France during 1993, the Bosnian tragedy was especially used to illustrate the bravery of General Morillon who, in Srebrenica, opposed the deportation of the city's inhabitants by the Serbs. But the upsurge of chauvinism that followed proves that the General's courage was used as a salve to our guilty conscience and makes us forget the ambiguous role our country played in this conflict. The rescuers must always be magnificent, and magnificent to the point of impudence. Sophia Loren comes to mind, posing in Baidoa next to starving children, and her paparazzi knocking down some little Somalians so they could photograph her with them. Such a scene is worth as much as an Oscar, for we like them, these starving people, these cripples, but we like them to be weak, disarmed, completely at our mercy; we want them to have the innocence of a child, the impotence of a child, the gratitude of a child. Nothing would offend us more than a poor wretch who was not overflowing with gratitude toward us: he must remain for all eternity an outstretched hand, a digestive tract, a wound that we bandage, an organism that we repair. He is still a man but also a little less than a man since he has been reduced to his biological needs, maintained in a state of survival. He never becomes an equal with whom we might possibly engage in a relation of reciprocity.[12] We take pleasure in the victim's need of us, as Rousseau[13] noted. The ontological scandal of charity is the inequality between the donor and the recipient who, unable to help himself, can only receive, without responding in word or in kind. Loving him only for that reason, cherishing his misfortune, is an expression not of noble-heartedness but of our will for power. We want to own the other's suffering, we collect it, we distill it like a nectar that sanctifies us.

So there is one charity that lifts up and prepares the emancipation of the one it helps, and there is another that degrades him, mires him in his infirmity, and asks him to collaborate in his own

---

* L'Abbé Pierre is the founder of Emmaüs, a sort of French Salvation Army.

inhumanity. Consequently the modern philanthropist is transformed not into a friend of the poor but into a friend of poverty: the poor suffer just to give him the chance to come and succor them and to extract from their perdition an ill-considered prestige.

Sainthood without the Hardship

As if the charitable ideal were too heavy to carry on our weak shoulders, there is a "soft" version that is built of small and inconsequential gestures. By a kind of degraded imitation of the knights of duty who are praised in the tabloids, each of us at his own modest level can effortlessly take part in the great festival of the heart. A secular version of the practice of indulgences in the Church, this way of discharging our neighbors' misfortunes is characterized by simplicity. We are satisfied to attend a rock concert against racism, world hunger, violations of human rights. Then the fight becomes a party, the virtues of sound and dance alone are sufficient to pulverize the evil, and the exercise of fraternity becomes both convenient and enjoyable. Nothing else is required but to writhe in unison at an event that is half party, half black magic: the miracle is accomplished, and hunger and racism imperceptibly diminish. And too bad if the weddings of pop, compassion and hedonism weave a parody of solidarity, too bad if the generous givers sometimes wake up to find out they've been betrayed, sorry to learn that their money went to support the causes of dictatorship. (As was the case of Bob Geldof's group Band Aid, the biggest moral swindle of the 1980's, that enabled the Mengistu regime to arm itself and to accelerate the herding of the rural populations into controlled zones. That is what happens when, through carelessness, we ignore the elementary law of any engagement: a minimal knowledge of the terrain, of the populations that one aims to help, of the players involved.) Better yet: our habits as consumers transform us, thanks to the products we choose, into instantaneous patrons. How many chocolate bars, coffee brands, fast foods, body lotions and jeans sponsor some humanitarian cause, taking part in the great crusade of the heart? By exercising a little care in our shopping, we can express our active benevolence from sunrise to sunset, we can sprinkle our benevolence over the world the way we mist a plant to refresh it. Do you want to help the homeless, for example? Wear an *Agnès B* T-shirt.[14] To protect an Amazonian tribe? Drink Stentor coffee. To stop violence, discrimination and spite? Buy Benetton. Then you will be doing good without even knowing it, the way Monsieur Jourdain made prose.

There isn't a moment of the day when we don't have an opportunity to express our all-consuming altruism. What object, even the most commonplace — pants, toothpaste, candy — couldn't be incorporated into the sphere of charity? Gone is the rigor of yesteryear, gone are our obsolete scruples: we act without having to lift our little finger. Everything I wear, use, drink or eat dispenses help and consolation somewhere around me, as if by magic. Alms are included in the purchase. This is a kind of absent-minded, automatic goodness that lavishes comfort in spite of us. The virtues of commitment are reconciled with the conveniences of torpor. This charity without obligation is the most pleasant thing there is: for now I can be selfish and generous, detached and engaged, passive and active. And how can we fail to appreciate the companies that guarantee to us that wearing their clothes, using their body lotion, eating their food can cure, even in a negligible way, the miseries of the world and discharge our concern?

You might say there is no harm in it, that this scattershot approach (inevitable when we are suffocating under causes) is preferable to inertia. But doing this very little bit becomes an alibi for not doing anything more.[15] The extraordinary abnegation of some (who are usually appointed to appease our remorse) must not make us forget the apathy or the tepidity of the majority. One should not confuse the avowed and publicized ideal with the accomplished ideal, we must work to reduce the distance that separates the two. In this respect our society is no worse than another; but it is characteristic of our time and its sentimental rhetoric that *we no longer dare to acknowledge indifference as such* and we speak the language of sacrifice, with hand on heart. Coldness, insensitivity return at the end of a speech inflated with fine words and great principles; *it is with the smile of love that we leave the other to die.* In this way we encourage a kind of peaceful selfishness that has digested its own criticism and believes itself to be eminently good.

Buying solidarity with a pair of jeans or a yogurt represents concern for others the way prostitution represents love. You will excuse me if I point out that charity cannot be amusing, that it must be "a little severe," as the founders of SOS-Sahel say, or risk degenerating into jokes and pleasantries. Applying the criteria and methods of consumerism to charity makes the ethical field look easy. When the market puts itself at the service of morals and claims to promote mutual aid and solidarity, it is morals that ends up serving the market, because it has become profitable.

When benevolence becomes mechanical, when generosity spreads everywhere like a gas, it disappears through dissolution, it ceases to wrench us out of our easy satisfaction. Having become ridiculous, this reflex "saintliness" brings discredit as well as confusion because it wins out over other more sincere attitudes. Through these counterfeits, our societies consume their ideals in the literal sense of the term, ridiculing them by celebrating them. And then our spirit of fraternity dies, not by drying up but by being drowned out in a simulacrum of brass bands and finer feelings.

3. EXTRANEOUS PEOPLE

The Pact of Tears

In the 18th century, they say, people liked to cry; Rousseau sang the praises of the liberating sob and the Encyclopédistes were not embarrassed to give in to tears in public — out of happiness and amazement more often than of sorrow. Still, we should review the history of tears in Europe, and study the famous "gift of tears" emphasized by Michelet in connection with St. Louis and celebrated as a spiritual exercise by Ignatius de Loyola,[16] the paradoxical joy of letting one's pain come bursting forth, the collective purification of a whole community. Our era has repudiated tears in favor of teary eyes: few tumultuous explosions of wrenching cries, but plenty of misty eyes, clouded, always on the verge of overflowing. It is an attitude of permanent humility vis-à-vis the blows dealt by fate, a kind of religion of sympathy that sympathizes with everything that lives, feels and suffers, with abused children and with abandoned animals. In all this revolving display, the losers pass by as in a parade, and anyone at all can play the role, provided he meets the two criteria of being spectacular and sentimental. Our goodness is avid for misfortunes, it draws up a kind of Top 50 of planetary suffering, it juggles victims (whom it consumes in great number), one day propelling to first place a little girl who was killed, only to dethrone her soon after in favor of another enticing disaster. Thus the High Mass of our commiseration sees in the multitude of suffering beings only a delightful occasion to wet a handkerchief. It's a twofold movement: only things that are going badly hold our attention and in discussing problems, the difficulties are emphasized, anything that moves our hearts. Looking for social topics to cover? Immediately the unemployed, drug addicts, the homeless, and restless youth are called desperate and are made into objects of compassion. If they conform to this stereotype and they are telegenic or radiophonic, and we can avoid other more political approaches: behind each particular case, we have to flush out something pathetic. As long as they remain unfortunate, we feel sorry for them; as soon as they rebel or protest, we fear them and hate them. The *reality-show* becomes the only lens for looking at the world: I'm interested in your misfortune. We do not want to be informed, only upset. We sniff out adversity with the zeal of a dog digging up truffles; we roll around in other people's troubles with a kind of enthusiasm and even a certain pleasure.

Why this everyday compassion? It certifies to a sense of cohesion in a world that is always in the process of crumbling. Emotion is our only real link with others and makes it possible to keep rebuilding a pretence of community, contrary to reflection, which suspects and separates. It is the idiom of the heart because it goes beyond the mediation of words or reason. In the spectacle of pain, we are seeking a little bit of that "warmth of the pariahs" that belongs, as Hanna Arendt put it, to the humiliated, a kind of superficial communication with the desperate from the comfort of our own armchairs. If there is any Utopia at the foundation of our charitable and media-based rituals, it is in this will to re-forge the social bond, to recreate fraternity through the most transitory feeling — commiseration for everyone who has been hurt. To cry over or, rather, to pity the others, means thanking them for having disturbed us, it means redeeming ourselves (without much cost) for our lack of interest in them; it means, finally, praying to the bad luck that has hit them and not us, holding them at arm's distance while pouring out our feelings. It's a deliciously passive position that engages neither our thought nor action. Every day we glorify the most appealing wretch: because under certain conditions and provided we all respect the laws of this dramaturgy, downfall and misery can be a festival. The detective novel has long since accustomed us to seeing crime and its refinements as a first quality enigma. And as we appreciate the crimes of assassins, so we also take a paradoxical pleasure in watching our neighbors suffer; we claim our daily ration of murder, accidents, attacks. There is a sadism of pity and we end up making a pleasure out of other people's tragedies by going over them too often. Such is the ambiguity of our expiatory ceremonies. The contract of commiseration that is played daily on the mass media mixes repulsion and pleasure in an ambiguous way: the sight or the account of other people's torments is terrifying but also entertaining. Now we watch all the victims and think, May the best ones win!

Compassion as a Form of Contempt

Charity and humanitarian aid have something in common, as they fill the gaps in justice and social policy: they prefer timely relief of a specific distress rather than a messianic expectation of complete salvation. Both express the same impatient generosity. However, charity always runs the risk of trying to replace the State as humanitarian aid vies with politics (at the price of being manipulated by the latter). The relation between these various authorities is not so much complementary as conflictual: they can paralyze each other but they can also egg each other on, cooperate, and improve each other.[17]

Charity plays a beneficial role in creating a scandal when it upsets entrenched egoism, challenges law and order, disturbs the peace of those who are comfortably seated; but it becomes scandalous in its turn when it claims to be sufficient on its own and does not look for ways to integrate itself into reality, in the long term, through legal or political mechanisms. It is scandalous when it elevates the intellectual or physical incapacities of the unfortunate into major qualities, when it venerates the defeated because he is defeated and cannot take care of himself. There is something terribly ambivalent in making misery a necessary plague, almost a virtue, in taking the poorest of the poor as the only measure of what is human, in exalting misfortune, sorrow and death as the worthiest foundations of the human condition.

Still, the humanitarian worker is an irreplaceable example of courage. Not satisfied with going straight to the victims, he serves an especially important role as witness since he can challenge the rule of confidentiality that governed the Red Cross. Moreover, humanitarian aid is founded on the idea that civil society alone is dynamic, that it alone has the resources to cut through bureau-cratic rigidity and inhuman rules. In its emphasis on individual initiative, in the will to short-circuit the procedures of politicking, humanitarian aid is our last fantasy of direct democracy. (That is why, in France, it was reinvented by former leftists — that is, by spirits broken by mistrust of the government apparatuses, media-tors and parties.) Therein lies its grandeur and beauty. It has all the allure of a Utopia, it sets up a new *internationale* of devotion that is a confirmation of the unity of mankind, of man abstracted from any religious, social or ethnic membership. But it becomes dubious when it refuses introspection on the excuse of some kind of blackmail of the oppressed that forces us to act, never to reflect; because it is the terrible truth of suffering, that it does not tolerate the least objection and strikes down whoever is opposed to it. It becomes suspect when it equates the crises of war with those of natural disasters, when it looks only at stereotypes (the poor, the refugee, the casualty) and refuses to name Evil, to name the tor-turers. And it is criminal when it comes in place of a solution that would have immediately saved thousands of lives (the ultimatum to the Serbs besieging Sarajevo in February 1994 did more in a few days for the inhabitants of the city than the 22 previous months of humanitarian aid that allowed them, at most, in their own words, to die with a full belly). Then it inevitably collapses in the defects that yesterday we criticized in the revolutionary ideologists: mes-sianism, vague universalism, the logic of all or nothing. Ignoring governments, national realities, and historical trends, it tries to intervene everywhere and pretends that with its own resources alone it can put an end to injustice immediately. In short, making impossible claims, it loses all sense of what is possible, the idea that failing to found a new paradise on earth, political solutions remain the choice of what is preferable over what is detestable. And this other-worldliness leads it straight to cynicism.

This is why humanitarian aid, like charity, should be contained inside strict limits and not be allowed to contribute to the confusion of the situation; while they are essential in their own field, these "moral countervailing powers" (Jacques Julliard) are harmful when they give in to the intoxication of their omnipotence and promote themselves as the solution to humanity's problems. What a disaster it would be if the UN and the democratic nations were, in their turn, to approach every major crisis from a strictly charitable standpoint, seeing only victims and never denouncing the culprits. A thousand admirable acts will never replace a real social policy. Raving over the prodigality and the virtue of the donors misses the point that they cannot adequately mitigate the deficiencies of the State. In this respect Abbot Pierre's dedication to the media, in France, is perhaps coincidental with the defeat of his ideal: it is because the French are generally resigned to mass poverty that they delegate to him the problem of redeeming their guilty consciences, of salving their hearts. These phenomena that we take for signs of triumph are in fact symptoms of a collective abdication.

Compassion is an admirable inclination, but it weaves between mankind a sense of solidarity only in pain, a dimension common to all living beings, human as well as animal (Brigitte Bardot sent a ton of dog food to Sarajevo — that still falls into the category of humanitarian logic; the gesture was not a blunder but was on the contrary fantastically revealing). It thus founds a purely negative communion; with it, no one is our peer, they only seem to be such. But it's not the heart and its accessories that are the source of real friendship between men and that make it possible to found a common home, livable for all, a world of reciprocal freedom; it is exchange and dialogue. While charity may alleviate a specific wound, it is only in the political sphere, where the confrontation is codified, in the public space, through interests and rights, that equals are made. Emotion must have its proper place and without the faculty of being affected by events, we would have no chance to be moral or immoral. But it is only a starting point and when it is over-stimulated, this vital jolt anesthetizes our sensitivity.

Compassion becomes a form of contempt when it is the only component influencing our relation with others, to the exclusion of other feelings like respect, admiration or joy. It is so much easier to sympathize abstractedly with the unfortunate, an elegant way of stepping aside; sympathy with happy people requires a greater openness of heart and obliges us to fight against the obstacle of envy. Making compassion the cardinal value of the City destroys the possibility of a world where men could speak with each other and recognize themselves as free people. Humanitarianism, like charity, only seeks out the afflicted, those who are dependent; whereas politics requires interlocutors, autonomous beings. One produces people on assistance, the other requires responsible people. That is why so many individuals or peoples in difficult situations resist allowing themselves to be dictated to like victims: they repel our pity because it humiliates them and they prefer to safeguard their dignity by revolt or fighting rather than to be the simple toys of universal mercy.

The Menu Approach

A few years ago, we thought we'd made a big step forward when we refused to distinguish between the good guys and the bad guys among the casualties of the Biafra conflict (a way of replicating Henri Dunant's gesture; the father of the Red Cross provided care to all the soldiers who were wounded in the battle of Solferino). Now everybody is eligible for our benevolence and the concepts of Right and Left, progressive and reactionary are no longer taken into account. Isn't this new ethics just substituting new criteria for the purely ideological divisions we used to observe? Contrary to the requisite other-worldliness, the political considerations remain paramount: in Bosnia as in Rwanda, humanitarianism was also a smokescreen behind which inadmissible diplomatic choices were hidden. In the one case, it was used to mask tacit support for Serbia, the only strong local power in the region; in the other, Operation Turquoise, as necessary as it may have been, was used by France to atone for earlier conduct, to make everyone forget its support for those responsible for the genocide, and worse yet to save them in order to hold onto a privileged position in the area of the Lakes. But above all, today as yesterday, we choose our charity cases the way we choose our lovers: we latch onto some people and we are stricken with aversion for others. It takes courage to admit that all nations, all ethnic groups are not equal before our solicitude, that some will be cherished more than others. It is not the misfortune that dictates our duty to us, it is we who decide who, among the needy, deserve our interest. In other words, it is less a morality of emergency than a morality of preference. And our response to the underprivileged is always the result of a complex choice.

With some 23 million refugees in the world (there were only 2.4 million in 1974) calling for assistance, when war is flaring up at our borders and causing exoduses and desolation that affect the civilian populations most of all, an emergency is presented to us every minute, every day. And our response is always partial, in both senses of the word. Why Somalia rather than Liberia or Mozambique? For every intervention there is somewhere that we do not intervene; and for every successful operation, we forget about ten others that were just as necessary. Not only do we all carve up the globe according to our affinities or our own interests, but some calamities are profitable for the media and others merit hardly a sad shake of the head. Definitely, some of the dispossessed will never become stars!

On the ethical level the only obligation is that which I take on, myself: only we judge, according to our whims, which situations are intolerable, and every country like every charitable organization has its preferred areas of activity. Even if we base our decisions on the moral imperative of the emergency, we cannot help being discriminatory: it is the prerogative of charity as well as of humanitarianism to apply itself to those of the needy that it has, to some extent, selected. (While history involves us against our will in crises or disasters that we cannot avoid, in the political realm the discontent form parties, movements, and trade unions that clamor for our attention; they put pressure on us to force us to look at them, to consider them.) There will always be some poor people, some beggars that we prefer over others: charity is selected from a menu. The reasons that guide our choices are all the more incomprehensible now that the Cold War is over and our approach is less explicitly ideological. The world order that succeeds the East-West division is no longer that of progressive inclusion of all the continents in the same economic and political space; on the contrary, it draws a new dividing line between the nations worthy of interest and the others who are rejected into darkness or anarchy. The first group receives our technology, our military support, our cultural exchanges. The others can hope for a little indulgence, occasional media attention, and some food. *We are only concerned with what threatens us or brings us benefit, not with what moves us.* As long as those who are forsaken in our countries do not fundamentally endanger the social structures, they will continue to be fodder for our altruism — that is, our inconstancy. And what is true for the outcasts inside our countries is all the more so for those abroad. Only regimes, groups, States can blackmail others, can represent a vital stake, can threaten the existence of the whole.

Revising History

We are no longer concerned with propagating democracy, human rights and civilization. The main goal of our pity and its institutional translation, UN troops and humanitarian organizations, is to relegate a certain number of populations to the margins, to draw a cordon around crisis areas in order to isolate them the way sick people are quarantined.[18] And when legally recognized States, having pleaded for military assistance from Europe or the United States, see humanitarian cargo planes full of food and drugs instead of arms and troops, they can legitimately think: the world has abandoned us. Humanitarian assistance, when it is substituted for political assistance, is the modern face of abstention, tempered by a few medical teams and airlifts. Ethnic groups and whole regions of the world — those that we have decided not to bother with or don't know what to do with — are strictly confined to the charitable arena, relegated to some extent to eternal purgatory. In short, while compassion *obliges* us, only politics *constrains* us. It will always be easier to neglect our moral duty than to ignore a specific danger that calls for our response under penalty of serious consequences.

There is one tragedy of action that even humanitarianism cannot evade. Every engagement is unique and can only be undertaken if a dozen other opportunities for action are forsaken. No aid can cover the whole planet; men do not have equal value everywhere at every moment. More than generosity or indignation, the logic of sacrifice is also at work behind our effervescence. And one wonders whether the recently proclaimed right to interfere is not being used as a discreet mantle for the inequality of treatment, if it is not actually the right to neglect certain people while pretending to help to them. The immense innovation of the duty of assistance theorized by Bernard Kouchner and Mario Bettati is to grant, on paper at least, *a right to those without rights and to limit a State's absolute power over its nationals.* By tackling the sacrosanct principle of sovereignty, by dissociating the citizen from the man, this duty defends "the natural right of victims" (François Ewald) and prohibits the crushing of a whole people by their government.

Actually, as many people have noted, the right of interference does not destroy the sovereignty of nations but limits that of certain States in favor of others (which are not exclusively in the North). And thus there is little chance that it will ever be applied in the great powers' zones of influence if it opposes their own interests. Even the plan for a world army that would be responsible for saying who is right, for protecting the weak and for preventing conflicts, forgets that the UN is in fact led by certain States who make the law there to the detriment of the smallest. The duty of assistance does not deprive the rescuer of this right to choose and to deal with the victims at its own discretion. That does not discredit it but it does show its limits, for the time being. Is the Utopia of a policy of human rights that is disengaged from the calculations of the States likely ever to see the light of day? It is too soon to say, especially since the two principal cases of intervention that have been carried out to date — Kurdistan and Somalia — are too ambiguous to be convincing. (Somalia is even a counter-example, since the military fiasco persuaded the Americans not to attempt another such expedition for a long time.)

We should not trust this inflation of dispositions that are so generous that they have little chance of actually materializing. It is a fundamental misinterpretation to call the duty of interference a new ploy of colonialism. What nowadays threatens a certain number of nations in Asia, Africa and Latin America is not neo-imperialism, it is pure and simple abandonment. Absolutely intolerable as it was, at least colonialism expressed a will to propagate the Enlightenment, to educate, to "civilize." The great powers are no longer inspired by a will for expansion, as they were at the end of the 19th century, but by commercial concerns and the desire to increase trade among themselves (the rich), while neglecting the other regions. Their official rhetoric is still universalist, express-ing equal concern for all the others; but the fictitious notion of a love that does not choose is a rhetorical formula that masks a cov-ert form of banishment. There is one humanity that is moving ahead and one humanity that is running in place, there are States that count, that embody Progress and Democracy, and others who have dropped out of the march of history. And now the interna-tional community, through the voice of its representatives at the UN, decides in all legality to sacrifice such or such group to pre-serve the peace of the ensemble. It is humanity as a whole that dictates this painful surgery: triage must be made. Not by war but by omission, by dismissing.

So, woe to the peoples and the minorities who do not have any strategic or economic leverage over the great powers of their day, woe to those who cannot defend themselves. For they will become an extraneous people, a people to reject, relegated to the wings, to the shadows. For they will depend on international charity, i.e. of a new form of arbitrary rule: that of the heart.

COMPARATIVE VICTIMOLOGY: ISRAEL AND PALESTINE

What precluded any possibility of agreement between the Hebrew State and the Palestinians until the autumn of 1993? The fact that each side considered itself the most aggrieved party. There was already only one land for two peoples; now they disputed the monopoly on absolute misfortune, too. In the name of the immense wrongs inflicted on the Jew-ish people, Israel considered every criticism to be a direct threat to its existence and every enemy to be a potential exterminator. Conversely the Palestinians, presenting themselves as the quintessential dispos-sessed, claimed for themselves all the titles of the Jews: the diaspora, per-secution, genocide. Thus the Israelis and Arabs began dueling for the title of world's greatest victim, saying, "We are the most aggrieved, therefore we have all the rights and our adversary has none." This rhetorical fear paralyzed the involved parties and led to the worst excesses. Two tragedies clashed on one tiny territory and it's another tragedy that both sides are right: since the war of independence in 1948, "free men, the Arabs, left in exile like poor wretched refugees; and poor wretched refugees, the Jews (many of whom were survivors of the Genocide), took over the houses of the exiles to begin their new life as free men."[19]

But Israel was also hated because, as a Western nation, it advanced under the mask of an immemorial insult and confiscated from people who had been colonized in the past the their sad-sack speech and turned it against them. It combined two irremediable defects: the arrogance of the Western imperialist and a usurpation of the role of the suffering. And the Arabs did not see why they should pay for the sins of the Nazis, committed in Europe by Europeans on other Europeans. Thus, invoking the distress of the Palestinians, a whole faction of the Western left could scold the Jews: you betrayed your destiny, which was to suffer and to testify through your martyrdom for all of humanity. The new Jew now speaks Arabic and wears the keffieh. By losing "the magistrature of martyrdom" (Charles Péguy), you monopolize a role that does not belong to you any more, you become deaf and blind to the miseries that you cause on this land that is not yours. By constituting yourselves into a nation, you have lost your singularity. In short, people were upset with the Jews for not conforming to the stereotypes of the victim: they were hated when they were unfortunate, and they were detested when they were victorious. Via the political dimension of the Hebrew State, they were held accountable for the least vexation inflicted on the Arabs and the word Judeophobia was given a new lease on life when it was merged into anti-Zionist rhetoric.

It is true that Israel, a country that embodies Western-Middle East misunderstanding, has long been building a double image as the persecutor and the persecuted — strong enough to win wars and repress the Intifada, weak enough to fear being surrounded, to fear being wiped off the map as its enemies swore it would be. Informed by millennia of persecution, Israel never counted but on anyone but itself and it built one of the most powerful armies in the region. This resolution, thorough sometimes to the point of extreme brutality, preserved the nation. "Certainly, we are paranoid, but we have good reasons for that," admitted the former chief of military information, General Shlomo Gazat.

The Shoah was too often invoked by the government to justify any reprisal, however disproportionate, against the Palestinian or Lebanese populations, against any ill treatment or racist act. "Our biggest mistake today," said the philosopher Yeshayahou Leibowitz, long an opponent of the policy of Greater Israel, "is in making the Shoah the central question in connection with everything that concerns the Jewish people. The only Judaïc element that many intellectuals find in their Jewishness is that they are interested in the Shoah."[20] "We must not transform the Shoah into a machine of political war . . . I do not want for Jews to share between themselves only the memory of atrocities," adds Professor Yehuda Elkana, himself an Auschwitz survivor.[21] "Thinking that the whole world hates us," the editorialist Boaz Avron wrote in 1980, anxious over Menahem Begin's extreme politicizing of the genocide, "we think we are ourselves exempt of responsibility for our actions in the world." It is the same Begin, who, during the Lebanon War, responded to criticism from the international community by exclaiming, "Nobody can make teach morality to our people." Later that summer he would say, "The Jews do not bow down before anybody except God." He often compared the charter of the PLO with Mein Kampf and promised to hunt down "that beast on two legs" that was Arafat-Hitler. Novelist Amos Oz responded to Begin, saying: "Hitler is already dead, Mister Prime Minister. . . Like it or not, it is a fact: Hitler is not hiding in Nabatyeh nor in Sidon nor in Beirut. He is indeed dead. Mr. Begin, you keep exhibiting a strange need to bring Hitler back to life in order to kill him again every day in the form of terrorists. . . . This need to revive and destroy Hitler comes from a melancholy that the poets must express but in a statesman it is a hazardous sentiment that can lead to mortal danger."

Conversely the Palestinian movement, long plunged into extremism, supporting the most insane political options (including Saddam Hussein's invasion of Kuwait), developed a blind terrorism, ready to strike anywhere in the world at the least symbol of Judaism, any school or synagogue, and to make every Jew the hostage of Israel. Many Arab countries picked up as a bloc the theses of European anti-Semitism, and moreover called "the Zionist entity" the ultimate misadventure of the Western crusade in the Levant. However, in the very bosom of the Hebrew State, which remained democratic in spite of the wars and a despotic environment, a broad sector of the population favored peace and called for dialogue with the Palestinians, certain that short of radical and repugnant solutions (such as the massive deportation of Arabs out of the country), concessions were inevitable. It is this same camp that was to bring together nearly 300,000 people in Tel-Aviv in 1982 to protest the massacres in Sabra and Chatila, committed by the Christian Lebanese Phalanxes under the benevolent eye of the Israeli army (no such demonstration of indignation was seen in any Arab country). It is this same camp, finally, that without giving up anything as to the security and the absolute right of the State of Israeli to live within its recognized borders, demanded that Israel give up its siege mentality (the morbid delight in believing itself hated by everyone) and agree to grant Palestinians the beginnings of autonomy. There are indeed in every Israeli two people who are split between a penchant for "nationalist isolationism" and "humanistic openness" (Tom Segev), one who says "Remember what they did to you," the other "Love your neighbor as yourself," as Hugo Bergman said during Eichman's trial. And, finally, it was the partisans of peace in Israel as well as among the Palestinians who allowed, at the cost of so much difficulty and with who knows what ulterior motives, negotiations to begin, who stretched out a hand to the other, to the one who just yesterday was seen as the devil and whom one now regards as a peer. That is an exemplary outcome, even if it is still likely to fail, and it proves that even after a century of confrontation, we can get out of what Nabil Chaath, advisor to Yasser Arafat, called "comparative victimology."

Footnotes

1. This is the thesis that Bernard Kouchner, for example, defends: "Without an image, there is no indignation: misfortune only affects the unfortunate. The helping hand of fraternity cannot be extended toward them. Photography and the initiatives that it sets off remain the essential enemy of dictatorships and underdevelopment. Let's accept it, without resign ourselves to it: this is the law of making a commotion. We should use it." (*Le Malheur des autres*, Odile Jacob, p. 194.)

2. It is equality, observed Tocqueville, that makes us sensitive to others' pain and that causes each of us, in the democratic centuries, to express a general compassion for all the members of mankind. "When the chroniclers of the Middle Ages (who were all members of the aristocracy by birth or by virtue of their practices) reported the tragic end of a noble, they express infinite pain, yet they relate the massacre and torture of the common people without a sigh or a raised eyebrow." (*De la démocratie en Amérique*, Folio, Gallimard, op. cit., volume II, p. 231.) Our interest in others is inversely proportional to the distance that separates us from them; journalists call this the law of the "sentimental mile." One death near at hand is a drama, ten thousand overseas is an anecdote.

3. Bernard de Mandeville, *La Fable des abeilles*, Vrin, 1974, p. 135.

4. The Polish science fiction writer Stanislas Lem imagined a monstrous book that would tell what happened in just one minute of humanity in every field, Bibliothèque du XX siècle, Seuil, 1989.

5. "When the USSR broke down, we Americans lost more than an enemy. We lost a collaborator in the search for meaning." (Richard Cohen, *International Herald Tribune*, October 27, 1993.) I also refer to the fact that democracy can die from its own triumph and that it requires enemies who revitalize it, in my book *La Mélancolie Démocratique*, Seuil, 1990.

6. Gina Lollobrigida in *Paris-Match*, May 4, 1993: "I share Mother Teresa's battle and I contribute to it in my own way." The most common photograph of Audrey Hepburn that was distributed the day she died was that of the actress visiting of the children in Somalia.

7. *Le Monde* presented an interesting series of articles on these "Adventurers of generosity" under the direction of Danielle Rouard (August 1993).

8. Quoted in Philippe Sassier, *Du bon usage des pauvres*, Fayard, 1990, p. 363.

9. Karl Jaspers made this inversion of values, this rupture with the accepted standards, the privilege of Christ's teachings. Christ opened a fatherland to those without a fatherland. "Since Jesus held himself at the

extreme margins of the world, because he is the exception, a chance is given to all who, according to the world's criteria, passes for the low, the lame, the ugly, all who are rejected, excluded from the established order; a chance is given to man as such under any condition." (*Les Grands Philosophes*, Presse-Pocket, 1956, volume I, p. 280.) We must also cite Rene Girard's work, the quintessential anti-Nietzsche whose so edifying second reading of the Bible and the Gospels opens enthralling perspectives on the contemporary world (even if Girard offers no other solution but the absolute leap, religious conversion).

10. According to the description given by Hannah Arendt in *Essai sur la Révolution*, compassion applies to the person, pity applies to the ensemble. "Compassion by its very nature cannot be inspired by the sufferings of a whole class. It cannot beyond what a single person suffers without ceasing to be what it is, by definition: co-suffering." (Gallimard, 1967, p. 121.)

11. Claude Coutance, who won the Nicéphore Niepce Prize in 1993, appearing at the palace in Tokyo, explained a report on Somalia this way: "I was looking in the faces for stereotypes of famine such as Westerners define them: thin people, a certain look, attitudes. I photographed not with my heart but with a cold, cynical machine that you have to know how to use. I was sometimes with inches of the faces. Sometimes I spent two hours to make an image. Without realizing it, we are making a casting call: for we seek the most touching scenes. There is nothing more touching than skeletons." (*Le Monde*, 1 June 1993.)

12. "All the humanitarian action in Bosnia is founded on the idea that there are people in Bosnia who cannot fend for themselves. The organizations in charge of the humanitarian aid expect to find something like the drought and the war in Somalia, or the Kurds in the mountaintops. Something like the Third World. As if the Bosnians were hit by some kind of natural disaster that made them forget how to read and write, to drive, to manage cities. As soon as they stop being victims, they start to be hated by the humanitarian organizations." (Erwin Hladmik-Milharcic, in Mladina (Slovenia), reproduced in *Courrier International*, April 15, 1993.)

13. Clifford Owin recalls this in an excellent article, "Rousseau et la découverte de la compassion politique, in *Écrire l'Histoire du XX siècle*, Gallimard-Seuil, 1994, pp. 109-110.

14. Cf. Agnes B, whose T-shirt sales benefit the homeless. Strong language: "These people who come into the store are doing humanitarian work. They are involved. That is normal, essential. I love Abbot Pierre. He is

super-important. He is almost the only one who is worthy of re-spect." (*Le Monde*, August 5, 1993.)

15. As the statistics testify: while the French give 7 billion francs to charita-ble organizations (partly for tax reasons), that is four times less than what they spend for cats and dogs. As for the 2 million volunteers, half work in fact in sports. Jacques Duquesnes, *Le Point*, December 19, 1992).

16. Roland Barthes has a very lovely text on this subject in "Pouvoirs de la tragédie antique,"in *Oeuvres complètes*, Seuil, 1993, volume 1, pp. 216 sqq., as well as in *Sade, Fourier, Loyola*, Seuil, 1971, p. 79.

17. Abbot Pierre puts it very well: "Charity has two roles: before the law, to force the law to progress; after the law, for try as one may, the law will never be enough." (*Autrement*, September 1991, p. 237.)

18. On the new division of the world, see Jean-Christophe Ruffin's premoni-tory book, *L'Empire et les Nouveaux Barbares*, Lattès, 1991.

19. Tom Segev, *Le Septième Million, Les Israéliens et le Génocide*, Liana Levi, 1993, P. 197.

CONCLUSION

A Narrow Door for Revolt

The game is not over, of course, and nothing says that immaturity and complaining must be the inexorable trend. Whereas irresponsibility was structural in the old communist bloc — the citizen owed subservience in the State that took him under its wing — our lack of responsibility remains sporadic and in theory can still be reformed. But when the exception becomes so frequent, it starts to become almost structural. Puerility and whining are not accidents but challenges that will always confront us. Just as democracy is haunted by totalitarianism that sticks to it like a shadow, the society of responsibility calls forth its opposite as a threat that is difficult to defuse. The free man's eternal penchant for resignation, his bad faith, can be thwarted or slowed down but will never be completely eradicated. It requires gigantic discipline not to give in to the temptations of weakness and it is difficult to count on such discipline — for the individual is a fragile construct that is held together by a certain number of counterweights — material abundance, the State of law and welfare, the exercise of citizenship. Remove just one brace from this scaffolding and it wavers, it falls.

A SENSE OF INDEBTEDNESS

We think we are helping the subject when we pamper him, when we relieve him of all that is not himself, when we lighten his duties and obligations so that he can devote himself entirely to his exquisite subjectivity. By doing so, however, we deprive him of guidelines, references and frameworks, we make him more anxious about himself, and we confuse independence with vacuum. Without meaning to, we increase the appalling defeatism of those who, crushed by their freedom, hasten to forget it and to trample it. Now, to reinforce the individual would mean to establish bonds and not to isolate him, it would mean relearning the sense of indebtedness — that is, of responsibility; it would mean enrolling him again in various networks, various webs of loyalty that make him one fragment in a vaster ensemble, opening him up and not limiting him to himself (provided that he agrees to these memberships voluntarily).

For Western man does not need to be protected or confined within the nursery or the old people's home. He needs courage to get him moving, challenges to keep him awake, rivals to spur him forward, the stimulation of some degree of hostility, of useful obstacles. He has to remain a being of discord, sheltering within himself contradictory ideals, a being whose conflict is a treasure and not a curse; he needs to keep a small civil war going on inside himself. Individualism will not be cured by a return to tradition or by increased permissiveness but by a more demanding definition of its ideal, by rooting it within something that is greater than itself. It is viable only when it is held in check by forces that seem to deny it but that actually supply it with hurdles and thereby enrich it. Deprive of constraints, it dries up; attack it, and it grows stronger.

We are never "men, simply men" (Hannah Arendt), but always the product of a specific situation, which cannot be conceived without a nation, a political regime, a people, a cultural heritage. Rather than conceiving the private individual as in a sterile combat against society, we should think of the two in terms of discrepancy, of fertile opposition, since each one generates the other. These are two points of view that are equally legitimate, that contrast concern for oneself and concern for the world. The private person marks the limit of the social order that circumscribes him, in its turn; he is the stumbling block that hinders mass recruitment and conformity (without degenerating, for all that, into a lack of interest in the common fate). He should be confronted with the germs of "communitarianism" that can destroy individualism but also can strengthen it; its antithesis must be a key component that revitalizes it through opposition. Just as the community meets an insuperable border in the will of each member, there is no true freedom except for that which is contained, that is, both extended and limited by the freedom of others, and deep-rooted in others. To slow down our puerile or victimist regression in all its forms, we must expose the subject to that which forces it to grow, to that which draws it out of itself toward a greater being.

Ultimately, there is only one way forward, and that is to continue to reinforce the great values of democracy, reason, education, responsibility, and prudence, to strengthen man's capacity to never bow down to established fact, to avoid succumbing to fatalism. It is up to us to show that democracy with its traditional weapons of debate and argument can still face up to its own contradictions; it is up to us to prove that the whining, narcissistic citizen is capable of making great strides (before reality takes it upon itself to punish him with all its impersonal rigor). Denouncing frivolity that is too often detrimental does not prevent us from having confidence in people, in their aptitude to correct their own errors and to impose limits upon themselves, to wake up and focus their minds at the smell of danger, to understand finally that under certain circumstances freedom is more important than happiness. Like democracy, only threatened freedom is precious; when we can take it for granted, it is natural that happiness again becomes our first concern. But then, by a perverse dialectic, freedom is again threatened. As a last resort, we must always bet on man's astuteness and grandeur. No difficulty is in itself insurmountable, the only danger lies in bringing old answers to new situations, in losing our sense of proportion, in translating the least nuisances into the Apocalypse. This is why optimism as well as pessimism are unsuitable: they both miss the bi-fold truth of our universe: a precarious balance between two extremes. Neither despair, nor bliss, but an eternal discomfort that demands that we fight alternately on several fronts without ever believing that we have won, without ever stopping to rest.

THE CHAOS OF MISFORTUNES

Minorities and oppressed peoples have only one right — but it is sacrosanct — and that is to stop being oppressed and to become once again the subjects of their history. And we have only one responsibility with respect to them, but it is absolute — to lend assistance. However, the fact of receiving assistance does not confer any metaphysical superiority on one category of human beings over the others. Looking at history from the point of view of the losers, as Walter Benjamin suggested, should not lead us to worship the latter. The idea that the exploited are always right, even when they react in blind violence, does not hold water. A cause is not inevitably right because men die for it. Fascism was a cause, Communism likewise, and Islamism is another. No group, by its history, is fore-armed against cruelty, and none, through the troubles it has endured, has acquired any kind of divine grace that would exempt it from paying for its actions and that would authorize it to maintain that its own interests are necessarily those of what is right and good. And none is appointed to the exalted mission of redeeming or leading mankind, designating itself as the new Messiah. The roles of persecutor and persecuted have become interchangeable; any community or private individual can adopt one or the other. So let's not hear anymore about these people *cum* archangels, these untouchable individuals who forbid others to judge them and cast a reproving eye on the world, reckoning that everyone owes them because of the insults that have been perpetrated.

Still, we cannot stop lending a hand to the precarious and the frail, we cannot abandon the victims of war and assault under the pretext that any revolution must be harboring the crime in its own midst; we must not content ourselves with replacing one tyranny by another. Legitimate mistrust for the lies of the century — and the worst of all, Communism — would only lead to an aggravation of injustice if it prohibited mutinies and uprisings, if it closed all exits and became just a painful conformity with the order of things. We must leave open a door to revolt, even if it is a narrow door. The right to resistance is inalienable for any threatened person or minority, and we should to welcome the myriad attempts of the offended and the humiliated to extricate themselves from their situations and to have others accord them their dignity. It is always right to revolt when what is at stake is one's humanity.

Not all the maltreated, however, have the same interests — it is impossible to put them in the same basket, to federate them under the same banner. While some regret Christopher Columbus' discovery of America as a disaster, others groan over the fall of Constantinople or the devastations of the crusades; others have never recovered from the wounds of slavery under colonialism or the catastrophe of the Holocaust. And what does the child prostitute in Thailand or the Philippines have in common with the people of Timor decimated by Djakarta, the Christian minorities oppressed in the land of Islam, the Gypsies in Central Europe and all the small peoples whose only crime is to want to exist and to maintain their own particularities, their languages and their cultures? There is no good subject of history charged with representing all the poor wretches, no nation or group that could take on, Christ-like, the immeasurable suffering of humanity. The complaints of the downtrodden form an immense cacophony, their wounds add up without being superimposed and their interests are not convergent. Evil is multifarious, cruelty shows several faces and when it comes to those who suffer, every distress is unique and requires a suitable answer. Our commitments thus are inevitably dispersed, competing, and irreconcilable.

And how can we ignore those populations whose entire history is founded on a succession of cataclysms (the native people of all the Americas, the Untouchables in India, the Jews — at least until the creation of Israel, the Blacks in the United States, Kurds, Armenians, etc.) and who remain haunted by a memory of exile, deprecation, conscription, lynching, pogroms, extermination? There are whole regions, even whole nations for which we must take into account a historical characteristic. But this clause of exception does not confer a right to immunity. And these same groups cannot take refuge indefinitely behind a painful past to excuse their present day brutalities or to claim a special status. It is a fine, even imperceptible, line that separates the moment when the dominated begin to suffer and must be helped, and when these same dominated start to kill, in their turn, inflicting upon the weaker the same treatment that they underwent earlier. Often the two situations coexist, and the slaughtered and the slaughterers are intermingled. Then it takes great wisdom to clarify the situation — great political intelligence, and a subtle weighing of the situation, a combination of comprehension and intransigence.

INEVITABLE DISAPPOINTMENT

How then can we avoid the devilish reversibility that makes today's victim tomorrow's predator, how can we escape the pitiless metronome that has regulated all of history? With democracy and the State of law, the only political systems that suspend hatred and revenge, allowing the expression of conflict while containing it within strictly codified forms. Getting out of the condition of victim, once the oppressor has been cut down and reparations have been made, means growing into the responsibilities that liberty implies, yielding to the moral and legal constraints that apply to all. One could say of democracy what Seneca said of institutions — that they result from the spite of men and that, at the same time, they cure it. Democracy is a spiritual and moral treasure shared by all of humanity and which, in each society, can be a device to hold evil at bay, to prevent the triumph of force and arbitrary power. The way in which a band of guerrillas or a liberation movement conducts its campaigns is in general revealing of the type of society that it will found; an inevitable fringe of violence and immorality notwithstanding, the choice of the means is already that of the ends. The right to insubordination must be counterbalanced by the duty to challenge terror and despotism as methods of government and the great brackets of chaos and absolutism — wars and revolutions — must be closed as quickly as possible. When those in misery aspire to the public light, they aspire to becoming men like the others, to returning to the common standard, and not to enjoying special exemptions.

The accession to freedom is thus the accession to "ordinary peccability," to the obligation to answer for one's actions, even those that are not too impressive. It must be acknowledged: history is a dirty business. Once the guarantee of martyrdom that justified their rebellion is lost, the victims will always disappoint us and seem to betray their promises. But they didn't promise us anything; it is we who ascribe perfection to them and we who are deprived of it; it is we who are wrong in expecting too much of them as though misfortune, Gehenna, would necessarily improve people, making them the instrument of redemption for the entire species. Using this disappointment as an excuse for not lending a helping hand to anyone who is groaning in chains is an unjustifiable sophism that adds complicity to ignominy.

However, there's no point in nourishing disproportionate illusions. The hope heralded by the Bible, the deliverance of prisoners, the relief of the oppressed, is not going to happen. Wrongs will not be righted, the malicious will continue to gloat, and the righteous will continue to weep. At least let us make note of unjustifiable suffering and eliminate it as much as possible. At least let us learn to discern, under the clamor of charlatans disguised as victims, of killers disguised as evangelists, the voice of all the afflicted that rises up in one appeal: help us!

But are the Western democracies still interested in defending rights and freedom beyond their own borders, now that the Cold War is over? Do they have the least ambition to foster civilization, to do anything more than seek their own immediate benefit, at the risk of slowly decaying through inanition? That's the question.

TABLE OF INSETS

Also from Algora Publishing:

CLAUDIU A. SECARA
THE NEW COMMONWEALTH
From Bureaucratic Corporatism to Socialist Capitalism

The notion of an elite-driven worldwide perestroika has gained some credibility lately. The book examines in a historical perspective the most intriguing dialectic in the Soviet Union's "collapse" — from socialism to capitalism and back to socialist capitalism — and speculates on the global implications.

IGNACIO RAMONET
THE GEOPOLITICS OF CHAOS

The author, Director of *Le Monde Diplomatique*, presents an original, discriminating and lucid political matrix for understanding what he calls the "current disorder of the world" in terms of Internationalization, Cyberculture and Political Chaos.

TZVETAN TODOROV
A PASSION FOR DEMOCRACY —
Benjamin Constant

The French Revolution rang the death knell not only for a form of society, but also for a way of feeling and of living; and it is still not clear as yet what did we gain from the changes.

MICHEL PINÇON & MONIQUE PINÇON-CHARLOT
GRAND FORTUNES —
Dynasties of Wealth in France

Going back for generations, the fortunes of great families consist of far more than money—they are also symbols of culture and social interaction. In a nation known for democracy and meritocracy, piercing the secrets of the grand fortunes verges on a crime of lèse-majesté . . . *Grand Fortunes* succeeds at that.

CLAUDIU A. SECARA
TIME & EGO —
Judeo-Christian Egotheism and the Anglo-Saxon Industrial Revolution

The first question of abstract reflection that arouses controversy is the problem of Becoming. Being persists, beings constantly change; they are born and they pass away. How can Being change and yet be eternal? The quest for the logical and experimental answer has just taken off.

JEAN-MARIE ABGRALL
SOUL SNATCHERS: THE MECHANICS OF CULTS

Jean-Marie Abgrall, psychiatrist, criminologist, expert witness to the French Court of Appeals, and member of the Inter-Ministry Committee on Cults, is one of the experts most frequently consulted by the European judicial and legislative processes. The fruit of fifteen years of research, his book delivers the first methodical analysis of the sectarian phenomenon, decoding the mental manipulation on behalf of mystified observers as well as victims.

JEAN-CLAUDE GUILLEBAUD
THE TYRANNY OF PLEASURE

Guillebaud, a Sixties' radical, re-thinks liberation, taking a hard look at the question of sexual morals -- that is, the place of the forbidden -- in a modern society. For almost a whole generation, we have lived in the illusion that this question had ceased to exist. Today the illusion is faded, but a strange and tumultuous distress replaces it. No longer knowing very clearly where we stand, our societies painfully seek answers between unacceptable alternatives: bold-faced permissiveness or nostalgic moralism.

SOPHIE COIGNARD AND MARIE-THÉRÈSE GUICHARD
FRENCH CONNECTIONS –
The Secret History of Networks of Influence

They were born in the same region, went to the same schools, fought the same fights and made the same mistakes in youth. They share the same morals, the same fantasies of success and the same taste for money. They act behind the scenes to help each other, boosting careers, monopolizing business and information, making money, conspiring and, why not, becoming Presidents!

VLADIMIR PLOUGIN
RUSSIAN INTELLIGENCE SERVICES. Vol. I. Early Years

Mysterious episodes from Russia's past – alliances and betrayals, espionage and military feats – are unearthed and examined in this study, which is drawn from ancient chronicles and preserved documents from Russia, Greece, Byzantium and the Vatican Library. Scholarly analysis and narrative flair combine to give both the facts and the flavor of the battle scenes and the espionage milieu, including the establishment of secret services in Kievan rus, the heroes and the techniques of intelligence and counter-intelligence in the 10th-12th centuries, and the times of Vladimir.

JEAN-JACQUES ROSA
EURO ERROR

The European Superstate makes Jean-Jacques Rosa mad, for two reasons. First, actions taken to relieve unemployment have created inflation, but have not reduced unemployment. His second argument is even more intriguing: the 21st century will see the fragmentation of the U. S., not the unification of Europe.

ANDRÉ GAURON
EUROPEAN MISUNDERSTANDING

Few of the books decrying the European Monetary Union raise the level of the discussion to a higher plane. *European Misunderstanding* is one of these. Gauron gets it right, observing that the real problem facing Europe is its political future, not its economic future.

DOMINIQUE FERNANDEZ
PHOTOGRAPHER: FERRANTE FERRANTI
ROMANIAN RHAPSODY — An Overlooked Corner of Europe

"Romania doesn't get very good press." And so, renowned French travel writer Dominique Fernandez and top photographer Ferrante Ferranti head out to form their own images. In four long journeys over a 6-year span, they uncover a tantalizing blend of German efficiency and Latin nonchalance, French literature and Gypsy music, Western rationalism and Oriental mysteries. Fernandez reveals the rich Romanian essence. Attentive and precise, he digs beneath the somber heritage of communism to reach the deep roots of a European country that is so little-known.

PHILIPPE TRÉTIACK
ARE YOU AGITÉ? Treatise on Everyday Agitation

"A book filled with the exuberance of a new millennium, full of humor and relevance. Philippe Trétiack, a leading reporter for *Elle*, goes around the world and back, taking an interest in the futile as well as the essential. His flair for words, his undeniable culture, help us to catch on the fly what we really are: characters subject to the ballistic impulse of desires, fads and a click of the remote. His book invites us to take a healthy break from the breathless agitation in general." — *Aujourd'hui le Parisien*

"The 'Agité,' that human species that lives in international airports, jumps into taxis while dialing the cell phone, eats while clearing the table, reads the paper while watching TV and works during vacation – has just been given a new title." — *Le Monde des Livres*

PAUL LOMBARD
VICE & VIRTUE — Men of History, Great Crooks for the Greater Good

Personal passion has often guided powerful people more than the public interest. With what result? From the courtiers of Versailles to the back halls of Mitterand's government, from Danton — revealed to have been a paid agent for England — to the shady bankers of Mitterand's era, from the buddies of Mazarin to the builders of the Panama Canal, Paul Lombard unearths the secrets of the corridors of power. He reveals the vanity and the corruption, but also the grandeur and panache that characterize the great. This cavalcade over many centuries can be read as a subversive tract on how to lead.

RICHARD LABÉVIÈRE
DOLLARS FOR TERROR — The U.S. and Islam

"In this riveting, often shocking analysis, the U.S. is an accessory in the rise of Islam, because it manipulates and aids radical Moslem groups in its shortsighted pursuit of its economic interests, especially the energy resources of the Middle East and the oil- and mineral-rich former Soviet republics of Central Asia. Labévière shows how radical Islamic fundamentalism spreads its influence on two levels, above board, through investment firms, banks and shell companies, and clandestinely, though a network of drug dealing, weapons smuggling and money laundering. This important book sounds a wake-up call to U.S. policy-makers." — *Publishers Weekly*

JEANNINE VERDÈS-LEROUX
DECONSTRUCTING PIERRE BOURDIEU
Against Sociological Terrorism From the Left

Sociologist Pierre Bourdieu went from widely-criticized to widely-acclaimed, without adjusting his hastily constructed theories. Turning the guns of critical analysis on his own critics, he was happier jousting in the ring of (often quite undemocratic) political debate than reflecting and expanding upon his own propositions. Verdès-Leroux has spent 20 years researching the policy impact of intellectuals who play at the fringes of politics. She suggests that Bourdieu arrogated for himself the role of "total intellectual" and proved that a good offense is the best defense. A pessimistic Leninist bolstered by a ponderous scientific construct, Bourdieu stands out as the ultimate doctrinaire more concerned with self-promotion than with democratic intellectual engagements.

HENRI TROYAT
TERRIBLE TZARINAS

Who should succeed Peter the Great? Upon the death of this visionary and despotic reformer, the great families plotted to come up with a successor who would surpass everyone else — or at least, offend none. But there were only women — Catherine I, Anna Ivanovna, Anna Leopoldovna, Elizabeth I. These autocrats imposed their violent and dissolute natures upon the empire, along with their loves, their feuds, their cruelties. Born in 1911 in Moscow, Troyat is a member of the Académie française, recipient of Prix Goncourt.

JEAN-MARIE ABGRALL
HEALERS OR STEALERS — Medical Charlatans in the New Age

Jean-Marie Abgrall is Europe's foremost expert on cults and forensic medicine. He asks, are fear of illness and death the only reasons why people trust their fates to the wizards of the pseudo-revolutionary and the practitioners of pseudo-magic? We live in a bazaar of the bizarre, where everyday denial of rationality has turned many patients into ecstatic fools. While not all systems of nontraditional medicine are linked to cults, this is one of the surest avenues of recruitment, and the crisis of the modern world may be leading to a new mystique of medicine where patients check their powers of judgment at the door.

DR. DEBORAH SCHURMAN-KAUFLIN
THE NEW PREDATOR: WOMEN WHO KILL — Profiles of Female Serial Killers
This is the *first book ever* based on face-to-face interviews with women serial killers.